Your Low-T... Dream House

by
Steve Carlson

A New Approach to Slashing the Cost of Home Ownership

Steve Carlson

BFR

Upper Access, Inc.
Hinesburg, Vermont

Upper Access, Inc.
One Upper Access Road
P.O. Box 457
Hinesburg, Vermont 05461
802-482-2988
1-800-356-9315

Illustrations by Thomas Ring
Photographs by Alden Pellett

Library of Congress Cataloging-in-Publication Data

Carlson, Steve, 1945-
    Your low-tax dream house : a new approach to slashing the cost of home ownership / Steve Carlson ; [illustrations by Thomas Ring ; photographs by Alden Pellett]. — 1st ed.
        p. cm.
    ISBN 0-942679-06-7 (alk. paper) : $17.95. — ISBN 0-942679-07-5 (pbk. : alk. paper) : $12.95
    1. Home ownership—United States—Costs. 2. Real property and taxation—United States. 3. Real property tax—United States-States. I. Title.
    HD7287.82.U6C37   1989
643'.1—dc20   89-22479
                                                                                    CIP

Printed on acid-free paper.

Contents

i

Section Two

Residential Property Tax Summaries

Builders and tax assessors have vocabularies of their own. If a word is unfamiliar to you, look it up here.

Introduction

Low Taxes and Affordability

When my wife and I began planning our dream house a few years ago, we wanted a great place to live for the rest of our lives. However, we didn't want to become locked into high costs for the rest of our lives.

Therefore, our dream house had to come with a modest mortgage, low taxes, low maintenance, and low energy costs.

We read every book we could find on construction techniques and energy efficiency. We also looked for information on how to hold down property taxes, but we couldn't find any. That seemed puzzling, since property taxation is one of the largest costs of home ownership.

We began our own research to find ways to reduce our tax burden without sacrificing the quality of life in our dream house. As it turned out, that was a piece of cake. Ideas for property-tax reduction were sitting around, waiting to be discovered.

We also made a serendipitous discovery. Many of the decisions made to hold down taxes also helped us to hold down mortgage payments, energy costs, and maintenance. In short, *a low-tax strategy became the basis for an affordability strategy.*

Once our dream house was completed, we didn't stop. We'd saved so much money that we bought a run-down house to remodel as rental property—testing new ideas for low taxation and total affordability. The project was so successful that we have been building or remodeling houses ever since.

We have been able to test our theories and findings in urban, suburban, and rural locations. Fine-tuning was needed to accommodate local conditions, but the result each time was a great house with low initial and continuing costs.

Meanwhile, I was elected as lister (local tax assessment official) in my home town. That's a thankless job, and I quickly decided not to make a career of it. However, it gave me a broader perspective on how tax assessment works in practice, compared to how it works in theory.

For the last year-and-a-half, I've been researching property tax systems throughout the United States. The lack of prior research has been a constant source of astonishment. Time and again, property tax officials responded to simple questions by saying, "Gosh, I've never been asked about that before."

This book explains the low-tax strategies that have worked well for us. It also compiles nationwide property tax information, so that you can adjust those strategies to your local assessment system.

I should emphasize—to avoid any misunderstanding that may be caused by the title—that the theme of this book is affordability, not just holding down taxes. Even in places blessed with spectacularly low tax rates, the strategies in this book should help to reduce, substantially, all costs of home ownership.

The information will be most useful to those who are building or remodeling a dream house. However, I hope it will also be useful to anybody else who is struggling with the high costs of home ownership. Knowing the optimal ways to hold down costs should help you to take advantage of features of the house where you live now, or the existing house that you may purchase.

One final note: there are many excellent books that explain the conventional wisdoms of cost-cutting. Before you begin a building or remodeling project, I hope you will read as many of them as possible. This book does not attempt to replicate the work of other authors; it concentrates on the information and insights that you will not be able to find anywhere else.

Section One

**Getting More House
for Less Money**

Chapter 1

Taking Control:
A Low-Tax Strategy

The process people go through to become homeowners has evolved little during recent decades.

Most people seek a house that will be ready to move into, with all the features they want. They check the want ads, the new developments, local contractors, and real estate brokers. They weigh the available alternatives on a balance-scale, with their desires on one side and their pocketbooks on the other.

That strategy worked well for my parents when I was growing up in the 1950s. Depending on location, a decent place to live could be bought for between $4,000 and $12,000. Thanks to the GI bill and FHA, mortgage rates averaged about 4 percent. Heating oil was about 14¢ per gallon, and electrical costs were measured in mills.

Since that time, housing costs have risen at an extraordinary pace. Average prices vary regionally, but regardless of where you live in the U.S., the cost of owning a house is a significantly higher percentage of income than it used to be.

No end to that trend is in sight. As a result, the strategy that served my parents well is no longer practicable for an increasing number of Americans. Many are priced out of the general housing market that was available to my parents. Others settle for housing that isn't consistent with their basic needs, let alone their dreams.

Those who do purchase dream houses often become locked into high payments that restrict all other choices in life. Family planning, career choices, and leisure-time activities become subordinate to the need to support the house.

The time has come to consider new strategies for home ownership.

Defining Affordability

The cost of home ownership is not the initial purchase price. It is the total of monthly, quarterly, and yearly bills. Few people pay cash for a house, so even the initial price is reflected in monthly mortgage payments.

Any realistic strategy for affordability must take into account all costs of ownership. Property taxes, energy costs, and maintenance can have as big an impact on the equation as mortgage payments.

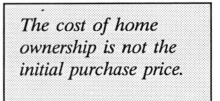

The cost of home ownership is not the initial purchase price.

Affordability is a relative concept. Some people start by figuring how much they can afford, then look for a house in that range. It's better to start by determining the least amount of money you can spend for a house that has all the features you want. If that's more than you can afford, you'll have to scale down, or perhaps defer some of the features until later. If it's less than what you can afford, you'll have money left over for other things.

Reducing Costs to a Percentage of the "Going Rate"

As the first step, find the "going rate" in your area for houses with the features you want. Check the want ads, the real estate agencies, or local developments to find a representative house that would meet your needs and desires. How much would it cost, on an annual basis, if you were to move in right now?

Suppose that the initial price of a typical house that meets your criteria is $100,000, and you have $10,000 for a down payment. You would have to finance $90,000. Where I live, the going rate for yearly costs, in 1989 dollars, might be computed as follows:

ANNUAL COST	
Annual cost of mortgage payments (at 11%, 20 years)	$11,156
Annual property taxes	$2,300
Heat (assuming a reasonably energy-efficient house)	$750
Other utilities (electricity, gas, water-sewer fees if on a municipal system)	$1,200
Estimated average annual maintenance	$500
TOTAL ANNUAL GOING RATE	$15,906

Since this is a rough estimate, you may want to round off the final figure to $16,000. This would be the going rate, on an annual basis, for ownership of a typical $100,000 house in my area, as of this writing. The annual cost could be reduced with a larger down payment (if you can afford one) or efforts to conserve heating and other utility bills. The figures might be different for a similarly priced house where you live, depending on property tax rates, heating and cooling needs, and other local or regional conditions.

Some of the items listed above are choices. For example, extending the term of the mortgage would slightly reduce monthly payments, but greatly increase the total payback cost. If you don't expect to live more than 20 more years, and don't like your heirs or assigns, that may be a good option. Using substandard materials might reduce mortgage payments, but it could add huge repair bills later. When making choices, it is important to consider the long-term costs as well as the immediate annual costs.

The objective of this book is to help you find ways to obtain a house with the features you want, while reducing short-and long-term costs. It's not unreasonable to plan to reduce the going rates by 30 percent, 40 percent, or even 50 percent. In other words, it may be possible to reduce the above $16,000 figure to $8,000. Even if you can afford $16,000, wouldn't you prefer to have an extra $8,000 a year to spend? If you became tired of your high-paying job during the next 20 years, wouldn't it be nice to be able to do something else, even if the salary is lower?

In the above example, the amount you would save over 20 years might be projected at $8,000 times 20, or $160,000. In practice, you might save far more than that. With good planning, you can insulate yourself from the "unexpected" events that are sure to occur over the next 20 years: surprise repair bills, national energy shortages, and skyrocketing interest rates on variable-rate mortgages, for example.

The extent of the savings will vary according to your situation and your dreams. They may not be as large as in the above example. Yet almost anybody can, with some effort, reduce the cost of a dream house far below the going rate.

Achieving those savings will require homework and active involvement. Fortunately, this can be enjoyable and satisfying. The effort will be minimal compared to, say, working a second job for the next 20 years to pay for a more expensive dream house.

What Is a Low-Tax Strategy?

The term "low-tax strategy," which I'll use throughout this book, needs some explanation. It is a strategy for total affordability. Taxes are among the largest costs of home ownership, but all other costs must be considered.

The key to developing a low-tax strategy is to emulate the role of a tax assessor. Conduct your own assessment while the house is in the planning stages. The tax assessor will wait until you complete the project.

Tax assessors use detailed checklists to value each feature of a house. The lists are good guides to cost. Options with low assessments usually cost less than those with high assessments. They sometimes have other advantages as well.

For example, if you choose a polished slab as a finished floor, it will be assessed at a lower rate than carpeting. The initial cost will also be lower, and it will never have to be replaced. A low-tax heating system, as discussed in Chapter 9, may be more energy-efficient than a high-tax system. If you were to choose those options, you'd do more than just reduce your property taxes. You'd also reduce your mortgage payments, your heating costs, and your maintenance.

Tax assessors usually ignore some items. An example is extra insulation. It can increase comfort and reduce heating bills without adding to taxes.

When planning your dream house, create your own checklists. What will each feature cost—not just initially, but during the time you expect to live in the house? Are there alternative features that can save substantial amounts of money? Would the quality of life in your dream house be just as good if you chose those less-expensive features? Take the time to do your own assessment before you make the decisions that will later be judged for taxes.

Holding down property taxes is a worthwhile goal in itself. That is an aspect of affordability not covered adequately in any other book or article I have seen. More important, it is an endeavor that can serve as the core of a larger strategy to hold down all costs.

Example of a Low-Tax, Low-Cost Decision

Here's an example. You and your spouse are sitting at a table, discussing what kind of roof your dream house should have.

> **You:** How about a steep roof with dormers, like the one over on Maple Street?
>
> **Spouse:** It's nice, but it might be cheaper to put on a shallow roof without dormers. We'd have the same amount of living space for less money.
>
> **You:** Yeah, but this is our dream house! If we want a steep roof with dormers, we should have a steep roof with dormers!

Too often, the conversation ends there. The decision is made without checking the initial cost, let alone the long-term costs.

A better procedure would be to make a couple of calls to get rough estimates. Then make a list. The list might look something like this. (The numbers used here are hypothetical, but typical for a new house in the area where I live.)

Extra Costs for the
Steep Roof with Dormers

Extra costs for proposed roof, over and above what we would pay for a shallow roof without dormers. Costs estimated over the 20-year period during which we expect to own the house.

1. *Initial construction costs.* Builder Bill's ball-park estimate of extra costs for labor and materials: **$12,000**

2. *Mortgage interest and bank fees.* The $12,000 would be added to our 20-year mortgage, at 12 percent interest, with bank fee of two points. Total extra interest and fees: **$19,977**

3. *Energy costs.* Builder Bill says the complex roof is less energy-efficient, so it's likely to add about $50 per year to heating and cooling costs. Twenty-year cost: **$1,000**

4. *Maintenance costs.* We won't be able to walk on the steep roof, and people we hire for repairs and maintenance will need extra safety equipment. Rough guess of extra cost for chimney cleaning, gutter cleaning, and roof repair over 20 years: **$500**

5. *Tax costs.* Steep roof can be expected to add $12,000 to "fair market value" assessment. Perhaps more, since it's a prominent exterior feature of the house. At $12,000 assessment, and effective property tax rate of $2.30, the steep roof would add at least $276 to the annual tax bill. Twenty-year cost: **$5,520**

6. TOTAL EXTRA COST OF STEEP ROOF WITH DORMERS, OVER 20 YEARS: **$38,997**

After making that list, it's time to resume the conversation:

You: I still like the steep roof with dormers. But I didn't know it would cost an extra $38,997!

Spouse: Dear, if you want the steep roof, you should have it. This is our dream house.

You: But the shallow roof isn't all that bad. We could buy something really nice with the money we save. Like a Volvo or something.

Spouse: Or we could eat out once a week for the next 20 years.

You: Or we could have a kid.

Spouse: Wait a minute. Kids cost more than $38,997.

You: Well, if we have an extra $38,997 to spend, we can probably find something we'd rather buy than a steep roof.

Spouse: I like the shallow roof better anyway.

The above script won't win a Tony award, and it makes arbitrary assumptions about your situation and your priorities. However, it illustrates the kind of educated review that should—but seldom does—occur when a dream house is planned. More often, people say they want the steep roof, the builder says it can be constructed, the cost is built into the estimate, and the homeowners have no inkling of how much extra they paid.

The Tax Assessment Shortcut

You and your spouse (or living companion) may not have time for detailed analysis of every feature of your dream house. A quicker approach to the above issue would be to check the manual used by your local assessor. You would see that the steep roof with dormers adds substantially to the assessment.

The manual probably also explains that there's a simple reason why the shallow, simple roof has a lower assessment: it costs considerably less. Knowing that, you can make a reasonably educated choice. You wouldn't know that the extra cost is $38,997, but you would know that the cost differential is significant.

Assessment manuals sometimes present issues in an overly complex manner. However, they usually have easy-to-read rankings of specific materials. For example, after choosing the shallower roof slope, you might want to check the relative expense of different roof coverings. The ranking might look like this:

**Slate
Wood Shakes
Asphalt Shingles
Metal
Rolled Asphalt
Tarpaper**

After going over the list, you can simply choose the option lowest on the list that is acceptable to you. That is largely a matter of taste. For aesthetic reasons, many people are willing to pay extra for asphalt shingles rather than rolled asphalt, for example. In a few (not many) locations, "snob zoning" regulations require shingles. If that aesthetic issue is not important, choose the rolled asphalt. It will reduce your initial costs and your tax assessment. As a side benefit, it will also provide better protection from leaks. You'll get more for less with rolled asphalt, if the appearance is acceptable to you.

Yet even if you can get a ranking from the tax manual, it is sometimes worthwhile to project costs in detail. If you have a mild preference for one option, paying a little extra for it may be reasonable. But how much extra? Your preference may change when you know how much money can be saved, or reallocated to other features of the house.

The Effect on Resale Price

Most people think of a house not only as a place to live, but also as a financial investment. If you save money now, will it damage your investment?

The answer is no.

I should qualify that answer slightly. Real estate markets are difficult to predict. Every situation is different. However, as a rule of thumb, sensible cost cuts will increase the rate of return on investment if you eventually sell the house.

Here's why:

1. The greatest appreciation in real estate value is not in the structure, but in the land the structure sits on. Even in a red-hot real estate market, land values may rise by 20 percent per year, while existing structures are rising in value by 2 percent per year. More often, structures depreciate while land is appreciating.

2. The most dramatic increases in the value of land occur in areas where prices are initially low. Higher-priced lots may have reached a plateau, or may decline.

3. Expensive improvements to a house almost never increase the resale value proportionate to their cost. If you spend $20,000 on

kitchen cabinets, you'll be lucky if the cabinets add $10,000 to the sale price.

4. Some features that can save money and reduce taxes have little or no effect on resale price. The tax assessor must give a lower rating for low-cost windows than for high-cost windows, for example. Yet if the low-cost windows look just as good, and are just as energy-efficient, they may not reduce the resale price at all. Resale prices are driven by the market, not by cost. (Assessments are often based on market values too, but assessors must use criteria that are more objective than the criteria used by buyers.)

Investment in "Quality of Life"

Let's return to the example discussed earlier in this chapter: the steep roof with dormers. The initial cost, you will recall, was $12,000 above the price of a shallow roof without dormers. The total extra cost over a 20-year period was projected conservatively at $38,997.

Suppose you had decided to go ahead with the steep roof with dormers. Suppose you had said, "Sure it's expensive, but it's an investment."

Let's flash ahead 20 years into the future. It's time to sell the house. Do you think the steep roof with dormers will add $38,997 to the sale price of the house? Do you think you'll get that part of your investment back with interest?

Fat chance. You may well get a handsome return on the house and lot. The steeper roof, however, isn't likely to add more than $12,000 to the sale price. The money you spend on the improvement will not increase with the rate of inflation.

Also, after 20 years you'll probably have to reroof the house before you sell it. The steep roof with dormers will cost at least $1,000 more to reroof than you would have spent for the same job on the shallow roof. Plan to spend at least $1,000 out of pocket in order to get back $12,000, in inflation-depleted dollars, for a $38,997 investment.

Perhaps you will have received 20 years of enjoyment from the steep roof, so there will be no regrets about the cost. You've lost $26,997, plus the extra cost of reroofing, but it was worth the price. In that case, you made an investment in quality of life. That's fine, but don't confuse an investment in quality of life with a financial investment.

Taking Control

A low-tax strategy requires that you take charge of the building or remodeling project that will become your dream house. It will require hundreds of large and small decisions.

It's worth listening to the advice of professionals. They have valuable knowledge and experience.

However, remember that the professionals with whom you deal have incentives that differ from yours. Most of their profits are percentages of what you will spend. The more you spend, the more the builders, designers, developers, real estate agents, and other professionals will get. They may be valuable, honorable people to work with, but it's your dream house—not theirs. If a builder refuses to cooperate with your desire to cut costs creatively, find another builder.

By taking control, you can keep the focus on your own priorities, rather than the features that the professionals consider "standard in a house of this quality."

Don't ignore the small decisions. They add up. Spending $4 less on a doorknob or $50 less on a window may seem like small potatoes. Yet 20 doorknobs and 10 windows, capitalized with 20 years of interest payments, plus the property taxes on those items, can have a significant influence on affordability.

As the late Everett Dirkson commented (in reference to the federal budget), "When you spend a million here and a million there, sooner or later you're talking about real money."

Before starting to plan your dream house, you may want to re-read *Mr. Blandings Builds a Dream House* (originally published in 1946, republished in 1987 by Academy Chicago Publishing, $7.95). Mr. Blandings relied extensively on professionals, most of whom were honorable people. He eventually spent $56,263.97 (in 1946 dollars) on his dream house, a figure that did not include all the optional extras, such as the cow. At the end of the book, Mr. Blandings fell asleep and had a pleasant dream about the house burning down.

If you take control, the story of your dream house will almost certainly have a happier ending.

Chapter 2

Tax Assessments: Deciphering the Smoke and Mirrors

There is nothing new about low-tax strategies for affordable housing. Such strategies have contributed to the architectural heritage of localities and regions throughout the world.

Mansard roofs, for example, evolved during a period of French history when space enclosed by the roof was not taxed. A mansard roof encloses the entire upper story of a house, so it provided a lot of tax-free living space.

Amsterdam, the Netherlands, once based property taxes on the street frontage of buildings. As a result, Amsterdam has a lot of tall skinny buildings. Charleston, South Carolina, once had a similar system, so builders constructed long rectangles with the shorter sides facing the street. If you admire the architecture of these charming cities, send a note of thanks to the tax assessors.

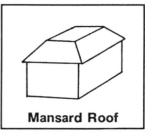

Mansard Roof

This chapter provides some of the background information on modern assessment practices that will help in planning a low-tax strategy in the U.S. today.

Fair Market Value

Most assessments are based, at least indirectly, on the concept of *fair market value*. Some states use other legal terms, such as *full cash value* or *true value in money* to describe the same concept.

The fair market value of a house is the price that a willing buyer would pay to a willing seller in an "arms-length" transaction. It is not the low price you might get from a relative, nor the high price you might get from a wealthy fool.

Unless your house is actually sold in an arms-length transaction, its fair market value is, of course, a hypothetical number. Since most of us are unwilling to sell our houses every year, assessors have to find arbitrary ways of guessing what the market value would be.

Understanding those arbitrary systems should help you to keep their official guesses on the low side.

The "Science" Of Estimating Fair Market Value

In any house sale, the price is influenced by factors that are difficult or impossible to quantify. Personal circumstances of the buyer or seller, emotions, interest rates, and sales techniques make a difference even in the most rational free-market sale.

Some factors, like supply and demand, can be examined with some objectivity. Yet even supply and demand are often difficult to chart with any precision, for a particular house in a particular location, at a particular time.

Three categories of professionals must, in the course of their jobs, attempt to make a science of the smoke and mirrors that determine market value. They are real estate brokers, bank appraisers, and tax assessors.

Their incentives vary. Real estate brokers usually work for sellers, so their incentive is to add up the factors in a way that will lead to a high price. It can always be reduced later, if necessary. Bank appraisers usually enter the picture after a price has been agreed on, so their incentive is to confirm that the price is appropriate.

Of course, brokers and appraisers have professional reputations to protect, so their estimates are usually within the ball park of what similar properties have sold for. However, it's a big ball park. Appraisals by top-of-the-line professionals can vary by many thousands of dollars.

Tax assessors have a more elusive task. They must pretend that there are two people who don't exist—a willing seller and a willing buyer. Then they must guess what price these imaginary people would agree upon.

The incentive of the tax assessor is to be fair. The property owner would be pleased by a low valuation, but if some owners pay less than their fair share of taxes, others end up paying more. As a result, tax assessors follow strict guidelines. They try to judge everybody's property by the same rigid standards. If you were to appeal the assessment, the assessor's best defense would be the manual that he or she is required to work with. The assessor does not want to tell the appellate board that "there are cheap features in this house that add a lot to resale value, even though the manual says they shouldn't." In a situation like that, you'd win the appeal, even though the assessor might be right.

Taking Advantage of the "Science"

Sometimes the dedication to objective standards can work to the advantage of a property owner.

For example, if the assessor's handbook says that vertical-board siding gets a lower rating than clapboards, the assessor will (or at least should) follow that guideline. The house with vertical boards will be assigned a lower value, and therefore a lower tax assessment.

But suppose the vertical boards look beautiful? Maybe they're perfect for this house. Maybe if the house were sold, a willing buyer would pay just as much as if the house had clapboards. A real estate broker or bank appraiser is likely to take those subjective judgments into consideration in valuing a house. A tax assessor will generally have less flexibility on that issue.

A homeowner in that situation may profit in three ways by using vertical boards. First, the boards cost less than clapboards, so the mortgage is lower. Second, the property taxes are lower. Third, if the house is sold, the real market value—determined by a willing buyer—may be just as high as if the homeowner had chosen more expensive siding.

Adjustments to Market Value

In some jurisdictions, the assessment is the same as the fair market value. In others, the assessment is a different, lower figure.

The systems for adjusting market values to compute assessments vary greatly. In some states the assessed value is a uniform percentage—10 percent, for example—of market value. In a few states the percentages are lower for owner-occupied houses than for rental or business property. Some systems (California's Proposition 13 and its offspring in other states) limit the increase in assessments to levels below the rate of inflation.

Even where the state law or constitution mandates assessments at 100 percent of fair market value, assessments usually do not keep pace with increases in property values. Often, there is a state equalization agency to determine the difference between average assessments and average sales prices. If assessments average 80 percent of sales prices, for example, an effort may be made to adjust all assessments to 80 percent of market value.

With a few minor exceptions, the property tax is not a state tax. Depending on where you live, property taxes may be collected by counties, townships, cities, villages, school districts, fire districts, or other local governmental units. Assessments are generally performed by counties or municipalities. However, assessment systems tend to be fairly uniform statewide, because they must be consistent with state laws and constitutions.

State governments tend to encourage counties and towns to make their assessment systems as uniform as possible. State aid goes to local governments for education and other services, often under formulas that take into consideration how "rich" or "poor" the locality is. Those comparisons can be made only if each locality uses the same system for assessing property. If the percentages of actual market value vary, the state tries to keep track of the differences, so that "equalized" values can be used in state aid formulas.

Tax Adjustments

In many states, farmland or other open land may be assessed according to its *current use*—what it could be sold for as a farm or as open land—rather than the price it would bring from a condominium developer.

Some states have *homestead exemptions*, so that a fixed amount of the value of all owner-occupied houses is tax-free. The exemptions range from the first $5,000 of the market value to as much as $75,000. (The latter, in case you're looking for a low-tax state to move to, is in Louisiana.)

In other states, similar relief is available through property tax *credits* or *rebates*. In many instances, this type of relief is available only to specific categories of residents: the elderly, veterans, disabled veterans, or families with low incomes, for example.

These and other important statewide provisions are summarized in Section 2.

How Tax Assessors Inspect Properties

The methods used to assess properties vary. In my town, the elected assessors (called *listers*) generally go through the entire house, from the basement to the attic. The outside dimensions are measured, the boundaries of the lots walked. Detailed notes are taken regarding almost every imaginable feature of the property.

In most places the physical inspection is less complete. In many localities, interior inspections occur only when the house is brand new, or when a building permit is granted for an improvement.

When periodic inspections are made from the outside, assumptions are made about what is inside.

The assessor will either observe or assume the quantity, quality, and condition of the electrical system, the floor joists, finish materials, plumbing fixtures, siding, roof trusses, and all other major components of the house.

This information is entered onto a card or sheet. The same sheet will contain information about the site, some of which is obtained from municipal or county records, and some from physical examination. The size of the lot, the neighborhood it's in, the attractiveness of the view, and many other factors will go into the final computation of your assessment.

Standard Approaches to Assessment

Once the information is gathered, there are three standard approaches that may be used to figure the fair market value: the cost approach, the market approach, and the income approach.

The cost approach attempts to determine how much it would cost to build the same house today. How much would that hardwood molding cost if you put it up today? How much would you pay for that kind of toilet? How much plywood and siding would be wasted with those angles and unusual spaces? What would be the labor costs of that drywall job? What would an architect or designer charge to come up with the plans? How much would you pay for permits, impact fees, and water-sewer hookups?

After all those costs are added up, "depreciation" is factored in to account for any wear and tear. If it's not brand new, it's not worth as much as if it were.

The costs in the formula don't necessarily reflect what you actually paid. Maybe you got a great deal on the hardwood flooring, but the cost formula will reflect the prevailing price. Maybe you taped the drywall yourself, but the formula will reflect what you would have paid somebody else to do it.

The market approach tries to compare your house to other houses that have sold within the last few months. It's a simple procedure if you have a condominium or tract house, and 16 identical units have been recently sold. If they've each sold for $121,900, that's likely to be the fair market value of your house.

Usually, there aren't many other properties identical to yours that have sold recently. Therefore, three or four "comparable" properties are selected. Since they aren't identical, the differences must be accounted for. If your house is on a smaller lot, has less kitchen-counter space, and less roof overhang than the comparable house, your valuation should be reduced accordingly. If your house has more square feet of living space, a more expensive heating system, and fancier bathroom fixtures, your valuation should be raised accordingly.

The income approach is not used for residential housing, except, in some instances, for rental units. This approach judges the value of commercial property by the amount of money it generates. A hot dog stand that nets $100,000 a year is worth more than a hot dog stand that nets only $20,000. The more successful stand could be sold for a higher price, even if the success is the result of secret sauces rather than the quality of the real estate.

Typical Assessment Practices

Most residential assessment methods are hybrids that incorporate features of both the cost and market approaches.

Typically, a market approach is used to determine the value of building lots. This is almost unavoidable, since a lot in one neighborhood may be considerably more expensive than a lot in another neighborhood. The difference in price usually has little to do with

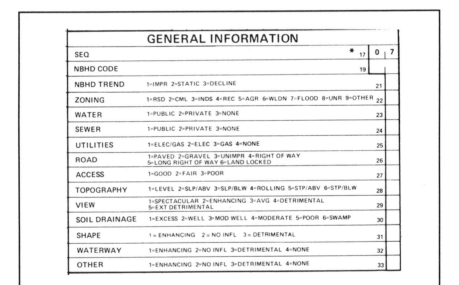

GENERAL INFORMATION		
SEQ		* 17	0	7
NBHD CODE		19
NBHD TREND	1=IMPR 2=STATIC 3=DECLINE	21
ZONING	1=RSD 2=CML 3=INDS 4=REC 5=AGR 6=WLDN 7=FLOOD 8=UNR 9=OTHER	22
WATER	1=PUBLIC 2=PRIVATE 3=NONE	23
SEWER	1=PUBLIC 2=PRIVATE 3=NONE	24
UTILITIES	1=ELEC/GAS 2=ELEC 3=GAS 4=NONE	25
ROAD	1=PAVED 2=GRAVEL 3=UNIMPR 4=RIGHT OF WAY 5=LONG RIGHT OF WAY 6=LAND LOCKED	26
ACCESS	1=GOOD 2=FAIR 3=POOR	27
TOPOGRAPHY	1=LEVEL 2=SLP/ABV 3=SLP/BLW 4=ROLLING 5=STP/ABV 6=STP/BLW	28
VIEW	1=SPECTACULAR 2=ENHANCING 3=AVG 4=DETRIMENTAL 5=EXT DETRIMENTAL	29
SOIL DRAINAGE	1=EXCESS 2=WELL 3=MOD WELL 4=MODERATE 5=POOR 6=SWAMP	30
SHAPE	1 = ENHANCING 2 = NO INFL 3 = DETRIMENTAL	31
WATERWAY	1=ENHANCING 2=NO INFL 3=DETRIMENTAL 4=NONE	32
OTHER	1=ENHANCING 2=NO INFL 3=DETRIMENTAL 4=NONE	33

Land Information: Features that affect the value of a building lot are recorded on this section of a typical data card used by some assessors.

the depth of the topsoil or other quantifiable features that are inherent in the land.

A common procedure is to establish a base price for building lots in a community, reflecting the prices paid in recent sales. The base price is adjusted according to the size of the lot. Then when a specific lot is assessed, that base price is multiplied by numbers that represent features that make it more or less valuable.

For example, if it's a corner lot, the base price might be multiplied by, say, a factor of 1.2. An enhancing view might merit a multiplier of 1.32. Less-than-average road frontage might merit a multiplier of 0.93. A toxic waste dump next door might merit a multiplier of 0.72.

Once those adjustments are made, the dollar figure is likely to be multiplied by a "neighborhood factor." If Neighborhood A is a pricey area, the base value might be multiplied by 1.88. If Neighborhood B is a little run-down, the base price might be multiplied by 0.76.

Each of these multipliers can have a sizeable effect on valuation. Often, a building lot is worth more, and adds more to the assessment, than the house that sits on it.

The structure is then likely to be assessed by a modified cost approach. That makes sense. After you buy the more expensive lot in Neighborhood A, it costs no more to build a house there than to build the same house in Neighborhood B.

Even then, cost is (or at least should be) adjusted by market experience. For example, it may cost $14,000 to install an in-ground swimming pool, but experience may have proven that pools never add more than $7,000 to the resale value of a house. If that is the case, since the assessment is the theoretical fair market value, the pool should raise the value by only $7,000.

Also, market experience may show that no house in Neighborhood B has ever sold for more than $80,000, under any circumstance. Therefore, even if the cost approach shows a value of $200,000, the market value should not be greater than $80,000.

Cost and market approaches are two different ways to arrive at the same hypothetical number—fair market value. While assessors often say that they depend primarily on a cost approach or a market approach, in practice, elements of each are incorporated into most residential assessment systems.

Shortcuts

Even the most thorough assessor won't count every electrical outlet or measure the linear feet of hardwood molding. Every assessment system incorporates simplified procedures to estimate

Your Low-Tax Dream House

BLDG NO. * 15			SEQ 17	1	0	CONST TYPE	1=STD 2=CSTM 3=CP/CTG 4=MTL 5=A-FR 6=CML 7=SHOP CNTR 8=MISC 9=PRE ENG 10=RESTR	19	

		TOTAL ROOMS				BEDROOMS				BATHROOMS		
	B	1	2	U	B	1	2	U	B	1	2	U
21												

COND CODES: 0=N/A 1=EX 2=EX/GOOD 3=GOOD 4=GOOD/AVG 5=AVG 6=AVG/BLW AVG 7=BLW AVG 8=BLW AVG/DILAP 9=DILAP

QUAL CODES: 0=N/A 1=EX 2=EX/GOOD 3=GOOD 4=GOOD/AVG 5=AVG 6=AVG/BLW AVG 7=BLW AVG 8=BLW AVG/LOW COST 9=LOW COST

QUAN CODES: 0=N/A 1=EXTENSIVE 3=MORE THAN TYPICAL 5=TYPICAL 7=LESS THAN TYPICAL 9=MINIMAL

SEQ * 17	1	1			SEQ * 17	1	2
UNIT STRUCTURE	CD	QL	QN	UNIT DESCRIPTION			
EXT WALLS 19				1=WD SH 2=CLPBD 3=SDNG 4=BRK 5=SHAKE 6=STONE 7=CONC BLK 8=ALM/VNL 9=LOG 10=OTHER 19			
EXT TRIM 21				1=WOOD 2=METAL 3=BRICK 4=STONE 5=OTHER 21			
ROOF CONST 23				1=GABLE 2=GAMBREL 3=HIP 4=FLAT 5=SHED 6=MANSARD 7=OTHER 22			
ROOF MATL				1=ASPH SH 2=SLATE 3=R R 4=MTL 5=WD SH 6=SHAKE 7=OTHER 23			
FND MATL 25				1=CONC 2=STONE 3=CONC BLK 4=BRK 5=OTHER 24			
BSMT EXTENT				1=FULL 2=3/4 3=1/2 4=1/4 5=FND ONLY 6=SLAB 7=PIER 8=NONE 25			
BSMT FLOOR 27				1=FULL 2=3/4 3=1/2 4=1/4 5=NONE 26			
FLR JSTS/SPTS 28				SIZE (in x in)/CENTERS (in)/SPAN (ft) 27 | X | | |			
INT WALS/PART 30				1=PLST 2=GYPBD 3=WOOD PANEL 4=LOG 5=OTHER 35			
INT TRIM 33				1=SOFTWOOD 2=HARDWOOD 3=WOOD PANEL 4=OTHER 36			
CEILING 36				1=PLST 2=GYPBD 3=COMP TILE 4=MTL 5=SUSPD 6=WOOD 7=OTHER 37			
HARDWARE 39							
DESIGN 42							
FIN FLR MAT 43				1=HARDWOOD 2=SOFTWOOD 3=LNLM 4=TILE 5=CRPT 6=OTHER 7=NONE 38			
FIN FLR AREA				SQ FT 39			
ELEC WRG AREA 45				SQ FT 45			
HEAT TYPE 48				1=HT WT/STM 2=ELEC 3=FHA 4=GHA 5=WALL/FLR 6=OTHER 7=NONE 51			
HEAT CNT				NUMBER 52			
HEAT FUEL				1=OIL 2=ELEC 3=GAS 4=WOOD 5=COAL 6=WD/OIL/GAS 7=SOLAR 8=OTHER 9=NONE 53			
INSULATION 50							
KITCHEN-PRI 52				NUMBER 54			
KITCHEN-SEC 55				NUMBER 56			
BATH-PRI 58				NUMBER 58			
BATH-SEC 61				NUMBER 61			
DORMERS 64				NUMBER/LN FT 64			
FIREPLACE 66				NUMBER/NUMBER OF STORIES 68			
ADD FRPL OPNS 69				NUMBER 71			

House Features: The condition, quality, and quantity of various components are recorded on this assessment card.

the cost and/or market value of those features.

Often the assessment card or sheet contains boxes to rate broad categories of components. Each category may have separate boxes to indicate quality, quantity, and condition of the component.

For the electrical system, for example, the assessor may make a mental note of the amperage of the breaker box, the number of outlets on a typical interior wall, and whether each room has a switched fixture. A big breaker box and many outlets and switches may lead to a high "quantity" rating. If the fixtures look like they came from a discount store, and the outlet boxes are sloppily installed, there may be a low "quality" rating. If they're new, with no wear and tear, the "condition" rating may be high. Each rating is on a scale, typically 1 through 5, or 1 through 10.

Those are not supposed to be subjective judgments. The assessor has a detailed manual explaining exactly what each numerical rating means. For example, the highest "quantity" rating for the electrical system may mean at least a 200-amp breaker box, outlets at least every seven feet, and a switched fixture in every room. The assessor's rating should reflect those specific criteria, rather than a subjective judgment that a house looks like it contains a lot of electrical work.

Everything Counts (in Theory)

In some systems, the categories are very broad. For example, there might be a single category for exterior walls—including siding materials, trim, windows, and doors.

Yet even within those broad categories, the assessor's manual will provide detailed criteria. Pine clapboards with five inches of exposure should get a much lower rating than cedar clapboards with four inches of exposure, for example. Double-hung wooden windows should contribute to a different rating than vinyl-clad casement windows. A paneled entrance door with stained glass should contribute to a higher rating than a flush metal door.

Therefore, even though your house may be assessed in broad categories, you should assume that anything you add to the house will add to the assessment.

In practice, conspicuous items have a larger effect on the assessment than do inconspicuous items. Assessors are busy people. They want to get in and out of your house as quickly as possible. Like the rest of us, they are more likely to notice obvious improvements than improvements that are difficult to see.

That's especially true in areas where most assessments occur from the outside, with assumptions about what is inside. A cute piece of workmanship on your outside trim may catch the admiring eye of the assessor, who will jump your "exterior trim" rating to the next higher level. If only the outside is viewed, the assessor will then make a higher estimate of the quality of the interior. In other words, the bathroom and kitchen may get a higher tax assessment because of the exterior trim.

> *A cute piece of work-manship on your out-side trim . . . will jump your rating to the next higher level.*

The same piece of trim might also lead to a higher "design factor" rating. The trim may have cost only a few hundred dollars, but by the time the process has run its course, it may add many thousands of dollars to your tax assessment.

Computer Programs

Computer programs are used for assessments in roughly half the jurisdictions in the U.S. They are becoming increasingly common, and the trend will continue. Computers can take much of the drudgery out of assessing, and I'd be surprised if, ten years from now, anybody is still doing assessments by hand.

Don't be intimidated by this. You don't have to understand computers to understand the assessment process. Humans still write down the information. You can inspect the paperwork to see if the information was entered correctly. The computer does the math— and computers are usually very good at math.

Of course, with computers, the chances are greater that silly errors will be made. Usually the person entering the information into the computer is not the assessor. The person hasn't seen your house, but has the job of punching in zillions of arbitrary numbers every day.

If you have a $50,000 house and the assessment comes back at $3 billion, you can be pretty sure that a computer program was used. In a case like that, the digit that meant "average view" may have been entered into the space allotted for "number of bathrooms."

Fortunately, computers are not only good at math, but also good at organizing information and printing it out. The printouts can be easier to decipher than some of the assessment sheets that are done by hand. In the above example, you may be able to scan the printout and notice quickly that the computer thinks you have 16,423 bathrooms. The assessors can then verify quickly that you have only two bathrooms, and the problem can be straightened out.

It's often easier to catch an error like that than to catch a simple, but less dramatic, math error made during a manual assessment.

Real Estate *vs.* Personal Property

In all states, real estate is subject to the property tax. Real estate generally consists of land and anything attached to the land (such as a house, for example).

Towns or counties in some states also tax personal property. There are vast differences in the categories of personal property that are taxed. Often, the statutes say "all property is taxed unless expressly exempt," or words to that effect. Then further statutes expressly exempt huge categories of property.

A common exemption is for "all intangible property." Intangible property consists of items such as bank accounts, stocks, bonds, etc. In a few states, however, there is a tax on some intangibles.

In many states, all personal property is exempt except for business property. In those states, the cash register and shelves in a store are taxed, even if they are not attached to the real estate. In some states, business inventory—the cans of beans on the shelf, for example—are also taxed. In some states, cars, boats, and airplanes are subject to property taxation.

The exemption from personal property taxation that is particularly important in this book is the exemption for "household goods and personal effects." The wording varies slightly from one state to another, but such an exemption exists in almost every jurisdiction that has a personal property tax.

It's a logical exemption. The assessor really doesn't want to sort through the socks and underwear in your laundry basket to estimate their value. Rather than specifically exempting dirty underwear and all the other miscellaneous items that assessors prefer not to fuss with, most states arbitrarily exempt all household items that are not physically attached to the real estate.

That exemption usually means that a free-standing appliance is not taxed, but a built-in appliance is. A table is not taxed, but a built-in counter is. A rug is not taxed, but a carpet is. More information and insights on this issue are included in Chapter 7.

There are two states where, at least in theory, the contents of your laundry basket are assessed and taxed. I'm not sure how thorough the assessment process is, but if you live in Arkansas or Oklahoma, you may want to avoid fancy name-brand socks.

Appeals

I recently asked a state tax equalization official what he thought the error rate was in his state. "In my experience, half the assessments are too high," he responded. "The other half are too low. I'd apologize for that, but it's probably about average for the rest of the country."

In every state, property owners whose assessments are too high have an opportunity to appeal. If you're too shy to take advantage of that right, you're likely to remain among the 50 percent of homeowners who pay more than their fair share.

The initial stage of appeal is usually called a *grievance.* It is often made to the assessor or assessment board. Further levels of appeal are possible, as outlined in Section 2.

Before deciding to appeal, be sure that your assessment is too high in relation to others. As a rule, your appeal opens the door for a fresh look at your entire assessment. The result could be an increase in the assessment, instead of the desired reduction.

Do your homework. In most jurisdictions, you, as the appellant, have the burden of proof. You're guilty until proven innocent.

Making Your Case in an Appeal

In most jurisdictions, you can win an appeal, and have your property taxes lowered, if you can prove one of three things.

1. There was an error. If the assessor said that you have three bathrooms instead of two, miscalculated the dimensions of your house or land, or assigned the wrong neighborhood code, chances are that the assessment will be straightened out quickly. In most jurisdictions you have a right to examine the data sheets, cards, or any other documents on which your assessment was based. If there are errors, the assessment should be corrected, and apologies extended.

Don't get upset about little errors. They exist on every assessment ever made. If there are a few mistakes that raise your assessment slightly, and a few others that lower it slightly, they'll cancel each other out. The errors that need straightening out are the ones that unfairly raise your property tax bill by a significant amount.

2. Your house was assessed too high in comparison with the assessments of other properties. If a comparable house near yours has expensive features that you don't have, your house should be assessed at a lower level.

If it's not, that means one of two things: your assessment is too high, or your neighbor's is too low. Usually, two or three "comparables" will carry greater weight in your appeal than just one. Five or six are better yet. The more you have, the easier it will be to convince the assessors to lower your assessment, rather than raising other assessments. If your complaint raises other people's assessments, they may stop sending birthday presents to your kids.

3. Your house was assessed too high in comparison with recent sales prices of other properties. If a house down the street that is identical to yours was recently sold for $80,000 by a willing seller to a willing buyer, then the market value of your house should be no higher than $80,000. If average assessments in your area are 50 percent of market value, then your assessment should not be higher than $40,000.

Appellate Courts and Boards

In some states, at certain levels of appeal you have a choice of appealing to a court or to an equalization board.

The rule of thumb is that the court may lower your assessment more, because a jury of your peers may be more sympathetic. The equalization board is usually more familiar with assessment procedures, and may have some sympathy for the difficult tasks faced by assessors. The board usually consists of former or present assessors.

However, you usually need a lawyer in court. You can represent yourself before the equalization board. You would need a very large tax reduction to pay the legal fees for a court appearance.

Appeals Are a Right

In a way, it seems out of order to be discussing appeals this early in the book. However, it's an important right that is not exercised often enough.

This book contains many suggestions that, if followed, should hold down your property tax assessment. There's no guarantee, however, that the assessor will notice the steps you have taken.

For example, the assessor may inspect your house from the outside only. The assessor may assume that you have fifty feet of kitchen counter space, three bathrooms, and a whirlpool spa. If you don't have all those things, you'll pay taxes on them unless you grieve.

A property tax appeal is not a last-resort act of desperation. It's a normal, expected part of the assessment process. It takes some effort, but it's one of the jobs that comes with home ownership, like mowing the lawn.

Chapter 3

Location, and How to Avoid It

As any real estate broker will tell you, the three things that influence real estate prices the most are location, location, and location.

Whether you're buying a building lot, acreage, or an old house to remodel, location is important. But what about "location and location"? Maybe they aren't so important. You might be able to save a bundle of money by avoiding them.

Real estate brokers and tax assessors tend to rate locations generically as good, bad, or somewhere in between. There are no objective, universal standards for those ratings. If you spend money to buy into a "good" neighborhood, you may pay for things you don't care about.

Determining What's Important To You

Below is a representative list of things that can add to the price and assessment of building lots, regardless of whether they already have houses on them. Some may seem important to you, while others may not.

Ten Things That Make Building Lots More Expensive

1. Proximity to job opportunities. People crowd into locations that offer exciting, high-paying jobs. Paying extra to live in such a place is worthwhile only if you have one of those great jobs.

2. Proximity to cultural activities. If theatres, concerts, and museums are part of your daily life, it may be worthwhile to pay extra to be nearby. If you partake of them only every other weekend, you may be able to save money by living farther away.

3. Security. It may cost extra to live in a place where you don't need seven locks and a peephole on your front door.

4. Schools. If you have young children, the extra cost of a location with good schools may be a great investment. Otherwise, you may be paying for the pleasure of watching other people's kids tromp through your garden.

5. Neat lawns. It will cost extra to move into an area where the neighbors will ostracize you if you fail to fertilize your lawn, mow weekly, trim edges and hedges, dig dandelions, and kill crabgrass.

6. Snob appeal. A house on Hoity-Toity Lane may cost twice as much as a nearly identical house on Proletariat Boulevard, two blocks away. The higher price entitles you to introduce yourself at the PTA meeting by saying, "I live on Hoity-Toity Lane." To your disappointment, the other parents probably won't swoon.

7. Lack of junk cars. If you're not bothered by inoperable motor vehicles, seek out a neighborhood where people keep them in their front yards. They'll reduce your purchase price and property taxes. Besides, you may have an occasional need for a used part.

8. Peace and quiet. Many of us are willing to pay extra to live in a place where teenagers aren't honking their horns and shouting obscenities at 3 a.m. However, if you occasionally enjoy playing the French horn after dusk, don't choose a neighborhood that is too quiet and peaceful.

9. View. If you can see mountains, lakes, or a historic district of a city from your window, you'll pay for it. The view may be worth the price, if you spend a lot of time looking at it.

10. Convenience. Paying a little extra to be near stores, churches, parks, and other services may save money in the long run by reducing transportation costs, if you use the nearby services.

In my own experience, I've found that features that raise property prices and taxes are sometimes irrelevant or contrary to my values and preferences.

One statewide property tax official I talked with recently said that the biggest single factor that affects property prices and assessments in his state is "the ethnic makeup of the neighborhood."

Translated into blunt terms, that means that a neighborhood populated by homogenous bigots is more expensive, and assessed at a higher level, than a neighborhood with cultural and ethnic diversity. Personally, I'd rather live in a diverse neighborhood.

I also prefer to live in a place where neighbors don't expect me to spend 20 hours a week poisoning the crabgrass in my yard. On the other hand, I would be willing to pay extra for a location with good schools, in a neighborhood where I don't need seven locks on the door.

Those are my preferences—yours may be different. But among the things that raise land prices and property tax assessments, some are probably important to you and others are probably not worth paying extra for.

Taxes and Prices

Property tax rates influence real estate prices. A low tax rate in a town or county makes property in that jurisdiction more desirable, thus raising prices.

Suppose you are comparing two lots for total value. One is in Mud City and the other is in Swampburg. The lots are equivalent. Either would be a fine location for your dream house.

The lot in Mud City is expensive by your local standards. Let's say it costs $30,000. However, Mud City has a good commercial base, so the property tax rate is low. Let's say it's $1.25 per $100 of market value.

The lot in Swampburg is half the price—$15,000. However, the tax rate is twice as high—$2.50 per $100 of value.

If the assessments of the two lots reflect the sale prices, the tax bills for the lots will be the same. The lower assessment in Swampburg will be offset by the higher tax rate. Once you build a house, the tax on the structure in Swampburg would be higher than the tax on an identical structure in Mud City.

So which lot is more affordable?

Take some time to work with numbers. In Swampburg, your initial costs—and therefore your mortgage—would be $15,000 less. If you have a 30-year mortgage at 11 percent interest, your yearly mortgage saving would be $1,715.40.

Compare that figure to your tax saving in Mud City. Let's assume that the house you want to build will be valued at $60,000, in addition to the value of the lot. This brings the total valuation to $90,000 in Mud City, or $75,000 in Swampburg.

With its $1.25 per $100 effective tax rate, the annual tax bill in Mud City would be $1,125. The bill in Swampburg, with an effective rate of $2.50, would be $1,875. The tax saving in Mud City would be $750 per year.

The mortgage saving in Swampburg exceeds the tax saving in Mud City by $965.40 per year. Swampburg is the more affordable choice, at least until the mortgage is paid off.

Of course, cost projections are never quite that simple. Maybe one of the two communities would assess the property at a lower percentage of true market value than the other would. Maybe the kazoo factory that provides Mud City's commercial tax base will close down or move to Swampburg. Maybe you'll win the state lottery and be able to pay off the mortgage. As the late Sam Goldwyn commented, "The one thing you should never try to predict is the future."

Nevertheless, it's worthwhile to make your best guesses, and punch them into your pocket calculator. Sometimes, paying a higher purchase price to live in a low-tax community will save money over time. Make the best calculations and projections you can before choosing.

Pink Trailers

The most affordable dream-house locations are "pink trailers."

That term is figurative. A pink trailer is a piece of land or a house that is hard to sell. It is hard to sell because most people planning dream houses don't have the objective vision that you have. They drive by and say, "EEUUGGHH! I don't want to live in a place like that!" Once a pink trailer has been on the market for an extended period, the bottom-line sales price becomes an extreme bargain.

The objective is to take advantage of the low price, then turn the pink trailer into your dream house. That requires looking at the property more methodically than the average shopper is inclined to do.

If the pink trailer is a piece of land, typical characteristics might be as follows:

• Ledgy land, if the property is in the country. A mound system may be needed for a septic tank. How much will a mound system cost? Will the saving on the land more than offset that cost? If so, the land may be a bargain.

• There's something unattractive next door. Will the unattractive view be in line with your windows? Will it detract from your enjoyment of barbecues on the lawn? If not, take advantage of the low purchase price and the low property taxes.

• The land was never surveyed, and the lawyer doing a title search says that there are questions about some of the boundaries. In a worst-case scenario, if the neighbors eventually claim part of your land as theirs, is the lot still adequate for your dream house? By taking that chance, you can sometimes save bundles of money.

Pink Trailer Structures

More often, a pink trailer is a house. Preferably, it's a house that you can remodel and/or add to. In many instances, the house and lot are cheaper than a bare lot would be.

Once in a while, the pink-trailer characteristics may be superficial. The house may be painted fluorescent pink, for example. Take advantage of the low price and re-paint the house.

Usually, the characteristics that have turned other buyers away are more fundamental. Perhaps the sills and subfloors have rotted out. The average buyer is frightened by toilets that lean at a 45-degree angle. It does take a lot of work to jack up a house to replace the sills and subfloors. Yet that can be done for a fraction of the cost of building a house from scratch, or buying an intact, ready-to-move-into house. Other typical features of pink-trailer structures include the following:

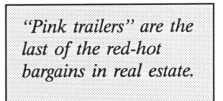

"Pink trailers" are the last of the red-hot bargains in real estate.

• Lack of off-street parking. If you don't drive, take advantage of that. Why pay extra for parking spaces you don't need? If you do drive, stare at the property carefully to determine whether remodeling can create parking spaces. If not, is the price saving substantial enough to offset the cost of renting a nearby space?

• The ceilings may be too low. I've bought three houses with that problem in as many years. They were cheap because people of average height looked at them, bumped their heads, and decided to buy something more expensive. Can the problem be rectified? Would a cathedral ceiling help? How about dormers? The solution may be beyond the "fixing up" ideas of most purchasers, but there may be a way to turn the house into a beautiful place to live.

• The property may literally be a pink trailer, or some other structure that you feel cannot be converted into your dream house. If the property is cheaper than a bare lot would be, what do you have to lose? Maybe you can sell the trailer for a couple of thousand dollars to somebody who will move it to another location. That would leave you with a bargain-priced developed lot.

Most structures have some features that can be salvaged, at a cost far lower than building from scratch. A foundation, water and sewer systems or hookups, a driveway, and an electrical hookup can be big parts of the cost of a new house. If they already exist, you can save big money. Also, if there's a house already on the lot, you may be able to avoid impact fees and some of the other permit costs of new construction.

If there's anything else in the house that can be salvaged—such as walls, floors, or parts of the electrical or plumbing systems—consider that to be an unexpected bonus.

Pink Trailers *vs.* Fixer-Uppers

Don't confuse pink trailers with what real estate brokers call "fixer-uppers." A fixer-upper is a place that needs some work, but its charm and its potential show through. A fixer-upper is almost never a bargain.

There are many people looking for charming old Victorian houses that need a little work. Buying one and fixing it up may cost more than buying a fixed-up house. What you want is a house that, at the time of purchase, looks really ugly.

The descriptive terms used in advertising of real estate are not precise. If you see a "fixer-upper" listed at an extremely low price, it may be a pink trailer. More often, pink trailers are advertised as "handyman's specials."

Pink trailers are still available almost everywhere, because most other people aren't looking for them. They are the last of the red-hot bargains in real estate.

Tax Implications of Pink Trailers

A typical pink trailer has been assessed at a low level for many years before you decide to purchase it. A building or remodeling project will, of course, raise the assessment.

Yet the assessment records will verify that the property was inexpensive to start with. Before you bought it, the assessors routinely checked off all the "cheap" boxes on their data cards and sheets. The new or improved structure you build doesn't give them any reason to upgrade the assessment of the land that the structure sits on.

Therefore, when you buy a pink trailer, it's sometimes possible to enjoy many years of inordinately-reduced tax assessments.

How to Find a Pink Trailer

There are so many different kinds of pink trailers that it's hard to describe what to look for. The examples above are common, but not necessarily descriptive of the pink trailer that is perfect for you.

There are two general criteria to look for. First, the property must be cheap. Second, the features that make the property cheap can be overcome, at reasonable cost, when you convert it to your dream house.

Begin with the first criterion. Find out what is cheap. Check the want ads. Go to a real estate broker who belongs to the Multiple Listing Service. Tell the broker you are interested in cheap property.

Don't take up a lot of the broker's time. Brokers' commissions are percentages of sales prices, so they don't stay awake nights thinking about ways to sell cheap properties. Perhaps the broker will allow you to spend time looking at the file cards and/or the MLS catalog, to find the cheapest properties on the market.

Then look at the properties, to see if one of them can be converted into your dream house. Ideally, you should drive to them yourself, to avoid using too much of the broker's time. If a piece of real estate looks promising, and you found it through a broker, you must go back to the broker to arrange a detailed inspection or to make a purchase offer.

At this point, the asking price may be more than what you are prepared to pay. Make mental calculations. At what price would this property be a good deal? Then make an offer. If the property has been on sale for a long time, your offer may be accepted, even if it is significantly below the asking price.

Mortgaging a Pink Trailer

If the pink trailer is a structure, banks may resist mortgaging it. Under the criteria used by banks, the things that made the property cheap may also make it a poor mortgage risk. The standards used by banks are extremely arbitrary. In my part of the country, for example, banks are reluctant to mortgage a house without central heating, even though the house may be efficiently heated with a non-central source.

If the property is so cheap that you can buy it with cash or an unsecured line of credit, that would be ideal. You can get a home improvement loan or a construction loan later.

One advantage of paying cash is that it gives you more leverage in negotiating the price. Most purchase contracts are contingent upon the ability of the buyer to obtain financing. The seller and the real estate broker probably know that the pink trailer is difficult to mortgage. They would rather have a cash sale than a contract that might fall through, even if the price is a little lower.

If, like most of us, you need a mortgage loan to purchase even cheap property, the bank may require you to combine it with a home improvement or construction loan.

Making Lists

Buying real estate can be an emotional experience, so it's a good idea to carry around a checklist of features that are important to you. That will allow more objective comparisons of properties, particularly if your search spans several months.

However, don't be too rigid about the items on your checklist. Real estate choices are limited to what is available. You're more likely to find bargains if you keep an open mind. A piece of property might lack a feature that you thought was important, but have another feature you that like even better.

If you are lucky enough to find a pink trailer, it won't meet all your criteria. That's why it's cheap. Go back to the drawing board, and figure out what it would take to turn the property into your dream house.

Neighborhood Trends

When you build or remodel a dream house, you probably expect to live there for a long time, perhaps for the rest of your life. Neighborhoods change, for better or worse. If, five years from now, the nice people next door sell their house to the local chapter of Hell's Angels, that could have a significant effect on your quality of life. It could also influence the resale price, if you decided to move.

There's no scientific way to predict neighborhood trends. Yet it's a good idea to solicit insights from real estate brokers, neighbors, tax assessors, or anybody else who is familiar with the area. Since they may have their personal biases, be sure to filter their comments through your own value system.

Your Dream Location as an Investment

People who think about housing primarily as a financial investment look for neighborhoods that are "on the way up." The ideal is a house that can be bought for $40,000 and sold two years later for $120,000.

The equation is slightly different for people who are investing in a place to live. If the market value triples in two years, the taxes will probably triple as well. You won't benefit financially until or unless you sell the house. Nevertheless, most people would rather live in a place that's becoming more valuable than a place that's becoming less valuable.

Almost without exception, the biggest increases in property values occur in areas that start out as modest neighborhoods. The high-priced neighborhoods have already been discovered by people who have unlimited money. How much higher can market values go? If you find an area where prices are low but the quality of life is high, other people will discover the area too, sooner or later.

One caution: don't over-build. If you build a $200,000 house in an $80,000 neighborhood, you won't get your money back if you sell. If somebody else has over-built in a neighborhood that you like, you might be able to buy the house at a bargain price.

From a property tax standpoint, a hypothetical argument can be made for building a lavish house in a modest neighborhood. Since the market value won't be raised, the assessment shouldn't be raised either.

However, it usually makes more sense to adopt a low-tax strategy that holds down all costs—including property taxes—without jeopardizing your return if circumstances change and you decide to sell.

Chapter 4

Timing and
Scheduling

Question: When is the best time to buy or build a house?
Answer: About 40 years ago.

The bargains of yesteryear aren't likely to come back. However, good timing is a key to the success of any investment, including an investment in a place to live. Shrewd decisions on when to buy, when to build, when to improve, and when to pay back debt can have a huge effect on the total cost of a house.

When to Buy

Although real estate prices almost always rise over time, it's not a steady climb. There are ups and downs.

A few years ago, mortgage interest rates rose above 17 percent. It seemed to most people to be a terrible time to buy real estate. People deferred their dreams of home ownership. At that time, in the area where I live, it was possible to buy a terrific building lot for $10,000 to $12,000. It was a buyers' market, so it was often possible to negotiate a price lower than that.

When mortgage rates began to descend, demand picked up quickly. Once rates fell below 10 percent, the floodgates opened. Everybody who dreamed of buying real estate said, in unison, "Now is the time."

Not surprisingly, prices rose to record levels. The building lots that hadn't sold for $10,000 a few years earlier suddenly sold for $25,000 or more. In retrospect, it was a big mistake to wait for lower rates. A $10,000 loan for a building lot, at 17 percent interest over 20 years, would have cost a total of $35,184. By buying the same lot with a $25,000 loan at 10 percent interest for 20 years, the total cost is $57,900. The lot was much more affordable when the initial price was low, even though interest was outrageous.

Of course, the real saving from buying the lot when the price was $10,000 would have been far greater than that. Almost all the 17 percent loans were at variable rates. When rates dropped, the payments on those loans dropped as well. Even those with fixed rates had the option of re-financing at lower rates.

When the prices of building lots jumped, all other costs of purchasing houses jumped. There were sudden, dramatic increases in the prices of existing houses, new houses in developments, and even manufactured houses. It was a sellers' market. Carpenters and other tradespeople, who had been eager for any work during the building lull, were suddenly commanding top dollar.

Many other conditions, besides interest rates, can temporarily depress housing prices in a given locality.

Prices fluctuate seasonally. Where I live, most people want to buy houses and lots between June and September. The best bargains are in winter, when the skies are gloomy, and the ground is covered with snow. The cycles are different in Florida, where the weather is more pleasant in February than in August. If possible, shop for real estate during the time of year when sales are slow.

Local economic conditions also affect prices. At this writing, depressed oil prices have held down real estate prices in oil-producing states. In any town where a major factory has just closed, real estate prices can be expected to fall. When the local economy improves, prices are likely to soar.

Of course, when the local economy is depressed, you may suffer financially to the same extent as everybody else. However, if it is possible to scrape together the money, that may be the best time to find a bargain in real estate.

When to Build: The Magic Assessment Date

Depending on where you live, the timing of your building or remodeling project can affect the amount of property tax you pay. This is especially true in the first year after completion of the project.

Virtually all states have fixed dates for tax assessments. The tax bill for the entire year is based on the condition of the property on the magic date.

In my state, the magic date is April Fool's Day. A house built on March 31 will be taxed this year. A house built on April 2 won't be taxed until the next year.

Houses aren't built in a single day, of course, but it's worthwhile to keep the magic assessment date in mind. Suppose you have a plot of land that will be your building site. Suppose the taxes on that land are $500 per year, but taxes will rise to $2,500 once the house is built. By deferring the project past the magic date, you'll save $2,000.

That's a one-time saving, but a substantial one. If the saving is used to reduce a 30-year, 11.5 percent mortgage by $2,000, the total saving will be $7,135.20.

In my state, many people take advantage of the magic date. Late March is a popular time to move mobile homes out of parks, for example, and early April is a popular time to move mobile homes into parks. There are many mobile homes moving along the Interstate on April 1. Similarly, many developers schedule the pouring of their foundations for April 2, or as soon thereafter as possible.

The assessment date varies from state to state. In the largest number of states, it is New Year's Day. In a few states, assessments all theoretically take place at 12:01 a.m. January 1. In practice, the assessors aren't likely to show up to inspect the quality, quantity, and condition of your bathroom fixtures at exactly that time. They're more likely to be blowing on noisemakers and singing "Auld Lang Syne."

Generally, assessors make educated guesses about what is there on January 1 (or whatever the magic date is in your state). They may make the guess ahead of time, or, more often, weeks or months later.

Often an assessor will ask a new homeowner how much of the project was completed as of the magic date. Unless there is strong evidence to the contrary, the assessor is likely to accept the word of the homeowner on that issue.

Some assessors, however, drive to all the building sites they know about within a few days of the magic date, and take Polaroid pictures. It's best not to try to fool these dedicated public servants. To cover your bases, take your own photos, and prepare to document how little of the project was completed.

The magic date for your state is listed in the state-by-state summaries in Section 2.

Seasonal Labor Costs

Most construction work takes place during warm weather. There are good reasons for that. During February blizzards, workers suffer from frostbite, asphalt shingles crack, and mortar sits for a long time before it sets.

Even interior work is more efficient in the summer. For example, the contact cement used for plastic laminates can be used safely only in a well-ventilated room. Ventilation is difficult when it is 20 degrees below zero outside.

But—and this is a big but—most people who work in the construction trades have a lot of time on their hands during the cold winter months. They're booked up in summer, because that's when most consumers schedule their projects. In winter, the work is welcome—even if extra precautions must be taken and even if the rate of pay is lower.

The lumber companies and building supply stores tend to offer lower prices in winter than in summer. The "once-in-a-blue-moon sales" are far better in February than they are in July.

In short, if you have a project, or part of a project, that can be done in cold weather, winter is the best and most economical time to do it.

Mortgage Interest

For most homeowners, the biggest single expense is interest on the mortgage. Timing and scheduling have a significant influence on this expense. Interest is such a large issue that a general discussion is in order, before outlining specific suggestions.

As noted above, it's not always wise to buy when mortgage rates are lowest. Low rates can raise purchase prices. However, don't underestimate the cost of paying off a mortgage.

A friend once commented that mortgage interest is "free" money, because it is deductible from federal income taxes. This is not a friend from whom I seek financial advice. You have to earn the money before you can make the payments. For income tax purposes, mortgage interest is the same as money you don't have. If the money isn't important to you, it's silly to spend the time and effort it takes to earn it.

Yet my friend's attitude toward mortgages is not unusual. Home buyers often choose expensive options, such as costlier carpets or appliances, with the rationalization that the expense "will just be absorbed into the mortgage anyway."

That is the worst possible excuse for buying something that's more expensive than you would normally buy. Anything that is absorbed into the mortgage will cost three times the nominal price or more.

Prevailing interest rates change from month to month. As I write this, rates are hovering around 11.5 percent. A year ago, they were down to 9.25 percent. There's no reliable way to guess what rates will be when you read this book.

To compare the cost of those rates, let's assume that you are taking out a $60,000 mortgage with a 30-year payback.

At 9.25 percent, your payments would be $493.80 per month, or a total of $177,768 over the 30-year period. This is quite a bargain; you'd be paying back slightly less than three times the amount of money you borrowed.

At 11.5 percent, your monthly payments would be $594.60, or $214,056 over the 30-year period. The higher interest rate would cost an extra $36,288 in payments on the $60,000 loan.

At 17 percent, your monthly payments would be $855, and the 30-year total would be $307,800. This is more than five times the amount of money you borrowed.

The above figures don't include "points" or other bank fees. If the bank charges two points, add $1,200 to the payback cost of a $60,000 loan.

Of course, all those numbers pale in comparison to the payback if you had to borrow, say, $100,000.

For most of us, interest is a necessary cost of owning a house. On the bright side, most financial advisors say that it makes more sense to borrow for real estate than to borrow for anything else. That's because of the income tax deduction, and because real estate, unlike most other purchases, tends to appreciate in value. It makes more sense to borrow for real estate than for a car or for a new suit. Also, interest is paid in inflation-reduced dollars, so a dollar paid in interest 20 years from now is worth less than a dollar paid now.

Nevertheless, any affordability strategy must keep the mortgage as low as feasible. Any justification for a larger mortgage than you need is a rationalization.

Reducing Mortgage Payments

Some of the methods of reducing mortgages are so obvious that mentioning them may seem like an insult to the intelligence of the reader. Yet they are important, so I'll mention them briefly, just to get them out of the way.

1. The larger the down payment you can make, the less you'll have to borrow.

2. It's worth shopping around. Interest rates vary from bank to bank, and a percentage-point difference is significant.

3. If interest rates are low when you buy, consider getting a fixed rate. If interest rates are high, a variable rate makes more sense. Nobody can predict future interest rates, so your decision will be a gamble. Get the best advice you can, then place your bet.

4. The faster you pay off the mortgage, the less interest you will pay.

Of the above points, the fourth seems, on the surface, as obvious as the first three. However, it is worth further discussion, because most people are unaware of the astonishing sums of money that they can save by speeding up the payment schedule.

47

Monthly Payments Per $1,000 Borrowed

	15 years	20 years	25 years	30 years
9%	$10.15	$9.00	$8.40	$8.05
9¼%	$10.29	$9.16	$8.50	$8.23
9½%	$10.44	$9.32	$8.74	$8.41
9¾%	$10.59	$9.49	$8.91	$8.59
10%	$10.75	$9.65	$9.09	$8.78
10¼%	$10.90	$9.82	$9.27	$8.97
10½%	$11.06	$9.99	$9.45	$9.15
10¾%	$11.21	$10.16	$9.63	$9.34
11%	$11.37	$10.33	$9.81	$9.53
11¼%	$11.53	$10.50	$9.99	$9.72
11½%	$11.69	$10.67	$10.17	$9.91
11¾%	$11.86	$10.84	$10.35	$10.10
12%	$12.01	$11.02	$10.54	$10.29
12¼%	$12.17	$11.19	$10.72	$10.48
12½%	$12.33	$11.37	$10.91	$10.68
12¾%	$12.49	$11.54	$11.10	$10.87
13%	$12.66	$11.72	$11.28	$11.07
13¼%	$12.82	$11.90	$11.47	$11.26
13½%	$12.99	$12.08	$11.66	$11.46
13¾%	$13.15	$12.26	$11.85	$11.66
14%	$13.32	$12.44	$12.04	$11.85

To compute full payment amount, multiply the figure found above times number of thousands borrowed, times 12, times number of years of mortgage.

Accelerating Mortgage Payments

Let's go back to the example of a $60,000 mortgage with an interest rate of 11.5 percent. Over 30 years, monthly payments are $594.60, and the total payback cost is $214,056.

Suppose you were to take out the same $60,000 mortgage, with the same interest rate, but with a 15-year payback. The monthly payments would be $701.40 per month. You'd have to come up with an extra $106.80 each month.

In exchange for the extra $106.80 per month, your mortgage would be paid off in half the time. If you're young now, maybe this would allow you to have an old-fashioned mortgage-burning party when you're still young enough to enjoy it. Maybe it would allow you to retire in greater comfort, because you wouldn't have to worry about mortgage payments.

In any event, the faster payment schedule would save big money. Total payments on the $60,000 mortgage, over 15 years, would be $126,252. That is $87,804 less than you would have paid for the 30-year mortgage.

The actual saving is likely to be even greater than that, because the interest rate is often lower for a 15-year mortgage than for a 30-year mortgage. Take along your pocket calculator when you talk with the bank officer.

There are many variations of the fast-payment strategy. Some banks offer mortgages with payments every two weeks, rather than once a month. The more frequent payments greatly reduce the total interest you pay, if the bank records the principal on the date of each payment. However, read the fine print before you sign up for this kind of mortgage.

Also, with most mortgages, you can pre-pay any amount at any time, to reduce the principal. Prepayments of even a modest amount, early in the life of a mortgage, can save huge sums in the long term. Suppose, hypothetically, that your mortgage payment is $400, of which $25 is applied to principal. By prepaying $50, you can eventually eliminate two payments of $400 each. Where else can you get a return of $800 on a $50 investment?

Prepaying whenever you can afford to do so is an attractive procedure, if you live on an erratic monthly budget. You may wish to avoid becoming locked in to higher monthly payments, but send extra money whenever you have it. When grandma sends a check for your birthday, or you get a refund from the IRS, send it to the bank. The returns are like lottery winnings, but the odds of winning are 100 percent.

If you enjoy going through the math, keeping track of your savings, and taking every possible step to maximize your return on

49

prepayment investments, you'll want to read the book *A Banker's Secret* by Marc Eisenson ($9.95, Good Advice Press, Elizaville, N.Y. 12523). If you prefer to just follow a rule of thumb, the rule is that *acceleration of mortgage payments is one of the best financial investments you can make.*

Building or Remodeling in Increments

When planning a dream house, it is sensible to consider your long-term needs. However, it is seldom wise to pay for any feature of a house until you are ready to use it.

Suppose you're newly married. You and your spouse expect eventually to have two kids, a girl and a boy. Should you build a house with two extra bedrooms and an extra bathroom? It would make a lot more financial sense to build a house that can accommodate an addition later.

By building the addition now, the full cost would be added to the mortgage. On average, that would triple the cash price. Delaying the project may allow time to save a down payment for the addition, so the additional mortgage (or other type of loan) would be reduced. Also, you will be able to avoid paying property taxes on the extra bedrooms and bathroom until you need them. Finally, if there are revisions in your plans later on—like deciding to have one kid, or three, or two girls who enjoy sharing a room—an addition designed at that time will be more appropriate to your needs.

Aside from additions, any finish work or other improvements can also be cheaper if done in increments, rather than all at once. Financially, the best strategy is to move into a "bare-bones" house that has as little finish work as you can stand to live with for the time being. That way, your mortgage will be minimal. Then put your mortgage savings into a bank account until you have enough to pay cash for the next improvement. By doing so, you can either get the same improvements for a third of the price (on average), or get three times as many improvements.

> *The time to pay for any house feature is when you are ready to use it.*

If you are a do-it-yourselfer, finishing the house in increments can make it practical to do more of the work yourself. Trying to finish off a whole house at once is an overwhelming task. A new improvement every few months, or every couple of years, can be manageable and enjoyable.

50

Tax Benefits of Incremental Construction

Incremental improvements may also have significant property tax advantages. The most thorough assessment occurs when the major construction is newly completed. If it's a bare-bones house, it will get a bare-bones tax assessment.

In most locations, future tax assessments will mostly take place from the outside. Therefore, interior improvements after the first inspection are unlikely to add to your assessment unless the projects are large enough to require building permits.

In a few states, by law, significant improvements can be made without adding to the tax assessment until the house is sold. Even where that's not the law, assessments rarely keep pace with improvements made after the initial inspection.

A good procedure is to get the improvements that are sure to be noticed—those on the exterior and those that require permits—out of the way first. Those improvements will inspire new assessments, which will cover anything else you have done to the house in the meantime. You can then make smaller interior improvements in increments that do not require permits, without adding to your tax burden.

There is one disadvantage of incremental building or remodeling. Construction work in space where the family is living can be inconvenient. Feeding a family is not fun in a room filled with sawdust. There may be days when you'll feel a need to go out to eat, or even spend the night in a motel. Go ahead. Indulge yourself. Go to a good restaurant, and reserve the honeymoon suite. Your savings in building costs, mortgage interest, and taxes will far exceed the restaurant and lodging bills.

Peroration

As reported in the Book of Ecclesiastes, for every thing there is a season, and a time for every purpose. I'm not a theologian, but that's great advice for anybody who plans to build or remodel on a limited budget.

There's a time to buy, a time to build, a time to improve, and a time to pay off mortgages. Timing and scheduling are crucial features of an affordability strategy.

Chapter 5

House Design: Keeping It Simple

The two issues that have the greatest influence on house construction costs are *size* and *design*. This chapter concentrates on design, even though it is not always separable from the issue of size.

If you need 2,000 square feet of living space, you will pay more for it than for 1,200 square feet in an otherwise similar structure. Good design can minimize your need for size. Several of the suggestions made elsewhere in this book will allow you to make better use of finished space, in addition to other benefits.

Three principles deserve passing mention here:

• An open design has many advantages. One is conservation of space. If the kitchen, dining area, and living area overlap, there will be more space for each function, with less total space than you would need for three separate rooms.

• If you add plenty of cheap unfinished space, you will need a lesser amount of expensive finished space.

• Don't add extra space in anticipation of future needs. Instead, design a house that will be easy to add on to, and build an addition when you need the space.

There are many other books that offer insights into efficient use of finished space. The best-known work on this subject is *Modest Mansions*, by Donald Prowler (Rodale Press, Emmaus, PA).

Yet when all is said and done, your dream house has to be large enough to serve your needs and desires. Unless your building lot is exceptionally tiny, there is no need to be fanatical about reducing square footage.

Prices and assessments of structures are often expressed in terms of "cost per square foot." Where I live, the cost of construction per square foot ranges from about $30 to about $200. Multiply those numbers by the square feet, and you have a significant range.

You'll save more by getting your cost per square foot down to the $30 range than by reducing the number of overpriced square feet. Your design should provide the space you need, with the features you want, at the lowest possible price.

Getting More Space for Fewer Dollars

The exterior faces of a structure are the most expensive parts to build. Therefore, the most cost-efficient design is one that produces the most interior space with the smallest exterior dimensions.

Mr. Pratt, who taught me geometry in junior high school, would say that the most efficient design is a sphere. Of all shapes, a sphere encloses the most space with the least amount of surface area. Unfortunately, spheres aren't easy to build, or practical to live in.

A hemisphere is a defensible alternative, thanks to the late Buckminster Fuller, who invented the geodesic dome. There are more than 300,000 geodesic domes around the world, including one that I lived in briefly.

However, as a practical matter, the shape that encloses the most *usable* living space at the lowest cost is a cube. Even a cube needs some modifications, which I'll discuss in the next few sections of this chapter. Pure math doesn't always take into account the practical aspects of home-building.

Advantages Of A Cube

The advantages of cube-like shapes can be illustrated with simple math. For this example, let's assume that you want 1,500 square feet of living space.

If you enclose that space in a square one-story house, each exterior wall will stretch about 38.73 feet. If each wall is eight feet high, the total area of the exterior walls will be about 1,240 square feet.

You could obtain the same number of square feet of living space by building the house long and narrow—12 x 125 feet, for example. The total surface area of the exterior walls (if they are eight feet high) would then be 2,192 square feet. That's almost twice as much wall area, to produce the same amount of living space.

A square one-story structure is far from being a cube, because the horizontal dimensions are far greater than the vertical dimensions. A two-story square house is closer to a cube. To provide 1,500 square feet of living space, each exterior wall would be 27.4 feet long. With eight-foot high exterior walls for each story, a two-story house would consume about 1,754 square feet of exterior wall materials. 27.4 x 27.4 x 16 still isn't a cube, but we're getting closer.

The two-story house has more exterior wall area than does the one-story house. But the top and bottom faces of the "cube," the areas covered by the roof and foundation, are only half as large. Each covers only 750 square feet, rather than 1,500.

Alternative Shapes

*Each of the following houses has
1,500 square feet of living space.*

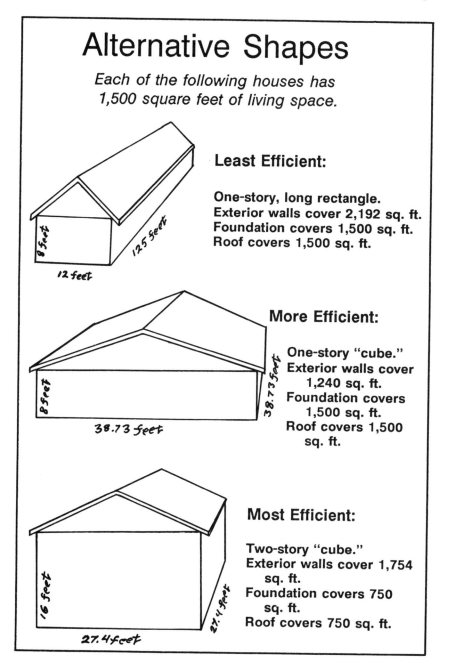

Least Efficient:

One-story, long rectangle.
Exterior walls cover 2,192 sq. ft.
Foundation covers 1,500 sq. ft.
Roof covers 1,500 sq. ft.

8 feet
125 feet
12 feet

More Efficient:

One-story "cube."
Exterior walls cover
1,240 sq. ft.
Foundation covers
1,500 sq. ft.
Roof covers 1,500
sq. ft.

8 feet
38.73 feet
38.73 feet

Most Efficient:

Two-story "cube."
Exterior walls cover 1,754
sq. ft.
Foundation covers 750
sq. ft.
Roof covers 750 sq. ft.

16 feet
27.4 feet
27.4 feet

Exterior walls are expensive, but foundations and roofs are, foot-by-foot, even more expensive. In choosing between a long rectangle or a square, or in choosing between one or two stories, *the cheapest design will be a square, two-story structure.*

One disadvantage of two-story houses is that they need stairways. Stairways add to expense and take up space. However, a simple, functional stairway, plus a little additional space, will cost far less than doubling the size of the roof and foundation.

Other Reasons for Cube-Like Designs

Besides efficiency of construction, there are other reasons to plan a square two-story structure. For example, it will take up a smaller portion of your building lot than would a one-story building.

If you have a ten-acre lot, the space taken up by the house may not be a big deal. However, with a small lot in a city or a suburb, you'll have more available yard space if the house takes up 750 square feet instead of 1,500. There will be more room for badminton, barbecues, gardening, or whatever you like to do on the lawn.

A cube is also the best design for energy efficiency. Heat travels through roofs and exterior walls. The smaller the size of those areas, the easier the house is to heat in winter and to keep cool in summer. Also, extra angles, corners, and cantilevers usually cannot be insulated as effectively as can straight walls.

In projecting maintenance costs, remember that roofs need replacement every 20 to 30 years. That's an expensive job. The smaller your roof is, the less expensive the replacement job will be.

Limiting Cubes to Two Stories

In theory, a three-story structure might be more practical than a two-story structure. It would be closer to a cube, since the vertical dimension would be closer to the horizontal dimensions.

However, a three-story house would require additional structural support. It might also need a fire escape, which can be an expensive feature. Because of the height, parts of the construction would take more time, and the workers would need additional safety equipment.

For a single-family house, two-story construction is almost inherently cheaper than three-story construction.

Accommodating Building Materials

You must also consider the dimensions of standard building materials. Studs, for example, usually come in eight-foot lengths. Longer studs can be bought, but the cost per foot is higher. If an

11-foot stud is needed, a 12-foot stud will have to be cut to size. That's extra labor, and a foot-long piece of wood will be wasted.

Many building materials come in 4x8-foot dimensions. Plywood, waferboard, drywall, and rigid foam insulation are common examples. It takes extra labor to cut these materials to smaller sizes. The material that is cut off is wasted. Waste is trucked to landfills, which are becoming increasingly expensive.

Making efficient use of these materials will result in huge savings. Ceilings, for example, should be eight feet high, minus the thickness of the flooring and ceiling materials. The dimensions of a house should, to the extent possible, be multiples of 4x8-foot building materials.

Let's go back to the example of the two-story square house with 1,500 square feet of living space. The length of each exterior wall, you will recall, was 27.4 feet. That's a wasteful use of 4x8-foot sheets of subflooring and sheathing.

If the dimensions are 28x28, there will be no waste of these materials, although one sheet of subflooring will have to be cut. You'll get a little more living space—it's now a 1,568-square-foot house—at a lower price than you would have paid for 1,500 square feet. If the dimensions are 28x32, the materials can be used without any cutting.

Limiting Spans

Also, you may save money by limiting the spans of floor joists and roof trusses. If you have a gable roof, for example, the standard—and usually the least expensive—type of truss to use is called a fink truss. The maximum practical span of a fink truss is 30 feet.

Therefore, it may become important to keep the width of the structure no greater than 30 feet, even though that may make the structure less cube-like.

Likewise, shorter spans allow use of floor joists with smaller dimensions, less support, or both.

Roof Slope

At least one more departure from the cube principle is in order. A true cube would have a flat roof. Flat roofs are not practical. To keep them from leaking, extremely expensive roofing materials and extensive maintenance are needed.

Don't depart too far from the cube principle in roof design, however. Steep roofs are never cost-effective. If you make the roof steeper than necessary, you will encounter the following disad-

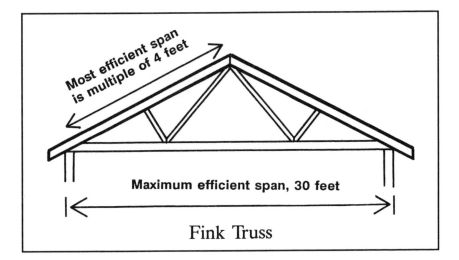

Most efficient span is multiple of 4 feet

Maximum efficient span, 30 feet

Fink Truss

vantages:
• The area covered with expensive roofing materials will be larger than necessary. A roof at a 45-degree angle, for example, uses 50 percent more plywood, felt paper, and asphalt (or other roof-covering materials) than a flat roof. Shallower roofs use less material.
• The trusses will be more expensive.
• Any interior space enclosed by the roof will be less useful as living space.
• In order to avoid bumping your head so often, you'll be tempted to add dormers, which are extremely expensive.
• Workers can't walk on steep roofs. Therefore, their work proceeds at a much slower pace than on shallow roofs, and they must spend large amounts of time setting up scaffolding and safety equipment.
• Routine maintenance, such as roof repairs and cleaning of the chimney and gutter, will also be more difficult, therefore more expensive.
• The materials for the end walls will have to be cut at sharp angles, with substantial waste.
A roof pitch is usually described in terms of the number of inches of rise per foot of horizontal span. For example, a "6 in 12" roof rises six inches per foot of span. Some people prefer to think in terms of feet instead of inches, in which case "6 in 12" means six feet of rise for every 12 feet of span.

The optimal roof is just steep enough to prevent leaking. The minimum pitch will depend on the roofing materials used and the design of the house. As a rule of thumb, if you use asphalt shingles or metal roofing, a pitch of 4 in 12 is adequate. Coincidentally, that's also the steepest pitch that can be safely walked on. Any pitch steeper than that provides only aesthetic benefits, at an extremely high price.

If you use double-coverage asphalt rolled roofing (commonly called "halflap"), you might be able to reduce the pitch to as little as 1 in 12. If you don't mind the aesthetics of a 1-in-12 roof with halflap, that's one of the most cost-efficient roofs you can buy.

Reasons for Deviating from Cubes

Once the cube has been refined to accommodate all the practical issues discussed above, it is by far the most efficient design for a house. However, efficiency is not the only design issue to consider when planning a dream house. There are sometimes good reasons to deviate from the cube principle.

If you plan to take advantage of passive solar gain, that may be a good reason to deviate. In a passive solar design, most windows are on the south side. The sunshine streams in during the day, and warms the thermal mass, so that the family still benefits from solar heat after the sun goes down or behind a cloud. To take maximum advantage of passive solar heating, you need a long, narrow house. The sunshine streaming through a south-facing window-wall will be most effective if it reaches as far into the room as possible. A long, narrow shape will increase construction costs and tax assessments, but those costs may be offset by energy savings.

If members of your family need privacy, that's another good reason to build a long narrow house. A cubical house, by minimizing exterior dimensions, also minimizes the distance between your bedroom and the kids' bedrooms. Inefficient dimensions may be less expensive than a divorce.

Sometimes, the shape of the building lot dictates the shape of the house. To meet the local setback requirements from the road and from neighboring properties, you have to build something other than a cube. Regardless of lot size, local planning and zoning requirements may affect the size and shape of a house, although cubes are generally accepted even by communities with "snob" zoning.

If you want a modular house, it may have to be long and narrow. Modules must be towed along the highway, so they can't be much wider than 14 feet. Even a two-module "double wide" is a far cry from a cube.

If you use a wheelchair, stairs are something to avoid. Even if you don't use a wheelchair now, it may make sense to build a single-story dream house. Stairs may become more difficult to deal with later in life.

If you are remodeling an existing house, it's usually most efficient to retain the original dimensions of the house. Keeping a funny-shaped structure—if that's what is already there—will be less expensive than tearing down and replacing.

This is your dream house, so if you have a good reason not to make it cubical in shape, go for it. Just keep in mind that deviations from the cube principle usually add to construction costs and tax assessments.

The Design Factor in Tax Assessment

Most tax assessment manuals refer to the "design factor," or some other term that means the same thing.

The design factor has a large effect on the assessment of a structure. After all other aspects of the house are valued, the dollar amount is multiplied by the design factor.

For illustration, suppose that the base figure is $100,000. If the design is fancy, the "design factor" multiplier might be 1.8, bringing the assessment to $180,000. With simple design, the multiplier might be 0.75, bringing the assessment to $75,000.

How can you hold down the multiplier? The manual used in my state begins its discussion of design factor by saying, "A cube is the cheapest design that a building can have. If the shape of the dwelling is such as to make its perimeter greater than a simple rectangle, design should be graded up accordingly."

A complex design wastes materials, raises labor costs and tax assessments . . . and reduces energy efficiency.

The manual continues: "If the roof overhang is notably more than standard, or the floors are built at more than the usual number of levels, or the ceiling is higher than usual, the design grade should be increased to account for the additional cost incurred."

Please keep in mind that these are quotes. Don't blame me for the grammar or sentence structure.

The description of an "excellent" design (i.e., a design that might be assessed at $200 per square foot) is as follows: "Generally (it) would be a building that required superb workmanship and extra quality material; such as high ceilings, complex roof, many corners or odd angle corners, or other items requiring excess material over the standard for that unit."

Angles and corners are key elements. A cube or any other simple rectangle has only four vertical corners. A house with six or eight corners will have a higher "design factor" rating. It may not be any better looking, but its assessment will be higher because it costs more to build. Every added complexity increases labor costs and wastes materials.

Assessment systems recognize the high hourly rates that carpenters charge to cut building materials and piece them together. They also recognize the high "tipping fees" paid when wasted materials are trucked to the landfill.

Environmental Note

Sometimes, saving money can also make you a better citizen of the Earth. The cutting of trees and production of other materials for your house affect the environment.

A simple design avoids waste. Besides saving money and keeping your assessment low, it also makes the most efficient use of the Earth's resources. You can do well by doing good.

Avoiding Making Assessors Crabby

Sometimes, extra corners and angles add even more to the assessment than they add to the actual cost. Why? Well, put yourself into the shoes of a tax assessor for a moment.

An assessor may have six houses to evaluate today. Among other things, he or she will have to measure the exteriors of those houses, compute the square footage, and make note of design features.

It's easy to compute the square footage of a rectangular house. If your house has eight extra corners and a few slants and curves, the computation will become a difficult math project. Add cathedral ceilings with dormers and the assessor will have to figure how much of the house is "two stories" and how much is "one and a half stories." It may take ten times longer to assess a complex house than to assess a simple rectangular house.

Mr. Pratt, the geometry teacher, might consider assessment of a complex house to be an interesting challenge. Yet if he had six houses to assess today, and one house took him six hours, even he might become a little crabby.

Of course, a conscientious assessor won't let his or her own problems affect the assessment. However, if you're playing the odds, it's safest to have a house design that does not make the tax assessor crabby.

Use of Cubes to Beat the System

During my own time as a tax assessor, I learned that it was impossible to assess a cube-shaped house at its true market value.

Many elegant houses have simple cubical designs, which don't deter buyers from paying top prices. Yet the formulas that I worked with didn't allow me to assess those houses at a level anywhere near the prices they sold for.

I've assessed houses for $125,000 after they sold for $250,000. I'm sure that the developers who built the houses saved big bucks with their cubical designs, but the savings weren't passed along to the home buyers. The developers didn't have to pass the savings along—cubical houses can be tasteful and beautiful. However, if you take charge of the construction project, *you* can pocket the savings.

Structural Cost Cuts

Design is a broad term. Besides corners and angles, it includes structural considerations. Most houses are not built with optimal construction methods.

For example, in stud-wall construction, studs are usually spaced on 16-inch centers. Yet for almost any one-or-two story structure, 2x4 studs on 24-inch centers provide all the support you need.

Many modern builders use 2x6 studs on 16-inch centers. That's wasteful. The 2x6 studs allow extra insulation, but they are not needed for support.

For insulation purposes, it makes more sense to put the 2x6 studs on 24-inch centers. They provide more structural support than you need, and the fiberglass insulation between the studs provides better insulation than would additional studs.

An even better, and more economical, design incorporates 2x4 studs on 24-inch centers. If you want more insulation—which is always a good idea—then add two inches of rigid foam insulation, either inside or outside of the studs. That will provide more effective insulation than will the wider studs, because the extra insulation is continuous. Studs are thermal bridges that cause heat loss.

A great many other design techniques exist that can reduce costs, if your builder is willing to use them. One such technique is to glue the subfloor to the joists. This significantly improves the amount of support provided by the joists. You can use lower-grade, smaller-dimension lumber for the joists, yet the floors will be less bouncy. You can get more for less.

Another technique to reduce materials used, without a reduction in quality, is the "two-stud corner." Older methods employed three studs on each corner, but any cost-conscious builder today uses two.

Tax assessment formulas, at least in theory, consider the dimensions and numbers of studs and joists. If you have 2x4 studs on 24-inch centers, the assessment should be considerably lower than for 2x6 studs on 16-inch centers. Similarly, 2x8 joists on 24-inch centers should be assessed at a lower rate than 2x10 joists on 16-inch centers.

The less expensive structural design features may not detract at all from the quality or resale value of the house. They are hidden features, so you may have to tell the assessor about them. *Make a point of doing so.* Hidden features have less effect on assessments than conspicuous features, but any money-saving design should lower your assessment if the assessor knows about it.

Other Reasons to Keep the Design Simple

Complex designs cause many problems. For example, they tend to reduce energy efficiency. It's almost impossible to provide a consistent R-value when insulating a house that contains a lot of corners, angles, floor levels, curves, and cantilevers.

A complex design also makes it harder to provide effective barriers for protection from outside air and inside vapor. Anybody building a complex house will devote a lot more time to these issues than will the builder of a simple rectangular house. Even so, the complex house may deteriorate more quickly and need more maintenance.

The edge of a roof is a key indicator used by assessors to judge the overall design of a house. Open rafters with minimal overhang will get a low-cost rating. Additional overhang and cosmetic features such as soffits and facias will add to the assessment. So will gutters.

Gutters will not only raise the construction cost and assessment, but will add to maintenance as well. Plan to spend a day or two every year to clean and repair gutters, particularly if there are tall trees that shed leaves or needles near the house. If you live in a cold climate, gutters may contribute to ice dams and structural damage to the house. Gutters are complex mechanisms that assessors think add value to your house. Their theoretical functions are better served by simple mechanisms—like proper slope and drainage of the soil next to the house—which the assessors seldom notice.

Backtracking a little, complex houses are also more expensive than simple houses in the design stage.

Maybe you designed your house on the back of an envelope, but if it has a lot of angles and curves, the tax assessor will assume that an architect designed it. Architect's fees generally add up to at least 10 percent of the cost of the structure, and often more. Therefore, if your house looks like an architect designed it, the assessor will add at least 10 percent to the valuation. If you do use an architect but the design is simple, the tax assessor is less likely to add the design costs to your assessment.

Summary

When you design your dream house, make it as cubical as possible, rounding off to make the best use of standard-sized building materials. Any extra angles, corners, or embellishments will add substantially to your initial cost and to your tax assessment.

Chapter 6

Exteriors:
Paying Taxes to
Please Tourists

A distant relative—not a particularly public person, so I'll call him Bob—built his house in a rural setting. Bob is a carpenter, so he did most of the work himself.

Outside, the house was unfinished and prematurely run down. Inside, it looked like a high-priced suburban house. It had white shag carpets, hardwood wainscotting, and a designer toilet.

During a visit a few years ago I asked Bob why he didn't fix up the outside. Bob, a man of few words, rolled his eyes to signal that this was a foolish question.

"The inside of the house is for the family," he explained, with as much patience as he could muster. "The outside of the house is for the tourists. They can fix it up if they want to pay the taxes."

How Assessors Look at Exteriors

Bob had a point. I wouldn't express it in such an extreme way—most of us get more enjoyment from a house if it is pleasant to look at from the outside. However, fancy exteriors are not only expensive initially—they also have a disproportionate effect on property tax assessments.

Often, assessors look only at the exterior. For example, in Maryland every house is assessed, from the outside only, every three years. In most other states the system is less specific in that regard, but assessments from the outside are common almost everywhere.

Where I live, houses are theoretically inspected throughout, but town-wide reassessments happen only every ten years or so. Even then, the inside is inspected only if the owner is at home and lets the assessors in.

An assessment from the outside assumes that the interior is equivalent in quality to the exterior. The theory is that if you have a particular kind of siding, you're likely to have a certain number of bathrooms and electrical switches.

Even when there is a thorough inspection, the assessor's first impression is based on the appearance of the ex-terior. If the siding looks ex-

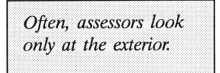

Often, assessors look only at the exterior.

pensive, the assessor may take more notice of high-priced interior features, or think they cost more than they did.

Expensive Symbols

In most communities, builders of high-end houses use certain symbols to distinguish their structures from others. In my town, for example, most of the more expensive new houses are sided with red cedar clapboards. Often, the cedar clapboards are arranged in fan-shaped patterns on the gable ends.

If you drive around my town looking at new houses, you'll learn quickly that cedar-sided houses usually have prices in the $200,000-plus range, rather than the $100,000 range. Obviously, the cost of the cedar is incidental to that higher price. It's good siding, but it's also a way to announce to people driving by that the price of the house is high.

For the developer, that may be a useful signal to potential buyers. However, after the house is bought, it's not the kind of signal most of us want to convey to the tax assessor.

The symbols in your area may be different. When planning your dream house, it may be worthwhile to drive by some of the high-end developments in your community. Are there any obvious exterior features that they share? Do they all have, say, red roofs, wooden gutters, or gargoyles? If so, you may be able to hold down your tax assessment by avoiding those features.

Exterior *vs.* Interior

In planning your house, keep in mind the tradeoffs. Spending more for one feature leaves less money for other features, or for groceries.

The tradeoffs made by Bob at the beginning of this chapter were rather extreme. Let's look in on some more typical (albeit hypotheti-cal) people—the Joneses and the Smiths.

The Joneses and the Smiths are each building new houses at the same time in the same neighborhood. Their lots are identical. They have both established the same budget; let's say it's $100,000.

The Joneses spend more money on the outside. They put up expensive siding, attractive masonry, a deck, high-tech windows, and colorful roofing shingles. After using up most of their $100,000 on the outside, they keep the interior simple and basic.

The Smiths put up economical siding, a metal roof with open rafters, and no design embellishments. From the outside, their house looks like a box with a roof. It's an attractive box with a roof, but nothing that people who drive by would exclaim about.

Since the Smiths are intent on spending $100,000 (to keep up with the Joneses), they have a lot of money left over for the interior. They put in solid interior doors, many electrical outlets, attractive flooring, sturdy cabinets, and designer toilets.

The two houses are not only equal in cost, but probably equal in market value. In the event of sale, the Jones house would look more impressive to people driving by. However, the Smiths would have a more impressive list of features to present to potential buyers.

Therefore, in theory, the Joneses' and Smiths' tax bills should be identical. In practice, the Joneses will almost certainly have a higher tax bill. In almost all jurisdictions, exterior improvements raise tax assessments far more than interior improvements of equal price.

Of course, the Smiths could have reduced their assessment even more by keeping the interior as simple and inexpensive as the exterior.

Building Component Costs and Taxes

Logically, the components that cost the most usually add the most to tax assessments.

In computing those costs, do-it-yourselfers must remember that their labor savings won't be reflected in tax assessments. Fieldstones might be collected from a field for free, but a fieldstone chimney will be assessed as if it had been built by a mason at a high hourly wage. Cedar shingles used as siding might cost the same as textured plywood, but the assessment will reflect the extra labor required to install shingles.

Although standards vary, the comparisons used in the following sections are consistent with the assessment manuals used in most parts of the country.

Siding Materials

Most Expensive: Masonry, particularly good-quality brick or stone. In some assessment systems, a masonry exterior raises assessments in two ways. First, the outside walls get a high rating. Then, after the rest of the house is assessed, the entire value is adjusted upward with a multiplier called a "masonry code adjustment." The assumption is that masonry construction inherently costs more than wood frame construction.

Next Most Expensive: Face brick or stone, cedar shakes, and good-quality cedar shingles or clapboards with narrow exposure. Contrary to popular opinion, good-quality vinyl or aluminum siding with backing often falls into this category, too.

Average: Pine clapboards with at least five-inch exposure, or wood shingles with at least seven-inch exposure. Other materials in this category include hardboard siding materials, stucco, and composite boards that resemble wood. At the low end of the "average" range are softwood board-and-batten siding, and softwood boards with shiplap edges applied vertically or horizontally. The same boards would be ranked at a slightly higher cost if applied diagonally. However, that extra cost is more than offset if the diagonal boards eliminate a need for structural sheathing.

Below Average: Textured plywood (often referred to by the trade name T-111), particularly if it is applied without separate structural sheathing. Low-cost aluminum siding, applied directly over the sheathing with no backing, may also qualify.

Low Cost: Asphalt rolled siding is usually in this category. At the extreme low end would be an unfinished exterior, with exposed sheathing or tar paper.

There are some exterior-wall materials that have values that are almost totally dependent on where you live. Stucco finishes and adobe walls, for example, get high ratings in some places and lower ratings elsewhere. As a rule of thumb, if a material is used in high-end houses where you live, it will be assessed at a high value. If it's common in low-end houses, the assessment will be lower.

The valuation of any siding material will, of course, be adjusted to reflect the quality of workmanship. A poorly built brick wall could get a low rating. The rating of clapboards will be lowered if they are applied crookedly and the nails are popping out.

In general, it is more sensible to reduce taxes by choosing materials from a lower category than by installing them in a defective manner. Siding that is properly installed requires less maintenance, and enhances the true market value if you sell the house.

Exterior Trim

In a highly detailed assessment system, "trim," "exterior doors," and "windows" may be three separate checklist items. More commonly, they are grouped together.

Trim: Fancy window casings and corner boards will cost much more than simple 1x4 boards. Soffits and fascias will cost more than open rafters. Brick trim along the bottom half of the front side of the house, extra trim boards on the roof line, shutters, and gargoyles will all add to your assessment—even though your neighbors might think the gargoyles are tacky.

Gutters add to taxes, although those of us who have struggled with them sometimes wonder why. If the ground slopes away from the house and there is sufficient soil drainage, gutters are usually superfluous. Slope and drainage are important in any event, so why bother with gutters?

Windows and Exterior Doors: Big bow windows and paneled entry doors with stained glass are costly. The more windows and doors you have, and the more expensive they are, the more you'll pay in taxes.

The cheapest windows are fixed glass. Therefore, it's important to decide which windows are for ventilation and which windows are for sunlight or view. An opening window will add much more to the initial price and taxes, even if you never open it. From an energy standpoint, a well-installed fixed pane allows no infiltration.

Casement windows are usually more expensive and add more to the assessment than sliders or double-hung windows. Regardless of what the window salesman may say, there is little inherent difference in energy efficiency among these types of windows.

High-tech windows with low-emissivity ("low-*e*") coatings are energy efficient and expensive. They have a slight tint, so assessors always notice them. You can get more energy efficiency with an insulated curtain, if you remember to close it at night. The curtain isn't taxed, but the window is. Also, on south-facing windows, low-*e* coatings can detract substantially from solar gain.

A single-glazed window with a storm sash provides about the same energy efficiency as a double-glazed window. It costs less, has a lower assessment, lasts longer (there's no seal to deteriorate), and is cheaper to repair if the kids throw a baseball through it. Despite all these advantages, hardly anybody chooses single-glazed windows any more. The assessor will interpret them as a symbol of low-cost construction.

Roof Materials

Quality differences in roofing materials are not always readily apparent to assessors. From the ground, an asphalt shingle with a 30-year limited warranty looks about the same as an asphalt shingle with a 15-year limited warranty. The longer-lasting shingle will cost far less in the long run, because it won't have to be replaced so soon. Yet it usually won't add to the assessment.

On the other hand, if you pay extra for shingles with funny shapes and pretty pink speckles, the assessment will go up.

The following categories are representative of the ratings used in most places.

Most Expensive: Slate, tile, copper, and sometimes wood shingles.

Slightly Less Expensive: Metal with standing seams, single-ply membranes, and asphalt shingles with intricate designs.

Average: Ordinary-looking asphalt shingles, and perhaps metal roofing with a baked-enamel coating.

Below Average or Low Cost: Asphalt rolled roofing and galvanized metal roofing. The extreme for low-cost would be an unfinished roof covered with tar paper.

The differences to a large extent are a matter of aesthetic preference. If you don't mind the look of rolled roofing, it will cost less and the assessment will be lower. Double-coverage rolled roofing (commonly called "halflap") will also provide better protection from leaks if you have a low roof pitch.

Again, the quality of the installation will also be considered. If your rows of shingles look like they went up after a few too many beers, your assessment will drop.

Other materials used on the roof are likely to be considered as well. Lead flashing is more expensive than aluminum flashing. Drip edges, ridge vents, or anything else you put on the roof will tend to raise the assessment.

It's hard to predict how your assessor may react if your roof is sod or thatched. Most manuals make no mention of uncommon materials. The assessor may consider the roof "weird" and give it a low rating. On the other hand, the assessor may know how much it cost.

Roof Construction

As noted in Chapter 5, prices and assessments for roof construction are based on design and slope. The simpler the design and the lower the slope, the less expensive it will be.

Most Expensive: Extremely complex construction techniques such as arched, monitor, sawtooth, or hyperbolic paraboloid roofs.

Next Most Expensive: Mansard roofs, hip roofs, and steep roofs with fancy dormers.

Above Average Cost: Gambrel roofs, modified gable roofs (such as salt-box styles), and gable roofs with steep pitch.

Average: A gable roof with average pitch and no dormers, or a double-shed roof.

Below Average or Low Cost: A gable or double-shed roof with more modest pitches than in the above category. The lowest cost would be a simple shed roof with a very shallow pitch, such as 1 in 12 (one inch of rise for every foot of span).

Roof Designs

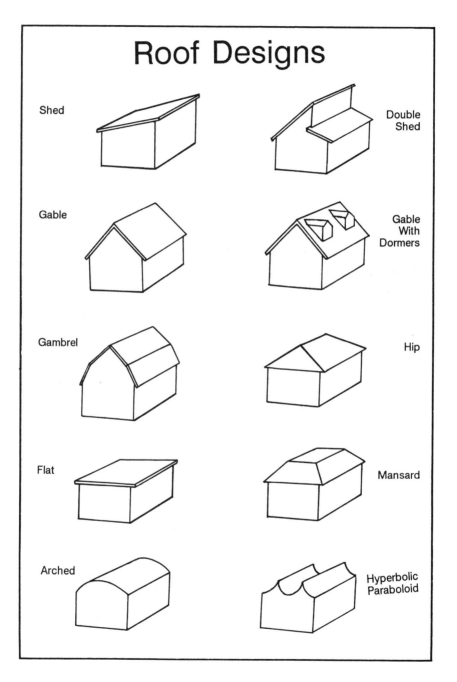

Shed

Double Shed

Gable

Gable With Dormers

Gambrel

Hip

Flat

Mansard

Arched

Hyperbolic Paraboloid

Although a flat roof might logically seem to be the structure with the lowest initial cost, it is not. Since gravity does not help to shed rain and snow from a flat roof, extra structural support is needed as well as extremely expensive roofing materials.

There is seldom any reason to invest in a design more expensive than a simple gable or shed roof. In either case, the cost and assessment will depend on the slope.

In one major assessing system, a base cost is set that reflects the style, size, and quality of construction of the roof. That base cost is then multiplied by another number that is determined by the slope. If the slope is 4 in 12 (four inches of rise for every foot of span), the multiplier is only 1.06. If the slope is 12 in 12, the multiplier is 1.42.

> *There is seldom any reason to invest in a design more expensive than a simple gable or shed roof.*

There are several considerations when choosing roof styles. Although a simple shed roof is the cheapest and easiest style, it must span from a lower wall to a higher wall. If the span is 12 feet, and the pitch is 4 in 12, one wall will have to be four feet higher than the other. Usually, a simple shed roof is practical only when the span and slope are modest.

A double-shed roof is quick and easy to build, and overcomes that limitation, if there is a supporting wall in the middle of the structure. Sometimes, double-shed roofs look so classy that assessors give them high ratings. If that happens, plan to grieve. Every assessment manual I've read acknowledges the low cost of a double-shed roof.

Gable roofs are the most common style for good reason. They are practical and attractive. If the span is 30 feet or less, you can use standard Fink trusses which are inexpensive because they are so common. Gables become expensive only if the pitch is excessive or if you add high-priced features like dormers.

Additional reasons for choosing a simple roof with a modest pitch are listed in Chapter 5.

Decks

A simple deck can be cheap and easy to build. However, like many other exterior features, it can add more to your tax assessment than it costs to build. Decks, for some reason, have become associated with higher-end housing. Therefore, a house with a deck is likely to receive a higher estimate of total value than an identical house without a deck.

A deck can be a sensible addition if it increases your living space during pleasant weather. It's far cheaper than adding enclosed, finished living space.

However, I've never understood why so many people build decks over level lawns. If the decks weren't there, the lawns would serve just as well, perhaps better, as locations for lawn chairs and charcoal grills.

Far too often, decks get added to house plans because they seem, abstractly, like nice things to have. Before investing in one, look at the terrain and ask yourself what you could do on the deck that you can't do on the lawn.

Landscaping and Other Exterior Items

Anything outside your house will be seen by the tax assessor, but the assessment practices for some items vary wildly from place to place.

Satellite dishes are considered taxable real estate in some jurisdictions and untaxed personal property in others. Some places tax above-ground swimming pools, and others don't. In-ground swimming pools are always taxable real estate.

"Landscaping" is a broad term, broken down into two categories by most assessment systems.

Category one consists of non-permanent improvements, such as marigolds and mowed grass. These are not assessed for taxation. However, if you live in a neighborhood where everybody has well-tended lawns and flower gardens, the "neighborhood factor" will be bumped up. You'll pay higher taxes because of the perceived quality of the neighborhood, not because of the specific things growing in your lawn.

Category two consists of permanent improvements. Examples include stone walls, garden fences, fieldstone patios, brick-bordered flower beds, and latticed grape arbors. Most assessment manuals say that they should be taxed. However, many of the assessors I surveyed said that in practice, such items are usually not taxed.

Regardless of the local policy, landscaping can affect assessments in ways that are indirect and difficult to measure. The slope, terrain, and soil quality are judged when the building lot is assessed. Those ratings will be upgraded if you bulldoze a lawn area and truck in topsoil for a flower garden. The view from your house will be assessed, and upgraded if the lawn itself is beautiful.

Dollar for dollar, in most jurisdictions, money spent on land-scaping will add less to your tax burden than money spent on the

73

exterior features of your house. The policies vary as much on landscaping as on swimming pools and satellite dishes, so talk with your local assessor if you are planning a major landscaping improvement.

Weighing the Costs and Benefits

Most of us begin planning a dream house with a picture in our heads of what it will look like from the outside. "My dream house will have vinyl siding, a mansard roof, high-tech windows, a stained-glass entry door, and a deck," for example.

It is important to begin with a vision. It's dangerous, however, to set the vision in concrete without comparing costs. If you begin by insisting on a mansard roof, you may never find out how much money you could have saved with a gable roof, for example. A small amount of research may make the gable roof seem more attractive.

Early in the planning stages, stand back and take a fresh look at each choice, to determine whether it is worth the extra cost. Visualize lower-cost alternatives, and consider whether they may be acceptable. Is it possible that vertical shiplap might look just as good? Would ordinary double-glazed windows with insulated curtains suffice? What could you do on the deck that you couldn't do as well in the yard?

Those are important questions that only you can answer. Perhaps it won't be your dream house unless it has some expensive exterior features. But if you find that some lower-cost options are acceptable, you can reduce substantially your mortgage payments and the tax bills. The appearance from the street might be slightly less impressive to people driving by, but you'll have more money left in your pocket to live out your dreams.

Chapter 7

Interiors:
The Moveability Rule

In gathering tips for a low-tax strategy, I polled the experts—tax assessors and their supervisors in every state. One of my questions was quite personal: "If you were building a house, and wanted improvements that would add to your quality of life *without* adding substantially to your property tax burden, what improvements would you choose?"

Many of the questionnaires came back without answers to that question. I wasn't surprised. This was a little like asking IRS auditors what they do to avoid income taxes. However, I did get 28 responses. The results were anecdotally interesting, if not statistically significant.

Every respondent listed interior features that might not be noticed, particularly when an assessment is done from the outside. One property tax official, presumably with tongue in cheek, suggested "a hidden room with a bar and a whirlpool spa."

Three-fourths of the respondents mentioned improvements that are not physically attached to the house or land. Examples included furniture, rugs, art work, and free-standing appliances.

In short, the experts on minimizing property taxes agreed that classy features should be inside, inconspicuous, and, when possible, moveable.

The advantages of keeping classy features inside were discussed in Chapter 6. Interior improvements, particularly if they are inconspicuous, are less likely to be noticed and taxed than are exterior features.

Moveability is a less obvious, less widely understood issue, but is a key element of a low-tax strategy. Although some of the specifics vary from location to location, the general rule is simple: *moveable things aren't taxed.* Until now, very few people other than tax assessors knew about that rule.

Real Estate *vs.* Personal Property

To put the moveability rule into perspective, let's review the distinctions between classifications of property.

The principal classifications are *real estate* and *personal property*. Real estate is always taxed (unless it is specifically exempted, as is church property, for example). For the typical homeowner, real estate consists of the house, the yard, and any permanent improvements such as a garage, a well, or a stone wall.

The general rule is simple: moveable things aren't taxed.

In some states, there is no tax on personal property. In others, there is a tax on some categories of personal property, with broad exemptions for other categories.

Under both systems, there is one category of personal property that is almost universally exempt: "household goods and personal effects." The wording is sometimes different, but the exemption usually includes all household items that are not real estate and that are not used to produce income.

The assessor must make a clear distinction between taxable real estate and non-taxable household personal property. The criteria for that distinction are sometimes explained in state laws or regulations. In some localities, the criteria have evolved over the years in the decisions of courts and appellate boards. Sometimes, local assessors have broad discretion and follow their own rules of thumb.

Moveability is the principal test used in most locations. If an item is nailed down or screwed to the wall, it's part of the real estate. Otherwise, it's personal property.

A second test is often used. It's called the "Would it go with the house?" test. If the house were sold, would the item logically be sold as part of the transaction? If so, the item—say a bookcase that was custom-built to fit a particular space—might be considered part of the real estate even though it is not built into the structure.

This second test tends to exempt some items that are temporarily attached to the real estate. A stuffed moose head, for example, might be nailed to the wall, but if you moved you'd probably take it with you. The people who buy your house would probably appreciate that. Therefore, the moose head is not taxed.

In some jurisdictions, the "Would it go with the house?" test gives a large amount of discretion to the local assessors. If you sold your house, would you leave the wood stove behind or take it with you? What about the satellite dish? Or the hot tub? A few localities assume that such items would go with the house, and tax them as real estate. Most localities assume that you would take them with you, and list them as untaxed personal property. If you are considering adding such items to your dream house, it may be worthwhile to check the local assessment practices in your town, county, or city.

In the statewide tax summaries in Section 2, I've tried to include the general criteria used in each state to distinguish between personal property and real estate. While there are substantial local variations, the descriptions that follow apply in most taxing jurisdictions.

Appliances

Built-in appliances are taxed as real estate. If you have a built-in range top, a built-in oven, and a built-in microwave, the cost of those units will be approximated and added to your assessment.

A free-standing range and a microwave sitting on a counter or table will not be taxed in most places.

Built-in refrigerators, besides being expensive, will always add to the assessment, while free-standing refrigerators will not. (The rare exceptions are in localities where assessors assume that free-standing refrigerators are sold with houses, and assess them as part of the real estate.)

Sometimes the distinction between a built-in or free-standing appliance is very arbitrary. A fancy cooking unit can sit in the space between two counters and appear built-in, when it's not. With a couple of screws, it would be built-in. In some localities, a couple of 10-cent screws can add a thousand dollars to your assessment. My advice is to omit the screws. Pull the unit out when the assessor visits to show that it is not attached.

Sometimes, built-in appliances have a lower purchase price than free-standing models. Examples include dishwashers and trash compactors. Portable units tend to be more expensive because they have finished sides and tops. However, if you add the costs of countertops and professional installation, built-in units become more expensive. Even if you save money by installing the appliances yourself, the assessment will reflect the price of professional installation.

Washers and dryers are never built in, and most jurisdictions consider them to be personal property. However, the washer hookup, the 220-volt circuit for the dryer, and the dryer vent may all be listed as real estate improvements.

Garbage disposals are not particularly expensive, but they are always built in, and sometimes increase assessments disproportionately. Many assessors will automatically assign a higher overall quality rating to a kitchen with a disposal than to an equivalent kitchen with a compost bucket. I personally prefer a compost bucket, but that's a subject for another book.

There may be instances in which built-in appliances offer enough convenience to justify the cost. In my dream house, we tried to live with a portable dishwasher. However, the kids started running away from home on the days when they were responsible for dishes. To keep the peace, we built in a dishwasher.

My wife used to be in the built-in vacuum cleaner business. She was still able to purchase a unit at a wholesale price when we were building our dream house. It's a real power sucker. In a house full of kids, it saves a lot of work. We have a modest installation; tax assessors differentiate greatly between a two-holer like ours and the six-holers found in some fancy houses. We figure it adds about $15 a year to our tax bill, but we probably save that much by not having to buy vacuum cleaner bags.

In short, building in appliances is not always a foolish thing to do, despite the arbitrary distinctions made by tax assessors. Each decision should be considered individually and realistically, with computations of the full cost—including mortgage interest, property taxes, and utility bills.

Kitchens and Bathrooms

Kitchens and baths are expensive. The judgments that assessors make about these rooms often carry symbolic importance and affect the valuation of the entire interior.

If you read books the way I do, you may be trying to read one chapter each evening before the lights go out. I don't want to keep you up all night, so I'll defer most of the details about kitchens and baths until Chapter 8. There are other things to think about tonight.

Carpets and Rugs

A carpet attached to a plywood subfloor is real estate in most localities, because it is attached. A plush carpet can cost as much, and add as much to the assessment, as a hardwood floor. Yet the hardwood floor will remain attractive for a lot longer.

A rug is usually untaxed personal property, because it is moveable.

If you have a plywood subfloor with a rug, you have an unfinished floor, regardless of how attractive the rug might be. The distinction can become less clear, however, if you have a room-size rug cut to fit the angles of the room. The assessor may assume that the rug would go with the house if the house were sold, and assess it as real estate.

An unfinished floor with a rug may not be consistent with your idea of a dream house, but it's worthwhile to consider alternative materials before deciding on carpeting.

Although carpets are taxed as real estate, they lack the durability of virtually all other forms of real estate. If you have kids and pets, you may have to replace carpets every few years. Another drawback of carpets is that they usually contain formaldehyde, a potential health hazard in a tight modern house.

Low-Tax Flooring Strategies

One tax assessor I know offered the following formula for putting in an attractive floor with a low assessment. "Just finish the floor around the edges, using whatever material you like. The price isn't important, because you won't need much of it. Leave the rest of the floor unfinished, and cover the particleboard with a room-size rug. Then when I come around to assess the house, roll up the edge of the rug to show me that the floor is unfinished. You and I are the only two people who have to know."

That may sound mildly devious, but there's nothing dishonest about it. It's simply a matter of taking advantage of the arbitrary nature of assessment systems.

A more straightforward approach is to install the cheapest finish flooring that is aesthetically acceptable to you, then jazz it up with rugs or other moveable adornments.

In our house, the first floor is an insulated concrete slab, the top layer of which is dyed and polished. It's attractive, permanent, and provides thermal mass that helps keep the house comfortable. Yet the local tax formula regards it as a "basement floor." There's no separate category for polished, dyed concrete. The appearance is enhanced by oriental rugs—family heirlooms that are not taxed because they are not attached.

(Note: in many other assessment systems, dyeing the concrete adds about 40¢ per square foot to the assessment. That's still cheap compared to carpets, which are assessed at between $1 and $12 per square foot, depending on their quality and condition.)

Our second floor is surfaced with wide softwood boards. In the region where I live, softwood floors can be found in some of the most beautiful older houses. Yet the material is relatively cheap and easy to install. Therefore softwood is assessed at a lower rate than carpeting attached to a subfloor.

In choosing flooring materials, be sure to remember the trap that do-it-yourselfers often fall into. Some cheap materials, like

79

flagstone, slate, and quarry tile, are expensive to install. Even if you save huge amounts of money by installing the materials yourself, the assessor will rate them as if they were installed by a high-priced professional.

Another caution: people my age (i.e., over 39) often assume that vinyl flooring is a low-cost, low-tax option. Not so. Today, vinyl flooring is expensive, and assessed accordingly. The squishy kind, which simulates the feel of rotted-out subflooring, is the most expensive.

If you like the colors that vinyl can add to a room, consider using a remnant to brighten up a lower-cost finished floor. The remnant is like a rug; it is untaxed because it is not attached.

Closets

It's possible to knock a few dollars off your tax bill by avoiding closets. The alternative to a closet is a piece of furniture that used to be called a wardrobe. Today, wardrobes are usually called *armoires*, particularly if they are sold at a high price.

Regardless of whether you have a cheap wardrobe or an expensive *armoire*, it will be classified as nontaxable personal property. A closet is taxable real estate.

Lack of closets may possibly have symbolic significance to tax assessors. They may feel that a house with no closets is a cheap house, and reduce other assessment factors accordingly. Therefore, if you have no closets, be sure that your assessor notices the deficit. Say something like, "Boy, it's hard to live in a house without closets! Those yuppies who pay $100,000 for a house sure wouldn't be interested in a place like this!" If you're lucky, the assessor might take pity.

However, if you have carved hardwood *armoires* with curved mirrors in each bedroom, don't count on the lack of closets to produce much tax relief. In practice, a simple, functional closet is cheap to build and usually doesn't add much to the assessment.

The mistake made in some dream houses is building closets that are too large. A closet is finished, heated space. All such space is expensive and assessed at a high rate. Don't dedicate any more of that space to closets than necessary. If you need space to lay out 102 pairs of shoes from which to choose each morning, a large walk-in closet may be useful. Otherwise, it's more efficient to have a smaller closet—and unfinished space to store the extra shoes.

80

Electrical Systems

Unless you long to return to an old-fashioned lifestyle with fewer gadgets, a decent electrical system will probably be a priority in your new house. It's annoying to live in a house where a fuse blows every time you try to pop toast and vacuum the floor at the same time.

A good, competently installed electrical system is also important for personal safety. There should be enough outlets so that you won't trip over extension cords. A ground-fault circuit interrupter in the bathroom may be expensive, and may add to your tax assessment, but it also may save your life.

Also, some electrical devices, like computers and refrigerators, ideally should be on their own dedicated circuits. Extra circuits are good insurance against damaged appliance motors or crashed disks.

When you're building, or when the walls are gutted for a remodeling project, adding circuits is easy and relatively inexpensive. Adding circuits later will be far more expensive.

That said, there's no useful purpose served by installing more of an electrical system than you need. A common mistake is to buy extra electrical capacity for potential future needs. Future needs aren't likely to increase; electrical appliances are getting more efficient, not less.

Unless you have electric heat—or some other extraordinary need

Overswitching: This switch bank was installed in the 1950s. It still adds to the tax assessment, even though only two of the switches are used regularly today.   Photo by Alden Pellett

for electricity—a 100-amp service panel with 10 to 20 breaker slots should be ample. If, for any reason, you need additional capacity later, you can add a sub panel at that time.

Keep in mind that your electrical system is real estate, but most of the things plugged into your electrical system are personal property.

A light fixture is real estate. A lamp is personal property. A swag light, which looks like a fixture but is plugged in rather than wired into your system, is personal property.

A light switch on the wall is real estate, even if it only activates an outlet for a lamp or a swag light. A switch or pull chain on a lamp or swag light is personal property.

A big bank of light switches next to your entry door is expensive. It takes a lot of wire and labor to connect those switches to lights scattered throughout the house. Your tax assessor knows that.

Is it important to you to be able to stand by your entry door and switch on an upstairs light? Do you need a switched ceiling fixture in every room? Might a swag light, or a floor lamp, suffice in some rooms? Might pull chains serve as well as wall switches in some rooms? Only you can answer those questions, but they're well worth asking.

Heating and Cooling

Although heating and cooling are discussed in detail in Chapter 9, the distinctions between personal property and real estate are worth underscoring in the context of this chapter.

Central heating and cooling systems are real estate. So are individual wall furnaces, although they are considerably less expensive real estate.

In most jurisdictions, a window air conditioner is personal property. Even if you have three or four of them, they won't add to your tax assessment. The 220-volt circuits they are plugged into might upgrade the assessment of your electrical system, however.

A wood or coal stove is usually (not always) personal property, although the chimney and hookup are real estate. A masonry fireplace is always real estate.

Miscellaneous Built-ins

I'm sure that you've seen magazine articles describing neat ways to build furniture into a house. Bunk beds and breakfast booths are common examples. The pictures are attractive, and there are usually step-by-step directions that are easy to follow.

Before running off to the lumber store for materials, consider the property-tax implications. A built-in bunk bed, unlike a regular bunk bed, will add to your assessment.

Even simple structures, like bookcases or shelving for stereo equipment, may add to the tax burden if they are attached. A moveable teak wall unit bought at the furniture store may serve the same function, and look just as good, as shelving that is built into the wall.

When structures must be attached, consider the possibility that crude structures may be aesthetically attractive in a rustic sense. Old and rough-textured boards may look beautiful, but will never add much to the valuation of a house. If you want fine craftsmanship, make sure that the fine craftsmanship is not attached.

Finish Trim

Simple trim can be attractive.

Inexpensive 1x4 pine boards are more than adequate for window and door casings, mopboards, and other interior trim features. They usually look best when painted the same color as the walls. Be sure to prime the knots with a special primer that prevents the knots from bleeding through. The most common such primer is *BIN* brand, but other companies make similar products.

For a more modern appearance, trim boards can be eliminated, and drywall with corner beads can be used for window and door openings.

If a rustic decor appeals to you, that can be accomplished cheaply—either with old weathered boards or new unplaned boards from a local mill. The effect can be stunning, as long as it's consistent throughout a room. If you have rough woodwork and intricately finished woodwork in the same room, they'll clash.

Excluding Personal Property from the Purchase Price

Personal property is included in many house transactions. While you're haggling over price, the seller is likely to throw in additional items rather than reducing the price. Appliances, furniture, snowblowers, and lawn mowers may become part of the deal.

That's a logical tactic on the seller's part. If the seller is moving a thousand miles away, it may make sense to get rid of big heavy items before the move. From your standpoint as the buyer, you might get a good deal on things that you'll need in your newly acquired house.

However, deals of that type should be separated from the agreed-upon purchase price of the house.

Purchase prices are public information. The assessors know how much you paid for the property. Their incentive is to assess it at that value, or the prevailing percentage of that value. If a snowblower is included in the purchase price, it will add to the perceived fair market value, even though the snowblower is not real estate and not assessed for taxation.

Indeed, many banks prohibit inclusion of personal items in mortgage loans. This is a case in which your own rules should be even stricter than the bank's rules. Even if the bank does approve inclusion of some items, like kitchen appliances, you're better off if the cost of the appliances is not added to the cost of the house.

If possible, arrange a separate transaction with the seller for the personal property. Take out a separate loan if you can't pay cash. If there's a question about how much any individual item is worth, it's in your interest to pay more for the snowblower in exchange for a reduced price for the house.

A Footnote about Personal Property Taxes

There are two states—Arkansas and Oklahoma—that do not have blanket exemptions for household goods and personal effects. A third state, Virginia, allows counties to tax household goods if they wish to do so.

Even if you live in one of those states, it may be important to distinguish between personal property and real estate. They are assessed and taxed separately, and depreciate at different rates. Everywhere else in the U.S., the advantages of personal property over real estate are more apparent.

One other issue to consider: localities in several states tax business personal property. Therefore, if you operate a business from your house, household items used to produce income may be taxed. More information on that subject is contained in Chapter 16.

Appeals

Since most assessments take place from the outside, you may wonder why I've devoted this much space to the issue of minimizing tax assessments of interior improvements.

The interior of a house is a big part of the assessment, even if the assessor has never looked at it.

When you undertake a major building or remodeling project, you will usually need a permit that outlines the details of your project. An estimate of the cost may be included on the permit. When you finish, a building inspector is likely to drop by to confirm that you did what you said you'd do.

In most localities, tax assessors work closely together with zoning administrators and building inspectors. Therefore, the assessor may have a good idea of what you've done even without entering the premises.

In many localities an assessor will walk through the interior of a house that has just been built or extensively remodeled. In some places, that's the only time an assessor will physically inspect the interior of your house. If, at that time, you have only two feet of built-in kitchen counter space, chances are that you'll pay taxes on only two feet of kitchen counter space for the next 30 years.

If the initial inspection contains errors, it's important to straighten them out quickly. Your assessments, now and in the future, will assume certain things about the inside of the house. If your initial assessment assumes—wrongly—that you have plush carpeting and oak molding, then set the record straight. Otherwise, you may be paying taxes for things you don't have for the next 30 years.

> *The interior is a big part of the assessment, even if the assessor has never looked at it.*

Suppose you have followed several of the suggestions in this chapter. The decor is rustic and the trim consists of 1x4 pine boards. There are no carpets. The first floor is a polished slab and the second floor is softwood. You have a 100-amp breaker box and only two overhead light fixtures in the entire house. Most of the appliances are free-standing.

Those economies are not typical of a new or extensively remodeled house. Unless the assessor goes through the house or receives detailed information from the zoning administrator, he or she will assume that you spent more money than you did. Plan to appeal.

Study in detail the first assessment sheets that come back after your project is completed. If you find errors, describe them at a grievance hearing. At that time, there will be a walk-through of your house. You should have a chance to point out that there are only 2 feet of built-in counter space, rather than 80. The records should be corrected immediately, assuring a lower tax assessment until or unless you later obtain a building permit to increase the amount of counter space.

If, for any reason, the records aren't corrected after the initial grievance, carry your appeal to the next level. In most states, there are one, two, or three levels of appeal that do not require the expense of a lawyer. Remember that tax officials are not accustomed to assessments of houses built with low-tax strategies. Their preconceptions will be challenged. Since you're right and they're wrong, you should prevail.

Classy Personal Property
vs. Classy Real Estate

A dream house is, by definition, a pleasant living environment. That environment is a combination of personal property and real estate. If you save money on real estate, you'll have more to spend on personal property.

The appearance of a wall might be enhanced by hardwood molding or by an oil painting. You'll pay for the painting only once. The molding will add to your tax bill every year.

Aside from tax advantages, personal property has many other advantages over real estate. Here are a few.

• Personal property tends to be less expensive than built-in items of comparable quality, because no installation is required.

• Personal property can be bought as you can afford it, whereas built-in items usually add to the mortgage. A built-in range top, financed over 30 years, will cost at least three times the nominal price. By contrast, a cheap second-hand stove may serve your needs adequately until you can afford to pay cash for a new one.

• You can move it around to change the decor any time you want. Rearranging built-ins is a major renovation project.

• Styles and tastes change. If you get tired of a piece of furniture, you can sell it at a garage sale and buy something else. Replacing a built-in cabinet is more difficult and expensive.

• Technology changes. When I was a kid, many classy new houses had built-in sound systems with vacuum-tube AM radios and 78-r.p.m. phonographs. These were paid for with 30-year mortgages, and are probably still hidden in the tax assessments of those houses.

• If you sell your house, you have the option of selling personal property to the buyer or taking it with you. Real estate goes with the house, even if the buyer plans to tear it out and haul it to the dump the day after closing.

In short, if you have needs or desires that can be met with either real estate or personal property, personal property is almost always a better buy. Most of the items that are inherently classified as real estate can be kept at modest levels of cost and assessment, without sacrificing quality of life. The fancy stuff should be moveable.

Chapter 8

The Wet Rooms:
Kitchens and Baths

The highest-priced interior regions of most houses are the "wet" rooms: kitchens, baths, and any other rooms that have running water.

Kitchens and bathrooms also have symbolic importance for tax assessors. If the kitchen looks like a photograph in *House Beautiful*, the assessor may upgrade the cost estimates of the rest of the house.

With careful planning and thoughtful choices, it is possible to build convenient, attractive wet rooms without exorbitant costs and assessments.

Clustering

The wet rooms should be clustered as closely together as possible. That will minimize the expensive materials and labor needed for your plumbing system.

Ideally, kitchens, bathrooms, and laundry areas should be built back-to-back or, in a multistory house, stacked on top of each other. Within a wet room, fixtures should be as close together as possible without sacrificing convenience.

Clustering will reduce the lengths of supply and waste piping. It also makes possible stack venting (with lines from each fixture running to the main stack) and wet venting (with one pipe serving as the drain for one fixture and the vent for another). These techniques not only save piping, but also reduce the number of holes in your roof—in turn reducing roof maintenance and heat loss.

Clustering produces other savings as well. A cluster of fixtures can be controlled by a single shut-off valve, rather than installing a separate valve for each fixture. A larger saving may be the ability to limit the areas of walls and flooring that need protection from moisture damage. Moisture-proofing is not cheap.

If you are considering a modular house with more than one module, clustering is especially important. A wet module (one with plumbing) is much more expensive than a dry module. All plumbing should be combined into a single module if possible.

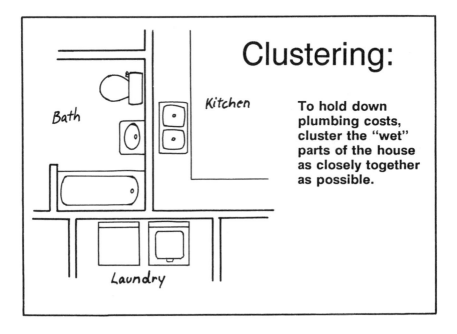

Clustering:

To hold down plumbing costs, cluster the "wet" parts of the house as closely together as possible.

Pipes and Fittings

Other plumbing savings can be achieved with economical piping and fittings. Under most codes, PB gray plastic pipe is acceptable for supply, and PVC is acceptable for waste. These materials can save huge amounts of money if you are a do-it-yourselfer who can install them yourself. They are easier to work with than copper supply pipe and cast iron waste pipe.

Many people, including me, prefer copper pipe for supply despite its higher cost. The price will depend on when you buy it, as copper prices fluctuate wildly. As for waste pipe, I've never heard a good reason to use anything more expensive than PVC.

If you use plastic pipe, be sure that the assessor knows about it. Plastic will always reduce the assessment of your plumbing system, even if the system functions just as well as one with metal pipes.

Regardless of what type of piping you use, price is a function of diameter. The smallest diameter allowed by your state or local code is usually adequate. The wider the pipe is, the more it costs. Most codes have reduced the required diameters of piping in recent years. The older rules were excessive. If your plumber chooses wider-than-necessary pipe out of habit, the extra cost will be significant and will probably not produce any benefit.

Cupboards and Counters

The typical American dream house contains huge expanses of cupboards and counters. They can add many thousands of dollars to the cost and the assessment.

One alternative is to use moveable furniture that serves the same function. The furniture can be as attractive as you want, or as you can afford. Since it's moveable, it won't add to your tax bill.

As an extreme example, a beautiful antique Dutch cupboard or hutch may be worth $10,000, while a row of veneered cabinets may be on sale at a discount lumber company for $500. The hutch, if you can afford it, will do more to make your living space attractive. When you're showing off your house to guests, they will be much more impressed by the hutch than by the cheap cabinets.

The hutch and cabinets serve the same function; they hold dishes. However, the tax assessor will list the hutch as non-taxable furniture. The cabinets, regardless of how ugly they may be, will be taxed as real estate because they are screwed to the wall. If you have beautiful cabinets that are worth $10,000, they will add that much more to your assessment.

Although I've used expensive antique furniture as an example, nontaxable furniture to hold dishes does not have to be expensive. Unfinished furniture stores often sell functional, attractive hutches and free-standing cupboard-counter units at lower prices than you'd pay for equivalent built-in items at a lumber store.

When you cook, it's handy to have sizeable horizontal surfaces to work on. A high trestle table (furniture) may be just as convenient a surface as a built-in counter (real estate).

If you're a do-it-yourselfer, or have the funds to pay a furniture builder, you might want to consider a portable island-type kitchen counter. We own two portable counters, which are just as convenient as built-in counters. They have drawers, cupboard doors, and large working surfaces on top. They're also on wheels. I make a point of pushing them to the side when the assessors come, to make it clear that they're not built in.

Shelves and Hooks

If portable furniture doesn't meet all your needs for storage of food and kitchen utensils, there are other low-cost alternatives.

Items that are used frequently may be stored conveniently on open shelves, located within reach of where you use them. Open shelves, even fancy ones, are astoundingly cheap compared to cabinets.

Moveable island: This counter is on wheels, so it's not taxed.
Photo by Alden Pellett

Pots and pans that are frequently used can be hung on the wall next to the stove. Sturdy, attractive hooks may cost 79¢ each, if you throw caution to the wind and buy fancy designer hooks. By contrast, a "cheap" cabinet to hold pots and pans costs hundreds of dollars. I've seen attractive country kitchens where pots and pans were hung on nails, which are even cheaper than hooks.

Pantries

Most people like to close doors on clutter. That's the attraction of cabinets. There is, however, a less expensive way to close doors on clutter. It's an old-fashioned feature that's due for a comeback; the pantry.

Pantries can hold huge quantities of food and utensils. In a well-arranged pantry, the foods and utensils that are used every day are within easy reach. The waffle iron you use once a month is a little farther back, but you know where it is. The spices you've been accumulating since 1968, and the slicer-dicer you ordered in a moment of weakness in 1972, are out of the way—but there if you ever decide to use them.

The advantage of a pantry is that it has only one door—rather than the 40 doors you'd need to store those things in cupboards and cabinets. By eliminating 39 doors, you can save thousands of dollars.

> *The advantage of a pantry is that it has only one door.*

In a remodeling project, it is often possible to convert a broom closet or an unused corner into a small pantry. It won't be big enough to serve the full function of a pantry, but it may eliminate the need for, say, five or ten cabinets. You'll have to find another location for the broom, however.

The Piggy Room—the Ideal Pantry

Some older houses had cold pantries. Grandma used hers to store lard and anything else that needed a cool temperature but wouldn't fit in the ice box.

The cold pantry was a good idea. It was a room with no artificial heat, so when the door was closed, stored food remained cool.

Many of the older cold pantries were not well designed. They were sometimes hard to get to, and often did not have sufficient insulation or thermal mass to provide consistent temperatures. However, if you start with the good idea and add good design, a cold pantry can be one of the most spectacular features of your dream house. It will also be cheap, and assessed at a low level.

The cold pantry in our house is called the "piggy room" because it has a picture of a pig on the door. I prefer that term, because our piggy room is so different from the cold pantry that grandma used. When you change the design of something enough, the name ought to change as well. However, I won't be insulted if you build a piggy room and call it a cold pantry.

Functions of a Piggy Room

A piggy room is located just off the kitchen—within two or three steps of where you prepare and cook food.

It contains the refrigerator, the freezer, and many shelves. The piggy room functions as a combination pantry, walk-in cooler, and storage area. If it's large enough, it can extend into a darker area that can be a combination root cellar and wine cellar.

During the colder months, the entire piggy room will remain at about the same temperature as your refrigerator. When the relatives come for Thanksgiving, you can store the turkey and fixings in the

Our piggy room door: The rustic appearance is not mandatory—you can use any insulated entry-type door.

Photo by Alden Pellett

piggy room without putting them in the refrigerator. Therefore, you can get by with a smaller refrigerator.

In the hot summer months, the piggy room remains cooler than the rest of your house (unless you have air conditioning). You probably don't keep as much lard on hand as grandma did, but anything with a marginal need to be kept cool will stay good longer in the piggy room than in the kitchen, even in August.

Aside from convenience, a piggy room saves energy. Mother Nature provides the cool temperature. Even the costs of running the refrigerator and freezer are reduced substantially, because they are in a cool room.

Piggy Room Design

The basic design of a piggy room is identical to that of a good root cellar or wine cellar.

OK, I know what you're thinking. Root cellars and wine cellars are in the basement, accessible only through trap doors or rickety stairways with great masses of cobwebs. A piggy room has to be bright, clean, and right next to the kitchen.

Ideally, the piggy room should be partially below grade. If you build your house into a hillside, you have a perfect opportunity to build the best possible piggy room. The cool earth outside the below-grade parts of the room will help to moderate the temperatures all year.

However, a very good piggy room can be built entirely above grade, if necessary. Ours is.

The exterior walls should be concrete or other masonry material to provide thermal mass. The floor should be a slab that is not

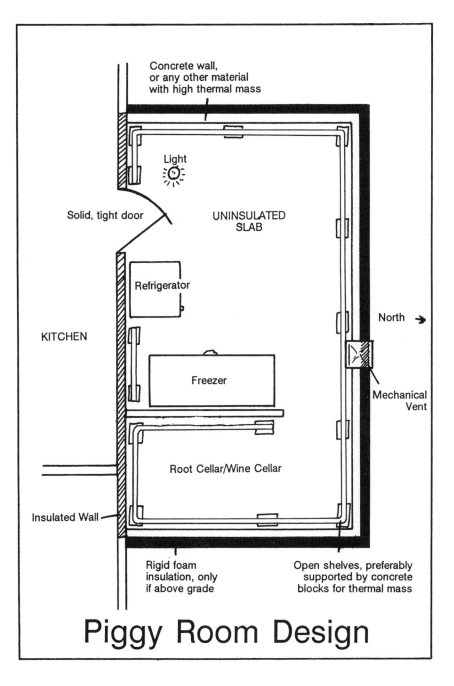

Concrete wall, or any other material with high thermal mass

Light

Solid, tight door

UNINSULATED SLAB

Refrigerator

KITCHEN

North →

Freezer

Mechanical Vent

Root Cellar/Wine Cellar

Insulated Wall

Rigid foam insulation, only if above grade

Open shelves, preferably supported by concrete blocks for thermal mass

Piggy Room Design

insulated underneath. (An earth floor would work as well, but earth is messy. A slab is classier and cleaner.)

Any parts of the exterior walls that are below grade should not be insulated. The parts of the exterior walls that are above grade should be well insulated on the outside. The wall and door separating the kitchen from the piggy room should also be well insulated, to block heat flow from the kitchen.

There should be an exterior vent that can be opened or closed easily. Close the vent in the winter and open it in the summer. In our piggy room, we use a door to the attached garage instead of a vent. That works fine, but only because we don't park cars in the garage. Cars emit fumes that should not enter into food-storage areas.

Thermal mass is important. Add as much of it as you can. In our piggy room, for example, we used concrete blocks as shelf-spacers. If you're unfamiliar with the functions of thermal mass, just tuck that suggestion into the back of your head for now. Thermal mass is discussed in detail in Chapter 9.

If you want to use the piggy room for storage of wine or root crops, make it long and narrow. You don't want to expose your wine and potatoes to bright light every time you walk into the piggy room and turn on the light. They must be kept at the dark end of the room, and should ideally be in an area that is partitioned off.

If these directions seem confusing to you, go to the library and take out a "build-it-yourself" book that covers root or wine cellars. The general principles are identical, except that a piggy room needs a more convenient location, and wine and roots are the only contents of a piggy room that need protection from light.

Bathrooms

Like kitchens, bathrooms are expensive and can have symbolic importance for assessors. Any assessor who inspects the inside of a house will spend time in the bathroom(s). If there's a beautiful bathroom off the master bedroom with designer fixtures and a whirlpool spa, dollar signs will flash before the eyes of the assessor. Those dollar signs may still be flashing when the rest of the house is assessed.

In bathrooms, there is little opportunity to substitute personal property for real estate. There are, however, a few options that may be worth considering. You could hang a medicine cabinet on the wall rather than building it in, or use a moveable bureau instead of an expensive built-in vanity to store bathroom items. You could hang a mirror from a hook rather than mounting it on the wall. Some elegant stores sell free-standing antique-reproduction toilet paper holders. They're expensive, but not taxed. Attractive towels and pretty shampoo bottles can improve the aesthetic appeal of a bathroom without adding to the tax burden.

However, the big-ticket items are toilets, sinks, bathtubs, and showers. They are almost always hooked into the plumbing system, and logically will go with the house if you sell it. Therefore, they are assessed as real estate.

In our home office, we have a portable composting toilet that qualifies as personal property. It works well and is environmentally sound. Unfortunately, guests are sometimes reluctant to use it, so their visits get cut short. Since we value visits from friends, we installed conventional toilets in our dream house.

While conventional facilities are always real estate, they can be modest real estate. Conventional new toilets, for example, range in price from about $50 (at a sale price at a discount home-supply store) to about $600. A $50 toilet works as well as a $600 toilet. It will flush whatever needs to be flushed just as efficiently. Cheap toilets tend to use less water than expensive toilets because they usually have smaller tanks. That can reduce your water bill.

The principal differences among toilets are aesthetics and price. Any assessor who inspects your bathroom will recognize the difference in price between an economy toilet and a designer toilet. The person using the facilities usually doesn't give a—well, I'm getting carried away here.

Bathroom Antiques

In our household, we have a taste for funky old fixtures that are obtainable for cheap or free. That has become a risky choice. Funky old fixtures have become fashionable. We put in an old clawfoot bathtub that we had picked up free of charge, before learning that clawfoot bathtubs have become valuable antiques. Fortunately, our assessor recognized that our particular clawfoot bathtub is not worth much.

We also installed old-fashioned faucets on the bathroom sinks. That's more than just an aesthetic preference; older faucets are more durable than most new ones. Antique faucets are chic now, and fetch a high price at salvage companies. Assessors recognize their value. We got ours free from a demolition project, and fortunately they don't match. If they matched, they would have added considerably to our assessment.

We've been lucky with the assessments of our older fixtures. If you fill your wet rooms with matching antiques, you may not be so lucky.

Half, Three-Quarter, And Full Baths

All tax assessment systems differentiate between a half bath, a three-quarter bath, and a full bath. Where the line is drawn is not always consistent. A bathroom without a tub or shower is almost always a half bath. A bathroom with a shower but no tub is usually either a half bath or a three-quarter bath. Those are literal terms in tax assessment; a half bath is assessed at half the value of a full bath of similar quality. The difference can amount to thousands of dollars.

If you need two rooms with toilets, do you also need two rooms with bathtubs? Think through your real needs, because unneeded fixtures are an unnecessary expense.

In our family, showers are more popular than baths. Therefore, one of our two bathrooms has a shower stall rather than a tub. The stall is more convenient for showers than a tub-shower combination would be. Yet it is taxed at a lower level. It's a good example of getting more for less. We're considering taking out the tub in the second bathroom. Since nobody uses it anyway, we're beginning to resent paying taxes on our "full" bath.

In a bathroom, the big extra costs occur when the fixtures and built-in decor are more expensive than they need to be. It costs nothing extra, in initial price or taxes, to arrange the fixtures in ways that make the bathroom convenient and easy to keep clean. And, as mentioned earlier, attractive moveable features can be added—colorful towels and pictures on the wall, for example—without adding to the tax burden.

Miscellaneous Wet Rooms

Many dream houses have wet rooms other than kitchens and baths. Ours, for example, has a laundry area and a darkroom.

I've read other books on affordable housing that advise people to build these functions—if they need them—into the bathroom. The logic, which is unimpeachable, is that building an extra room adds to cost.

In our family configuration, it is terribly inconvenient to fold sheets or develop photographs in the bathroom. People with bathroom needs have priority use of the space, and tend to want privacy.

Separating space is not expensive—walls are cheap if they're not fancy. In our case, we saved money by creating unfinished spaces for laundry and photo finishing. Bathrooms are expensive finished spaces, which shouldn't be wasted on activities that can take place just as well in unfinished spaces (see Chapter 10).

That principle may not hold true for all miscellaneous wet rooms. For example, some dream houses include recreation rooms that have bars with running water. If that's where you entertain your friends, it should be finished space.

In any event, other wet rooms—whether or not they are finished—should be clustered as closely as possible with kitchens and bathrooms. You'll save on plumbing, and your friends at the wet bar will appreciate the proximity.

Revival of Old Ideas

While reading parts of this chapter, you might have gotten the impression that I'm a sentimentalist who longs for a return to the good old days. Not so. However, we shouldn't automatically reject the things that our grandparents figured out.

Our grandparents used portable furniture—like hutches and Dutch cupboards—to store dishes. They had pantries, and sometimes even cold pantries. They watched their dollars, and designed features that minimized property taxes as well as mortgage payments.

It's true that most of our grandparents did not have convenient kitchens. Grandma spent about eight hours a day preparing three good meals. If she hadn't spent much time cooking, grandma might have been able to write the Great American Novel. Very few people today want to spend eight hours a day cooking food for the family. We've rebelled against the old ways for good reasons.

Yet the rebellion has not always been a rational one. The pantry, the cold pantry, the open shelves, the hutches, and the hooks were good features—even if they weren't always well designed. The rational approach would have been to improve the designs and the layouts, and keep the good, time-tested features. Instead, modern designers have insisted on big expanses of expensive built-ins. Much of the "solution" has nothing to do with the problem.

Similar arbitrary changes occurred in bathrooms. In the houses where my generation grew up, the water heaters often lacked adequate capacity. That was inconvenient. We expressed our anger by demanding built-in medicine chests and designer toilets.

The bathroom door we grew up with was often next to the dining table, so embarrassing noises were overheard by people who were trying to eat dinner. All we needed to do was to move the door, but instead we moved the bathroom, tripling the fee we paid to plumbers. In our desire to overcome real problems, we insisted on changes that cost more money, with no increase in comfort or convenience.

I have no desire to return to the old days. But at a time when housing costs are getting out of control, let's take another look at some of the features that have been thrown out in recent decades. Some of them are worth retrieving and repairing.

Wet Room Designs

If cooking is a major priority in your household, spend some time designing the kitchen to achieve maximum convenience. Other authors have explored these issues in detail, so I won't try to replicate their work. One book that will provide useful insights is Sam Clark's *The Motion-Minded Kitchen* (Houghton Mifflin, $9.95, 1985). With some forethought, it's possible to have a convenient, aesthetically pleasing kitchen that is not an expensive, high-tax, plastic-laminate jungle.

Bathroom design is far less complex than kitchen design. There aren't many variations in the things we do in bathrooms. The toilet paper should be within reach of the toilet. The towels should be within reach of the shower or tub. The floor and wall materials should be water-tight. If people who will use the bathroom need high fixtures and wall-grips, then install high fixtures and grips. You don't need a degree in architecture to design a bathroom. Just figure out what you need, and include it in the design.

A convenient layout doesn't have to add anything to the cost or to the tax assessment. It costs no more to put features in convenient locations than it does to put them in inconvenient locations. All you need is a little extra thought and reflection during the planning stages.

Chapter 9

Cheap Heating,
Cheap Cooling

Heating and cooling are issues that arouse nearly as many emotions as kitchens and baths when dream houses are discussed. Many people have vivid memories of winters (or summers) of discontent.

I once lived in a drafty house heated with a single, inefficient wood stove. We competed to see who could stay in bed the longest on cold mornings, because the first one up had to build a fire and thaw the water pipes.

A friend once told me about a period when his family had to resort to burning furniture. He had particularly vivid recollections of a blizzardy "three-chair night."

The horror stories about lack of air conditioning in more southern climates are just as bad.

Comfort and convenience are important objectives. There is a popular notion that they are inherently expensive. Fortunately, there are ways to cut energy costs without returning to three-chair nights.

Avoiding Central Systems

Central systems are dinosaurs. You don't need them. I know that I'm treading into controversial territory by saying that. Central heating and cooling have joined baseball and apple pie on the list of things that Americans cherish. Nevertheless, I hope you will bear with me for the next few pages. If you like to do things before they become trendy, now is the time to choose a non-central system.

There was a time when central systems were necessary to assure comfort. That has changed. Houses have become tighter, better insulated, and more open in design. Meanwhile, individual heating units have become safer and more efficient. Comfort and convenience are no longer dependent upon central systems.

A central system is one of the most expensive components of a house. It adds substantially to the mortgage bill. Tax assessors recognize how much it costs, so the more expensive a system you have, the more it will add to your tax bill.

In the cold climate where I live, it's not uncommon to hear the owner of an expensive new house boast that he or she spent "only" $1,500 on heating bills last winter. That figure represents only the fuel costs. The mortgage payments and property taxes paid on the heating system may add up to another $1,500 per year. For most of us, $3,000 a year is a substantial amount of money. In my 2,000-square-foot dream house, that's the ten-year cost of heating, not the one-year cost.

In warmer regions, heating fuel costs tend to be lower, but the costs of installation and property taxation are not sensitive to climate. Also, the lower costs for heating fuel are usually offset by higher cooling costs.

Big savings can be achieved by not installing a central system. To assure comfort, the house must be designed and built to accommodate a non-central system. Keep in mind that heating and cooling are provided by systems, even when they aren't centralized.

Basic Design Issues

Six general principles should be observed in designing a house with a non-central system.

1. The house should be well insulated.

2. It should be tight.

3. It should contain as much thermal mass as possible.

4. It should be designed in a way that allows heat to circulate to any part of the living space.

5. The design should allow venting of hot air when it's not wanted, and air exchanges for healthy living.

6. Solar gain should be taken advantage of during winter and avoided during summer.

How Heat Works

You don't have to be an architect or an engineer to design a house that will stay comfortable without a central system. The concepts are fairly simple.

Heat always tries to average itself out. When you pour cool cream into hot coffee, the cream gets warmer and the coffee gets cooler. If you sit on a cold toilet, it will draw heat from your body and eventually warm up, while you cool off. Similarly, the cold air in one room will try to average out with the warm air in the next room.

Heat spreads in three ways: conduction, convection, and radiation.

Conduction occurs when two things with different temperatures touch each other. When you fry an egg, the heat conducts from the burner to the frying pan to the egg.

Convection is a method of transferring conduction from one place to another. A liquid or gas touches something that's hot, then goes somewhere else and warms up whatever it touches. In a typical central heating system, air or water is heated, then ducted or piped somewhere else, where the heat is transferred to the air in the room, which in turn warms the occupants.

Radiation occurs when heat travels directly from one thing to another, even though there may be some distance between the two. When you're warmed by the sun, the process is radiation.

Conduction can be a convenient means of personal heating or cooling in a few limited situations. Examples would be warming a brick on the wood stove and putting it under your bed covers, or cooling off with a bag of ice on your head.

Radiation is nearly as efficient as conduction. If you sit next to a radiant heater such as a wood stove, the heat will radiate to your body without any need to warm the air in between.

Central systems rely mostly on convection. They warm the air, rather than radiating heat directly to the occupants of the room. Even a hot-water "radiator" relies more on convection than radiation.

Any heating system makes some use of all three methods of heat transfer. Convection starts with conduction. Any convection system will eventually warm up the walls, which will eventually radiate heat back to the occupants of the room. A radiant system will eventually warm the air. (A thermometer in direct sunlight is not accurate because it may record temperatures twice as high as the air temperature. However, if the sun shines long enough, the temperature recorded on a shaded thermometer will rise.)

A system that emphasizes radiation is more efficient, and arguably more comfortable, than one that emphasizes convection. This is because a comfortable temperature can be achieved without warming all the air in a room.

Pipes and ducts emphasize convection. The most practical alternative system, which emphasizes radiation, is called *thermal mass*.

Thermal Mass

Thermal mass works as a heat bank. It sucks up heat, preferably from a radiant source, and stores it for later, gradual release. To some extent, any building material will provide thermal mass. However, dense materials, such as concrete, bricks, tile, and plaster, will suck up much more radiant heat than will lighter materials such as plastic or wood.

An example of a house with large amounts of thermal mass would be one with brick walls and a flagstone floor. To be effective for distributing heat, the bricks would have to be insulated on the outside, and the flagstones would have to be insulated underneath. Without insulation, thermal mass would suck heat from the inside and transfer it outside.

To the extent possible, thermal mass should be directly exposed to a heat source. That source doesn't have to be constant. A slab exposed to south-facing windows or a masonry wall near a wood stove make efficient use of thermal mass.

> *In a house that is high in thermal mass, comfort depends more on the temperature of the thermal mass than on the temperature of the air.*

When heat isn't being absorbed, it is released. The heat can be released by conduction to the cooler parts of the wall or slab. It can be released by radiation to other materials with high thermal mass, or to the occupants of the room. It will eventually warm the air as well.

In a house that is high in thermal mass, the comfort level depends more on the temperature of the thermal mass than on the temperature of the air. If the room smokes up because you burned the toast, you can open the windows and clear the air without putting on your winter jacket or wasting a lot of heating fuel. Once you close the windows, the house will feel warm again.

Simplifying Science

I need to pause a moment to add a caveat to the discussions of heat transfer above and below.

If my seventh-grade science teacher, Mr. Saterlie, were reading this chapter, he'd find some technical inaccuracies. For example, he would point out that thermal mass cannot radiate heat to a human body unless the thermal mass is warmer than 98.6 degrees. Comfort depends on heat transfer away from the body. We're too warm if it doesn't transfer fast enough, and too cold if it transfers too fast.

Therefore, when I talk about a concrete wall sucking up heat and releasing it to the inhabitants of the room, that's not exactly the way it happens. The thermal mass really just sucks up enough heat

Polishing a slab: A worker puts the finishing touches on a low-cost, low-tax floor that is high in thermal mass.

to balance the radiant heat flow from the human body at a comfortable level. However, without an occasional over-simplification, we'd digress at length into issues that are more appropriate to science texts than to a book on affordable housing.

Thermal Mass and Erratic Heat Sources

The benefits of thermal mass are most dramatic with a radiant, erratic heat source such as a wood stove or sunshine. When excess heat is available, it is absorbed, so you won't get too hot. The heat is released later when you want it.

Thermal mass makes heating with wood convenient, because you don't have to fuss with the stove to keep it at a constant temperature. A short, hot fire has the same effect as a long, slow fire. We heat our house with wrapping paper on Christmas day, and with the Christmas tree on New Year's day. (Actually, the Christmas tradition of burning wrapping paper was discontinued last year because of toxic chemicals in some of the paper.)

Every house has some erratic heat sources. Examples include the heat from cooking, lighting, body heat, popping toast, running the dishwasher, blow-drying hair, and venting the clothes dryer indoors. In most houses, these heat sources will not contribute to the comfort level of the occupants. In a house with lots of thermal mass, they will.

Thermal Mass as a Central System

From a property tax standpoint, no assessment manual I know of considers thermal mass to be a central heating system. If you don't have pipes or ducts running all over the house, you can expect that thousands of dollars will be knocked off your assessment.

Yet properly used, thermal mass can provide as much comfort as any central system at a much lower cost. This is true regardless of the heat source you choose.

Suppose you have a gas wall furnace. Without substantial thermal mass, the heat from the wall furnace might be adequate but not very comfortable. You might feel too hot when you stand in front of the heater and too cold when you're in another room. You might feel too hot when the heater snaps on and too cold when it snaps off. By adding thermal mass, you can make the same gas heat even and consistent. Although the wall furnace is a convector, the thermal mass would absorb some of the heat and release it through radiation.

For the same reason, thermal mass would also make a central hot-air system more comfortable, but the most cost-effective way to use thermal mass is to eliminate the need for costly pipes and ducts.

Thermal Mass and Solar Gain

Most books and articles on energy efficiency mention thermal mass only as a heat bank for solar gain, even though it serves the same function with any heat source.

There are several important specific issues to address if solar gain is all or part of your heating plan.

The winter sun must shine directly onto a sizeable amount of thermal mass. To absorb the sun rays, the thermal mass should ideally be dark in color and dull in texture. This is more important for solar heat than for other types of heat. A glossy white concrete wall, for example, may provide useful thermal mass when you heat with a wood stove, but not for storage of solar gain. (A darker, less glossy wall will work better with the wood heat too, but the difference is less pronounced.)

A high thermal mass floor, such as an insulated dyed slab, will store solar gain. Dye it charcoal gray or brick red, and don't give it a waxy sheen. Another possibility is a concrete or brick interior wall, within reach of the rays of the winter sun. The darker the color, and the less shiny the surface, the better service it will provide.

To maximize solar gain, the best design is a long, narrow house with many windows on the south-facing wall. The rays from the low winter sun should strike directly as much thermal mass as possible. To some extent, that solar gain will conduct or radiate to other thermal mass in the house.

Solar Glazing

Some of the earlier solar houses had slanted or overhead glass. This is less common now, but is sometimes seen on new sun-room additions. It is usually a huge mistake, for the following reasons:

1. Heat rises. Therefore, when the sun goes down, it will escape even more quickly through a slanted or overhead pane of glass than through a vertical window. Insulated drapes are much easier to install, open, and close on vertical windows than on overhead glass.

2. Slanted or overhead glass often leaks around the edges. It's also vulnerable to hailstones. (For that reason, much of the overhead "glass" produced today is actually plastic.) Maintaining it, to prevent leaks and structural damage, can cause headaches.

3. Slanted or overhead glass will provide more heat in the summer, when you don't want it, than in the winter, when you do

105

want it. The sun is much higher in the summer than in the winter. With vertical windows, the sunshine will pour in during the winter, but not in summer.

4. For some reason, despite all the problems, tax assessors consider overhead glass to be a classy feature. For the purposes of taxation, it adds significant "value" to a house.

Double-glazed windows are usually the best option for solar gain. Triple glazing or high-tech glass with low-emissivity coatings will insulate better, but should be reserved (if you want to spend the extra money) for non-south-facing windows. Ordinary double-glazed windows let in more sunshine.

Insulated curtains are essential. Otherwise, all the heat you gained during the day will radiate back out of the house as soon as the sun goes down. A passive solar system is an owner-active system. It works only if you open the curtains when the sun is shining and close them the rest of the time.

Passive solar principles can and should be considered in any house design. For example, in any house you'll lose less heat through south-facing windows than through north-facing windows. However, if passive solar gain is a significant part of your heating plan, put in the extra effort to make it function well.

Water as Thermal Mass

Different materials absorb and release heat at different rates. Even air will hold heat temporarily before releasing it to you. However, it happens so quickly that you need a constant heat source to keep the air warm.

Water holds heat longer than air does. Some of the early solar houses of the '60s had barrels of water to hold the solar heat after the sun went down. Although the water warmed up quickly, unfortunately it also released heat quickly. Therefore, that system didn't do much to keep a house warm overnight, or through a cloudy winter week. The barrels of water also took up much expensive, finished, interior space.

A hot-water central heating system relies on the same principle as the barrels of water. Warm water releases its heat more gradually than warm air does. This moderates the swings of temperature between too-hot and too-cool. However, the heat source still must be virtually constant.

Masonry works more slowly. It takes its time sucking up and releasing heat. Therefore, it minimizes temperature swings more effectively than water does.

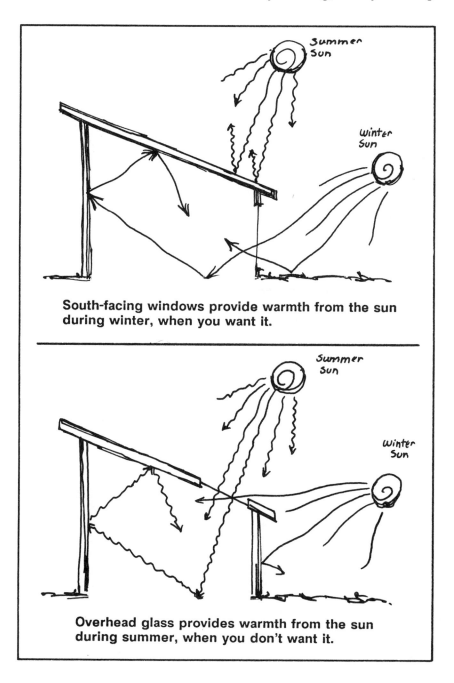

South-facing windows provide warmth from the sun during winter, when you want it.

Overhead glass provides warmth from the sun during summer, when you don't want it.

Miscellaneous Forms of Thermal Mass

The first floor of our house has a dyed and polished slab, concrete walls, and many south-facing windows. It's finished to resemble a conventional house, but has a lot of hidden thermal mass, extensively insulated on the outside.

That's a nearly ideal configuration, but I haven't been able to replicate it in the houses I've renovated. It would be silly to tear down good stud walls and hardwood floors and replace them with concrete.

Even with new construction, southern exposure is not always possible, and not everybody likes concrete floors. Thermal mass comes in many forms. The more you can add—considering your tastes and what you are working with—the better.

Drywall and plaster provide thermal mass. Five-eighth-inch drywall will provide more thermal mass than half-inch drywall. If you have potted plants, the damp soil in them will provide thermal mass. You can add to that by using clay pots instead of plastic pots.

Wood is not a good thermal mass material, but if you have enough of it—for example big, heavy posts and beams—it will help.

Ceramic tile in the bathroom provides thermal mass, but will also add to your tax burden unless it's really ugly. The same is true of slate, tile, and flagstone floors. I sometimes use quarry tile to finish the tops of tables and other furniture; it's not expensive, but is taxed at a high level if attached to the house. (I've also used it on countertops, as the tax assessment is no higher than for plastic laminates, which are less sturdy and provide no thermal mass.) If you're at a tag sale and see a marble slab that would make a neat bread board, get it.

Bookshelves built with decorative bricks or cinder blocks add thermal mass. So do coffee tables made with slices of petrified wood. (Thermal mass does not discriminate according to taste or environmental awareness.) Pottery, stoneware, and china dishes will add thermal mass, but plastic dishes won't. Among the things that your kids buy, marbles and china dolls will add thermal mass, but Barbie dolls and video games won't. I could go on; I love word processors, but unfortunately disks provide far less thermal mass than some of the older technologies, like stone tablets.

Some heating units have their own built-in thermal mass. The best examples are Russian fireplaces, which are sometimes called Scandinavian masonry heaters. They contain massive masonry work that efficiently absorbs the heat from a short, hot fire. They were developed in response to firewood shortages in northern and eastern Europe 500 years ago, and are still unsurpassed for energy efficiency. Unfortunately, the cost of masonry work has risen dramatically in the last 500 years, and is now taxed at a high level.

A more affordable option may be a wood stove clad in soapstone. These are expensive when new, but used models are sometimes obtainable at affordable prices. Our home office has very little thermal mass in its structure, so we bought a second-hand soapstone stove for $200. It has greatly increased the comfort level, and reduced the time we have had to spend fussing with the stove to keep it at an even temperature. The date of publication of this book would have been delayed by two months if I hadn't had the soapstone stove.

Thermal Mass and Cooling

Even though I live in a colder climate, my first draft of this chapter occurred in the midst of an extraordinary hot spell. We went through two weeks of daily temperatures that reached at least 95 degrees.

Our house got warmer than I'm accustomed to, despite its thermal mass. The high-low thermometer says it got as high as 80 degrees. But that's still a lot cooler than the outside air, and we have no air conditioning.

During hot periods, the hot air that comes into the house during the day is absorbed by the thermal mass and/or vented through high windows. At night, when the air cools, the venting continues and the thermal mass cools. In the summer, thermal mass can suck heat away from your body as effectively as it can keep you warm in the winter.

We would have designed our house differently if we lived in a hot climate. We probably wouldn't have put in as many south-facing windows, and probably wouldn't have insulated under the slab. Maybe we would have put in a basement, with no insulation below grade. The earth is cooler than air on hot days, so if cooling were the primary consideration, it would be foolish to place insulation between the house and the earth.

Yet regardless of where you live, thermal mass will help you keep warmer on cold days and cooler on hot days. I've read books and articles that go through detailed calculations to determine the "optimum" thermal mass for a given structure at a given latitude. That may be a fun exercise for

> *There's no such thing as a house with too much thermal mass.*

mathematicians and engineers, but it's not necessary for a person designing a dream house. The rule is simple: the more thermal mass you have, the more comfortable your house will be. There's no such thing as a house with too much thermal mass.

Unwanted Radiant Cooling

Window coverings were mentioned in the context of solar design, but must be a part of any plan to hold down heating costs. Radiation through uncovered windows is a terrible way to lose heat from the house in the winter.

If you don't believe me, stand in front of a large closed window on a cold night. The air in the room may be at a comfortable temperature, but the side of your body facing the window will be cold. That's not because you forgot to caulk the window. No matter how tight it is, the window will pull radiant heat from your body at a rapid rate. You are the radiant heat source.

When you lose heat through infiltration, you get the benefit of fresh air. There is no benefit at all from radiant heat loss.

If you cover the window with anything that is light in color—a sheet or a newspaper for example—the radiant heat loss will be reduced dramatically. Something shiny, like aluminum foil, will work even better. Even if the material has no R-value at all, it will contribute dramatically to the energy efficiency of the house.

Insulated curtains are better, because they add R-value to reduce heat loss from conduction. However, don't leave the windows uncovered on cold nights just because you are still saving up to buy expensive insulated curtains one of these years. Cover them with something, anything, to retard the radiant heat loss.

Heat Flow

Hot air rises. Within a house, hot air hangs around the ceiling for a while and eventually cools a little. It then sinks, and is replaced by hotter air.

That simple principle assures a predictable pattern of air circulation within the house. Another predictable pattern is the one mentioned earlier in this chapter: hot and cold air try to find each other, to average each other out, regardless of elevation.

In any event, the circulation that occurs from natural patterns can allow a single heat source to heat an entire building.

If you have a heat source in the basement, the heat will rise, cling to the ceiling, cool a bit, and fall as it's replaced by hotter air. During that cycle, a significant amount of the heat will conduct through the ceiling, walk up the stairway, or both. That will start a

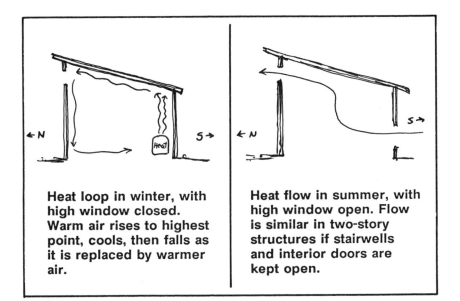

Heat loop in winter, with high window closed. Warm air rises to highest point, cools, then falls as it is replaced by warmer air.

Heat flow in summer, with high window open. Flow is similar in two-story structures if stairwells and interior doors are kept open.

similar pattern in the living space above the basement. If you have a second and third story, similar loops of rising hot air and falling cool air will occur on those levels of the house.

A sloped ceiling on the highest story of the house can expedite the flow of heat through the loop, if the high part of the ceiling is on the north side. The air will cool more quickly there, even in a well-insulated house, and fall to be replaced by warmer air.

If you have a room that is off to the side somewhere, not within the theoretical heating loop, the heat will try to find it anyway. If it has a hard time, there are ways to encourage it. For example, you could leave the door to the room open on cold days, or install a quiet little blower fan in the wall.

Heat will circulate best if you have an open design. Closed doors make circulation more difficult. In rooms where doors tend to remain closed, it's a good idea to increase the gap between the door and the floor. If the gap is an inch and a half, some circulation is possible with no intrusion on privacy. If the air flow is still not sufficient, a vent or fan can be installed in the wall later.

Venting Unwanted Heat

During the cooling season, you will want to break the heating loop. You don't want the heat to circulate back down to the living area; you want it to leave. The cheapest and easiest way to do that is with high windows. When high windows are above a connected roof, they are called clerestory windows (although the word is misspelled as "clearstory" about 80 percent of the time).

Since heat rises, high windows will allow the hottest air to exit. To push the hot air out, you will need a source of cooler air from an open window or door at a lower level.

Opening skylights can serve the same function as clerestory windows. When you open them, heat whooshes out. However, skylights have all the drawbacks that were listed above for slanted and overhead glass. Skylights are sometimes practical to let natural light into a house where a window is not appropriate. In most instances, though, a high window is a better choice for venting of air.

Another option for venting air is a whole-house fan. It works like a bathroom exhaust fan, but is bigger and ducts air from several high points in the house. A whole-house fan is more expensive than a high window, but cheaper than central air conditioning. Unfortunately, whole-house fans tend to interrupt the ceiling insulation. As a rule, they make houses easier to cool in summer, but harder to heat in winter. If they interrupt the vapor barrier, they may also cause structural damage. If you have a relatively open design, a fan blowing air out of a high window will serve the same function, at far lower cost, with none of the drawbacks.

Cooling Units

If your need for air conditioning is marginal, you can avoid it with thermal mass and high windows. However, if the outside air stays at 105 degrees for a few weeks, you may want more cooling power. Incoming air at that temperature will not feel comfortable, even if it is constantly moving and hotter air is constantly expelled. If I lived in a climate like that, I'd want air conditioning in my dream house.

Window air conditioners are always cheaper than central systems. What rooms do you have to spend time in during unbearably hot periods? Installing window units in those rooms will be less expensive than installing a central system. Also, the operating costs will be significantly lower, because you will cool only the rooms you are in at any particular time.

The property tax assessor will almost always consider a window air conditioner to be "personal property." It will not be taxed (although the 220-volt outlet may add to the valuation of the electrical system). A central system is always listed as taxable real estate.

If you have a lot of thermal mass, your air conditioner(s) will work less hard. If your electrical rates are lower during off-peak hours, you can save money by cooling the thermal mass during those times and turning off the air conditioning during the expensive peak periods.

Multiple Heating Units

Depending on your lifestyle and the design of your house, you may want more than one heater—even if one is sufficient to heat the whole house.

Most of us don't need to have every room at the same temperature 24 hours a day. If one room is used only for ping-pong or weight-lifting, we don't want it to be as warm as the room where we sit quietly to read. If the master bedroom is used only at night, it doesn't have to be warm all day. In a well-designed house, the ping-pong room would be off to the side of the major heating loop of the house, while the reading room would be well within the loop.

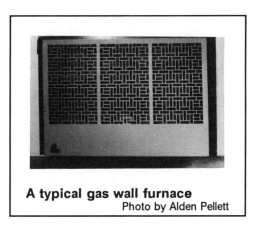

A typical gas wall furnace
Photo by Alden Pellett

However, if part of the house needs to be warm during certain times of the day or night, and another region needs warmth at other times, a second heater is worthwhile.

For perspective on this issue, let's pause for a moment and consider the history of central heating.

In older times, houses were drafty and poorly insulated. The only way to heat was to build a fire in an inefficient stove or fireplace. Most of the heat went up the chimney. Therefore, to get heat into every room of the house, people had to build a fire in every room of the house and constantly tend to the fires. If they wanted comfort throughout the house, they didn't have time for anything else. Central heat was a big advance. It allowed people to heat every room with only one fire. They had time to write books, earn money, paint pictures, and gather firewood. (I'm making some of this up, but history, like science, sometimes has to be simplified for illustration of larger truths.)

113

Modern construction norms and modern heaters have made it possible to heat a whole house with one fire. This eliminated the *raison d'être* of central heat. In the meantime, however, central heat had become a big industry. To justify its continued existence, the industry came up with something new—zoned heating. This allows setting the heat in different rooms at different temperatures. Zoned systems provide the advantages of the old "fire-in-every-room" system without the inconvenience.

Yet if zoning is important, it's more practical to put individual heaters in different parts of the house.

Most modern heaters, such as wall furnaces, are controlled by thermostats that are as convenient as the thermostats for zoned central heating. Additional "fires" are more energy efficient than pipes and ducts. It is easier to pipe fuel to a separate heater than to pipe heat to a separate location.

Another advantage of separate heaters is that you can add them in increments. Start out with one—which should heat the house adequately. Then add a second, or even a third heater if, through actual experience, you decide they would be useful. By contrast, a multizoned central system is installed all at once, and you pay for it even if you decide later that it exceeds your practical needs.

There are other reasons for choosing multiple heating units. If your cheapest heat source is a wood or coal stove, you may want a wall furnace that will snap on whenever you get tired of stoking the stove. If the house is empty during the day, keeping the wall furnace on at a low level will keep the water pipes from freezing when the stove isn't fed. If you don't mind feeding the stove during the day, the stove might be in the living-room area and the wall furnace nearer to the bedrooms.

Healthy Infiltration

As houses have been tightened up for the sake of energy efficiency, indoor pollution has become a significant health hazard. Dangerous substances like formaldehyde and radon weren't much of a concern in leaky old houses, but can rise to toxic levels in tight new houses.

It's worthwhile to try to avoid known carcinogens and allergens when you build a house. In our house, for example, we avoided use of any plywood or particleboard in the interior, used no carpeting, and tested the concrete aggregate and water for radon. Unfortunately, it's almost impossible to avoid bringing toxins into a house. Formaldehyde has probably come into our house via the stereo speaker cases and the veneer on my desk, not to mention the last batch of sports jackets I had dry cleaned.

Scientists are finding or suspecting new dangers all the time. Potential toxins exist in virtually all forms of insulation, paint, varnish, caulk, and sealers. They exist in cleaning compounds, cooking fumes, art supplies, personal copiers, computer printers, fax machines, and flakes of skin. Future scientists are sure to find dangers that are not even suspected today.

Reducing air changes makes a house easier to heat, but your family's health is more important. You need fresh air for protection from things that we know about, things we suspect, and things that may not be discovered until a hundred years after they've killed you.

How can you get sufficient air exchange while keeping your heating system efficient? The high-tech answer is an expensive device called an *air-to-air heat exchanger.* It keeps air circulating in and out of the house at a preset rate, and transfers heat from the outgoing air to the incoming air. That's a great idea, and sometimes it works well.

I prefer low-tech methods of exchanging air. I crack open a window periodically, and restrain the urge to nag at the kids when they hold the door open on cold winter days. I don't worry too much about the damaged weatherstripping on the entry door, or the windows that aren't quite as tight as they were advertised to be.

No matter how tight your house may be, it will lose some heat on cold days. For the sake of health, to the extent possible the heat loss should be through infiltration, rather than conduction or radiation.

The level of comfort in our house depends more on the temperature of the thermal mass than the temperature of the air. Therefore, we can allow infiltration of healthy outside air without sacrificing comfort or wasting huge quantities of fuel. That's one of the biggest advantages of thermal mass over other heating systems—it remains efficient during healthy air changes.

Combustion Air

Air changes aside, it's important to provide intake air for any source of combustion. A wood stove, a gas cook stove, a gas or kerosene wall furnace, a gas water heater, or an oil furnace will need combustion air drawn from the outside. Otherwise, in a tight house, the combustion will consume oxygen that you need for healthy living.

One horror story may be worth relating here. On the first Thanksgiving day after we built our house, I learned that I could not run the wood cook stove and the heating stove at the same time. It turned out that each stove had been drawing replacement air down through the chimney of the other stove. When both stoves

115

were lit, there was not sufficient combustion air for either. I hate to think about the filthy air that passed down the chimneys and through our house before we discovered this design flaw.

Modern gas and kerosene wall furnaces draw their combustion air from the outside, then vent the exhaust outside. That's an ideal system, as long as you don't have an opening window (or the intake for an air-to-air heat exchanger) located above the exhaust. Many other modern combustion devices, including some wood stoves, similarly draw their combustion air from the outside. If that's not the case with your heat sources or appliances, make sure that you crack open a nearby window or have some other means to supply combustion air.

Combustion air is needed only when something is combusting. If the air for a furnace in the basement comes through a leaky second-story window, it will cool the whole house en route. The source of air should be as near as possible to the combustion, and should be shut off when the combustion stops. One option is a small mechanical vent near the appliance, opened only when the appliance is operating.

Tight Construction

In the old days, houses were ventilated by a system of random leaks. The attraction of that system is that it's easy. Just don't do anything to tighten up the structure, and random leaks will provide all the air changes you need for healthy living.

Unfortunately, that system also made houses feel drafty and uncomfortable, while burning excessive quantities of heating fuel. A house is much more energy efficient if you can control the air intake.

You'll need more air changes when your house is full of guests who are playing the piano with their feet than when you're sitting home alone reading a book. If everybody goes to work or school during the day, no air changes are needed during that time. The same is true if you vacate the house for a week to visit grandma. If ventilation depends on random air leaks, you'll waste a lot of heating fuel during times when few or no air changes are needed.

Tight construction, with good vapor barriers, also helps to prevent moisture condensation in the walls or attic, which can cause structural damage and reduce the effectiveness of the insulation.

Some quality builders have an almost fanatical dedication to tightness. They invest extra days of labor on specialized construction techniques, installation of expensive gaskets, and sealing the edges of the vapor barrier with an unpleasant compound that is commonly called "black death."

Most builders take a more moderate approach. If they have any concern for quality, they install vapor barriers, and give extra attention to parts of the house that are particularly vulnerable to moisture damage. For example, a vent pipe that goes through the roof must be tightly sealed.

Those steps represent prudent common sense. You do need air exchanges, but they should be controlled rather than random. Tight construction can add to the quality of life. As an added benefit, it's hidden, so it contributes little if anything to your tax assessment.

Insulating Walls

If you have a concrete (or any type of masonry) wall for thermal mass, the most common method of insulating the outside is with thick rigid foam. Usually, simple stressed-skin panels are used: foam with particle board laminated to the outside so that siding can be nailed on.

If you have a timber-frame house, you'll want stressed-skin panels with drywall laminated inside. With a structural stressed-skin house, the foam is sandwiched between two layers of particle-board. The panel *is* the exterior wall, and the insulation is continuous.

In a house built with stud walls, the usual practice is to place fiberglass insulation between the studs. Many newer houses are built with 2x6 studs, which allow thicker fiberglass than 2x4's. This, by itself, is not an efficient insulation technique. The wooden studs are not good insulators. They act as thermal bridges; heat blocked by the insulation travels through the studs. In a typical wood-frame house, the fiberglass insulation may cover only about 80 percent of the exterior wall area. In such a house, the real R-value is nowhere near the R-value announced by the insulation manufacturer.

I should repeat that for emphasis, because you'll read in other books that 2x6 studs with six-inch insulation provide the best *nominal* R-value for the dollar. That's true. But nominal R-value doesn't keep you warm. *Effective* R-value keeps you warm. If your insulation is interrupted by studs (or anything else), the effective R-value is nowhere near the nominal R-value.

The easiest and cheapest way to rectify the problem of thermal bridging is to supplement the fiberglass with a layer of rigid foam. The foam covers the studs and the cavities, adding to the insulation and substantially reducing thermal bridging. The rigid foam can be placed either inside or outside the stud wall. Outside is generally more convenient, and therefore more common.

Some experts advise against using rigid foam outside of a stud wall. The foam forms a vapor barrier, and one of the basic principles of construction is that the vapor barrier should be inside, not outside.

Those who defend rigid foam on the outside of a stud wall say it is such an effective insulator that temperatures within the wall cavity don't reach the dew point. Therefore, they say, condensation doesn't occur. They also note that most houses are sheathed with plywood or particleboard, which forms a vapor barrier anyway, so the foam doesn't make the situation any worse. If you raise the subject in a room full of carpenters, you can expect heated arguments. I've put rigid foam on the outside for some projects and on the inside for others, without any apparent problems either way. But I'd leave that judgment to you and the experts you're consulting.

The most economical application of rigid form is when it is used *instead* of plywood or particleboard sheathing. The foam costs no more than the other sheathing materials, so you get more insulation for the same amount of money. The rigid foam does not provide bracing for the walls, so diagonal braces are needed. Structural bracing, however, is cheap compared to the cost of structural sheathing.

Insulating Ceilings

The most cost-effective way to insulate a ceiling is to pile loose-fill insulation as high as possible in the attic area.

If you have a cathedral ceiling, you won't have an attic area. The most common technique to insulate a cathedral ceiling is to stuff fiberglass between the rafters or trusses, then apply stressed-skin on top. This technique also ignites heated discussions among people in the building trades about vapor barriers, dew points, ventilation, etc. The controversy is even more complex for roofs than for walls. Asphalt roofing doesn't last as long if there is no ventilation underneath. If you're concerned about that, some of the stressed-skin manufacturers now offer panels with grooves to allow air flow between the foam and the sheathing. As an alternative, you might want to consider metal roofing, which is self-ventilating.

The R-value of the ceiling insulation should be greater than the R-value of the walls. If not, the heat blocked in by the wall insulation will simply travel to the ceiling and escape there.

Adding Extra Insulation

There are diminishing returns from adding more insulation. R-11 insulation will save huge amounts on your heating bill compared to no insulation at all. Upgrading it to R-22 won't save twice as much. R-66 won't save three times as much as R-22.

However, insulation is relatively cheap. Whatever you add—unless you carry it to an extreme—will pay for itself quickly. Our walls are about R-45 and our ceiling is about R-80. If we had less, our heating bills would be higher and our house would be less comfortable.

Extra insulation adds little or nothing to assessments, according to most (not all) of the tax officials I surveyed in every state. With rare exceptions, you can save on energy bills without paying extra in property taxes.

At the risk of stating the obvious, insulation helps to keep a house cool on hot summer days as much as it helps to keep a house warm on cold winter days. The cost-benefit ratio for upgrading of insulation may vary somewhat between hot and cold climates. Yet regardless of where you live, it's worthwhile to err on the side of more, rather than less, insulation.

Radiant Barriers for Heating and Cooling

Earlier in this chapter, I emphasized the need for window coverings to retard unwanted heat loss through windows on cold nights. However, some radiant heat travels through even a well-insulated ceiling or wall. This adds to the heating load in winter and the cooling load in summer.

At the time I'm writing this, the wizards of energy efficiency are battling among themselves on the subject of radiant barriers to block this unwanted heat loss or gain. They all agree that radiant barriers are good, but argue about how good they are and where they should be installed.

Radiant barriers are layers of shiny foil installed next to an air space to reduce the radiant flow of heat into or out of a house. The foil is sometimes used by itself, but is more often glued to cardboard, fiberglass, or rigid foam insulation.

The data are inconclusive on the extent of savings, but a properly-installed radiant barrier will reduce your cooling and heating load.

This is not a new idea. Insulation faced with foil has been available for as long as I can remember. However, the idea has attracted renewed attention among energy efficiency experts in recent years.

The savings seem to be most dramatic in southern regions,

when a radiant barrier is placed in the attic space to reduce the cooling load. The data on radiant barriers in walls, and on the extent of heat savings in northern states, are less conclusive.

I'd be wary of any dramatic claims made by a manufacturer. More testing is needed before you can accurately predict energy savings. However, radiant barriers are not expensive—and there is no doubt that if properly installed, they will reduce your heating and cooling load.

The barrier *must* face an air space. Therefore, if you install foil-faced rigid foam inside the studs and rafters, *don't screw drywall directly to it*. Nail wooden straps over the foil, and screw the drywall to the straps.

This system has some additional potential advantages. The straps may provide a firmer backing for the drywall, so there will be less danger of cracked seams. The space between the straps can also be a convenient location for electrical wiring, which can be installed without interrupting the insulation. However, some codes require that wiring be placed deeper in the wall.

In the attic space, where a radiant barrier apparently does the most good, some sources say it should be below the insulation. Others say it should be above the insulation. In my opinion, you should put it above if you live down south and want to keep heat out, and below if you're in the north and want to keep heat in. When both heating and cooling are important, radiant barriers above and below the ceiling insulation may be helpful.

Radiant barriers must be placed in a location where they will not accumulate dust. Dust dulls the reflective surface and reduces the benefits.

Research is continuing, so seek out the most up-to-date advice you can get. My only contribution to the discussion at this point is that radiant barriers are almost never noticed by tax assessors.

Doors and Windows

While windows and doors are discussed in other sections of this book, several points relating to energy consumption deserve mention here, even at the risk of repetition.

From an energy standpoint, an insulated entry door with a high R-value is a good investment. Such doors come in plain designs at relatively low cost. If you take advantage of the "once-in-a-blue moon" sales that occur at your local lumber store every other week, a good insulated entry door may cost about $140 in 1989 dollars. If you spend more, it will be because of aesthetic preference, not energy conservation.

The entry door should ideally open into an entry *room*. This is usually an unheated "mud room" or enclosed porch, where people wipe their feet and hang their coats before entering the main house. An entry room works like a low-tech air-to-air heat exchanger. The air from the entry room that follows you into the house is moderated by the warmer air that escaped last time the door was opened.

Fixed panes of glass are both cheaper and tighter than opening windows. For energy efficiency, you should have only as many opening windows as you need for ventilation.

Double-hung and sliding windows are reputed to be slightly less tight than the more expensive casement windows. However, any infiltration you get from them will be only a tiny portion of the total air change you're going to need for healthy living.

Single-glazed windows with storm sashes are cheaper than double-glazed windows, with equivalent energy efficiency.

High-tech windows with low-emissivity coatings can be useful in some situations. The technology is improving and prices are coming down. If you shop around, it's possible to get double the R-value of ordinary double-glazed glass, at a price that is only 20 percent higher. Also, the low-*e* coatings significantly reduce radiant heat loss through the windows at night if you forget to close the drapes. If you decide to invest in low-*e* windows, look at the models that are filled with argon. Argon is an inert gas that can substantially improve the R-value of a low-*e* window at a very small additional price.

However, low-*e* windows reduce solar gain. At least on south-facing windows, you'll achieve more energy efficiency by using ordinary double-glazed windows and closing the curtains at night. The low-*e* coatings also tint the glass, giving the view an unnatural color besides letting in less sunlight.

In a climate where heating is the major concern, I would use high-tech glass only on non-south-facing windows where there is no view and where it is difficult to close the curtains at night. The clerestory windows on the north side of the house that are used for summer ventilation might be good candidates for low-*e*. Where cooling is the major concern, high-tech windows might be useful on any side of the house that does not have a view.

Keep in mind that tax assessors always notice, and duly record, the distinctive tint of low-*e* coatings.

Alternative Energy Sources and Water Heating

You may have noticed that in discussing heating and cooling, I made no mention of photovoltaics, other types of active solar systems, closed-loop-earth-coupled heat pumps, or other alternative energy sources such as windmills.

The problem is that at the time I'm writing this (1989), such systems cost more than conventional systems for heating and cooling. In the meantime, solar collectors are practical for heating domestic water—the largest component of the average monthly electric bill. Solar collectors on your roof won't pay for themselves in a single year, but they will usually do so long before their usefulness expires.

Although collectors no longer qualify for federal income tax credits, many jurisdictions exempt them from property taxes. Nobody who knows anything about energy supply doubts that we will have another energy crisis sometime in the next few years. The federal government refuses to acknowledge that prospect, but many local governments do.

In colder climates, solar collectors won't give you a year-round source of free hot water. They must be supplemented by another heat source, particularly in winter.

My wife's solution to this problem was to loop a copper pipe from the water heater through the firebox of our wood cook stove. We use the cook stove more in the winter than in the summer, as it heats the house while it heats the food. Cooking with it also heats the domestic hot water, at a time of year when the solar collector isn't doing much.

There are many other ways to reduce the cost of domestic hot water. They include timers (particularly if your electric company reduces rates during nonpeak hours) and insulation on the tank and hot water pipes. Gas, especially natural gas where it is available, is far less expensive than electricity.

Domestic hot water costs can also be reduced with technology to cut water use—like shower flow restrictors and front-loading washing machines. (Front loaders are one of the nation's best-kept secrets. They use a third to half the electricity, water, soap, and bleach of a top loader, and get clothes cleaner. If one of the few companies that still make front loaders adopted a decent advertising campaign, everybody would want one.)

Other Energy Savings

A wood cook stove like the one we use is not the only way to reduce cooking costs. Gas stoves are more economical to use than electric stoves. Microwave ovens use less energy than conventional electric stoves. Electric frying pans, crock pots, and coffee makers use less power than equivalent units placed on top of electric stoves. An outdoor cooking pit, particularly one that burns scrap wood rather than charcoal briquets, can provide a pleasant way to reduce cooking costs in the summer. (*Don't burn scrap plywood, painted wood, or wood that has been treated in any way. The fumes from burning pressure-treated wood are particularly dangerous.*)

Gas dryers are less expensive to run (though more expensive to purchase) than electric dryers. The cheapest alternative to a clothes dryer is a clothesline. Keep in mind that a clothesline is unlikely to be used if it is not convenient. If possible, the laundry area should be located next to a door, with a clothesline immediately outside the door. If the tax assessor comes when clothes are hanging outside, the assessment is likely to be reduced. Clotheslines are signs of thrift. If you have one, the assessor should understand that you don't spend money frivolously.

Another energy-efficient design feature is a cool location for the freezer, and preferably for the refrigerator as well. The ideal is a piggy room, as described in Chapter 8.

Energy conservation is a day-to-day activity. However, in the hectic pace of modern family life, good conservation practices are more likely to be employed if they are supported by the design and infrastructure of the house.

Don't Wait for Technology

Alternative technologies are constantly becoming better and less expensive. Closed-loop-earth-coupled heat pumps, for example, have become competitive in price with standard central heating and cooling systems, and are arguably much more efficient. If I were to invest in a central system, that's what I would choose.

Once the market grows large enough to allow mass production, photovoltaic cells and other technologies will become increasingly affordable.

There may well come a day when earth-coupled heat pumps and photovoltaic cells are the most practical and economical energy sources. Some day, maybe, cold fusion or other technologies will make energy too cheap to meter. But a couple of decades ago, that was the promise we heard from the people promoting nuclear fission. They were as wrong as anybody gets, so I'll remain skeptical of other breakthroughs until they happen.

Meanwhile, there have been huge advances in building methods and materials. Houses today are tighter and better insulated than ever before. There have also been major improvements in the design of individual heating units. "Space heaters" used to be substandard clunkers; today they are as safe and efficient as any heating system. Some of the simple technologies, like thermal mass and radiant barriers, are under-used but available. Those advances are accessible here and now. By taking advantage of them you can avoid central systems and save big money.

Chapter 10

Unfinished Space: Low-Cost Luxury

When you're framing walls and putting up roof trusses, you make dramatic progress each day. Rough carpentry proceeds at a fast pace. The work is heavy, sweaty, and noisy, but at the end of a day you can sit back and marvel at how quickly the house is taking shape.

By contrast, finish carpentry is slow, painstaking, expensive work. People with specialized skills go over the interior surfaces inch by inch, foot by foot, until the appearance is just so.

Unfinished space is cheap to build because it is functional rather than pretty. If you need electrical or plumbing work in an unfinished space, installation is quick and easy because you don't have to hide the wires and pipes. If you need shelves you can nail up scrap boards rather than fussing with fancy woodwork and ornate brackets. Nothing needs to be sanded with three grades of sandpaper, or coated with four layers of varnish in a temperature-controlled, dust-free environment.

On average, finished space costs three to four times as much per square foot as unfinished space. Even if you do all the finishing work yourself, the tax assessment will reflect the price you would have paid to a professional contractor.

Of all the activities that will take place in your dream house, which would be enhanced by taking place in finished areas? For which activities would an unfinished area suffice? You can save big money by addressing those questions honestly.

Storage

I've been in modern houses that have no unfinished space for storage. None. Bicycles were stored for the winter in closets. Paint cans and tools were stored in kitchen cabinets. Bags of outgrown children's clothing were stuffed into any available corner, awaiting the day when they may be given away to the Salvation Army.

125

Any of those items could be stored just as well in an unfinished space, built at a fraction of the cost. The cheaper space would be more convenient because stored items would not be in the way of daily activities.

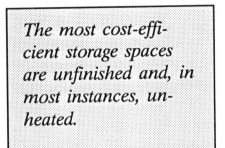

The most cost-efficient storage spaces are unfinished and, in most instances, unheated.

Also, energy costs could be reduced. No useful function is served by heating and cooling storage space for bicycles and old clothes. Even the paint cans don't need a comfortable temperature, although they should be protected from freezing and extreme heat. The most cost-efficient storage spaces are unfinished, and, in most instances, unheated.

Working Spaces

In most houses, some areas are set aside for strictly functional purposes. They are not used for entertaining guests or for other leisure-time activities. They are working spaces.

In our house, the working spaces include the laundry area, the workbench, and the darkroom. Some houses have separate sewing rooms, or areas to pay the bills and catch up on book work without constant interruptions from the kids. These are important spaces that can improve the quality of life, but they don't necessarily have to be pretty.

Working spaces should be well designed for the functions they serve. Form follows function. If the space is laid out well for the job, it will look fine, without any finish work.

A laundry area should have a washer and dryer, a place to store dirty clothes, and a horizontal surface to fold clean clothes. The area should be accessible and easy to keep clean. We never entertain guests in our laundry area. When I use it, my attention is focused on the task, not the workmanship of the surroundings. By keeping the area unfinished, we were able to make better use of space by recessing the washer hookup and dryer outlet into the cavity between the studs. Why would we want to spend a lot of money on finish work?

When I work with tools, I prefer to do it in a shop area that is simple, sturdy, and unfinished. In a finished area, you have to constantly worry about protecting the surroundings, rather than the project you're working on. Less is more.

My darkroom is a great luxury. I can develop photos whenever I want without competing with kids who need to go to the bathroom. Since the lights are off most of the time, I forget that the room is unfinished.

Finish work, like drywall and molding, would not make the working spaces in our house any more useful or enjoyable. Yet if we had chosen to turn them into finished areas, the cost and the tax assessments would have increased dramatically.

That's strictly a personal judgment. If you dream of a beautiful finished area for laundry, go for it. If your home business is photo finishing and you like to show off the darkroom to clients, perhaps your darkroom should be beautiful. But finish work is expensive, so it should be reserved for the parts of the house where it will be appreciated.

Garages

Regardless of whether you use them to park cars, garages can be handy unfinished areas. You can use them for storage, woodworking, and even for raising geese if that's allowed by the local zoning ordinance.

Our garage holds the electric train board that comes out only at Christmas, the old furniture that we'll give to our kids when they move out, and the antique lamp parts that my wife thinks we might have a use for some day.

It also contains my roll of antique linoleum, which the Smithsonian Institution will undoubtedly inquire about one of these years. My wife and I have running discussions about the lamp parts and the linoleum, but fortunately we have plenty of storage space for both.

A simple unfinished garage is cheap to build and assessed at a low level. If you insulate it, heat it, apply finish materials, and install automatic door openers, you will defeat the function of a garage. Some garages cost as much per square foot, and are assessed as highly, as the finished parts of a house.

Basements

Basements, whether they are finished or not, are costly. Excavation is expensive, so if you're building on a reasonably level lot, a slab will be a more cost-effective foundation.

Nevertheless, some basements are good living space that are well worth the extra cost. If you insulate the basement *outside* the concrete and install a wood stove, the thermal mass might help to keep your whole house comfortable. If local zoning limits you to two stories and you need three, it may make sense to put one story underground and call it a basement. In a hot climate, a basement might stay pleasantly cool without air conditioning. If your house is built on a hillside that faces a view, a basement with one exposed wall can be the most pleasant living space in the house.

Because of the expense, it almost never makes sense to build a basement to use for storage. To the extent possible, any basement should be used as quality living space.

If you're remodeling, chances are that you already have a basement. It may be damp and ugly. It may have low ceilings. It may be half filled by a big antique furnace coated with asbestos. In the old days, when excavation and concrete were cheap, basements were put in with no thought of making them into good living spaces.

If it's not practical to convert an existing basement into living space, it can, and usually does, serve as storage space. It may be a great place to store half-used cans of paint. Basements, unlike garages, usually don't freeze. An ugly basement may also be a good place to store the lawn furniture and bicycles during the winter. They're made for outside use, so they won't be damaged by moisture. Perhaps, with a little extra work, a portion of the basement can be turned into a root cellar or wine cellar. Another portion may be usable as a laundry room or tool bench. All is not lost if you have an ugly basement.

However, a basement that can't be converted to decent living space is usually damp. Therefore, be careful about what you store there. When I left my parents' house to go to college, I stored my old collection of baseball cards in the basement. Of course, the cards turned green. If I'd been able to salvage even the six Hank Aaron rookie cards, I'd be a rich man today.

In most old basements the kids' clothing won't survive in good enough condition for donation to the Salvation Army. Your first draft of the Great American Novel, the collection of family photos, and the box of love letters from your spouse will self-destruct.

Attics

There was a time when most houses had attics. Some attics even had stairways leading to them. Younger readers will find this hard to believe, but it's the honest truth.

For people who like tag sales, 1973 was a great year. During the energy crisis, most homeowners filled their attics with insulation and sold the valuables that they had been storing. Houses built since then have generally used trusses instead of rafters. The cross pieces on most trusses make the attic space unusable.

In new construction, it is usually most economical to avoid attics. Trusses with minimal roof slope are almost always the most cost-efficient configuration. Whatever space there is between the ceiling and the roof should be crammed as full of insulation as feasible to hold down energy costs.

The most common alternative is a steep roof with a cathedral ceiling. That provides useful (and expensive) living space rather than an attic.

That said, if you're remodeling an older house with an attic, and if there's no reasonable way to convert the attic into living space, it can provide good storage space. If it functions well as an attic, it will be dry and have plenty of ventilation. Your old love letters, baseball cards, and the paintings you did in Art 101 will survive indefinitely in a real attic.

The $6,000 Woodshed

Two years ago, my wife and I hired a professional carpenter to build a new woodshed. By the time the project was completed, we had spent about $600, which seemed like a lot of money for a woodshed. But the shed was functional and attractive, so we had no regrets.

That is to say, we had no regrets until the tax assessors came around. The assessors really admired the woodshed. They added $6,000 to our assessment—ten times the amount we had paid.

I was pretty upset. At our town's tax rate, the $6,000 assessment added $150 to our yearly tax burden. That seemed like a lot of tax money to pay for an item that cost $600. Beyond that, I felt insulted that anybody might think I'm the kind of person who would spend $6,000 for a shed to hold $225 worth of firewood.

We went through three levels of appeal. It turned out that the assessors had mismeasured the shed, and that an incorrect multiplier had been used in the computerized assessment. The assessment was brought to a more realistic level, but it still far exceeds the $600 we paid for the shed.

One specific lesson I learned from this incident is that some unfinished areas should not look particularly beautiful. Our woodshed is fancier than necessary. It exceeds the norms for woodsheds in our community. The assessors interpreted it as a symbol of luxury. Since we spent more than we had to spend for that conspicuous item, they figured we wouldn't mind spending a little extra on property taxes.

We could have adequately protected our firewood without adding anything to the assessment. We could have piled the wood neatly and put a couple of pieces of metal roofing on top. That would not have been real estate, so it would not have been taxed.

If we'd wanted something a little more convenient and permanent, we could have pounded posts into the ground to hold up the metal roofing. Maybe the assessors would have listed that as real estate, and maybe they wouldn't. But under no circumstances would it have been listed as fancy real estate. Any influence on our tax bill would have been modest.

Real Estate Sheds
vs. Personal Property Sheds

Storage sheds, whether they're used for wood, garden tools, lawn furniture, or anything else that you want to keep out of the rain and snow, often fall into a gray area between real estate and personal property.

Sheds that are on foundations and/or attached to the house are almost always listed as real estate. If you buy a little prebuilt metal shed from a discount lumber company and set it in the yard, without building a foundation, is it real estate? In my town, the answer would be yes. In most other localities across the country, the answer would be no. It's a judgment call, influenced as much by the opinion of your local assessor as by the state statutes.

The best advice is to have unfinished storage capacity that serves your needs to the extent possible, but meets only the minimum aesthetic standards you can live with. Additional flourishes can encourage an assessor to list a shed as real estate instead of personal property, or to list it as expensive, rather than cheap, real estate. Those distinctions can make a dramatic difference in your tax bill, regardless of how much or how little you spent on the shed.

Common Walls

In most instances, garages and sheds are most cost efficient if they are attached to the house.

As noted in Chapter 5, exterior walls are expensive. When you attach a garage or shed to the house, the common wall reduces the cost and the assessment. Only three additional walls have to be built, instead of four.

There are sometimes good reasons not to attach a structure to a house. If your home business is demolition, it's probably wise to put the dynamite shed as far from the house as possible.

While the dangers may be less dramatic, an attached garage, in some instances, can be hazardous to your health. Exhaust fumes are more likely to travel into the house if the garage is attached.

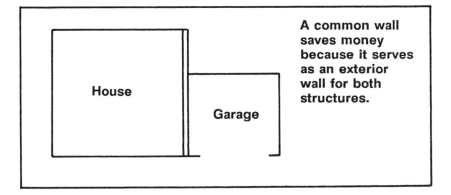

A good solution to that problem is to attach the garage to the house, but avoid a connecting door. The moderate inconvenience of exiting the garage before entering the house could possibly save your life. Cost and assessment will be reduced by a common wall, and will be reduced even more if there is no common door. Less is more.

Before making a final decision on that issue, check with your insurance company. Some insurance companies charge higher premiums if a garage is attached. They reason that the cans of gasoline and mineral spirits in a typical garage are fire hazards, which can jeopardize the house if the garage is attached. The increased insurance premiums can, in some instances, wipe out the tax savings that are made possible by the common wall.

One more caution about common walls: anything attached to your house will be listed as real estate. If you are building a modest shed without a foundation, and hope to have it listed as nontaxable personal property, then don't attach it.

Despite all those caveats, a common wall usually will save a significant amount of money. The best policy is to attach a garage or shed to the house unless you have a reason not to.

Making the Most of Finished Space

Reducing the square footage of finished space is a key to cost cutting. Lower numbers in that category mean lower mortgage payments, lower property taxes, and lower energy costs.

Other design ideas discussed throughout this book also make the use of finished space more efficient. For example, an open design allows for more cost-effective heating and cooling and more efficient use of each square foot of space.

Planning unfinished spaces into your dream house is another way to get more for less.

As noted earlier in this chapter, unfinished space costs a quarter to a third of the price of finished space. It saves big money if it replaces finished space. If you need 1,500 square feet, but decide to leave 300 square feet unfinished, your mortgage bills and tax assessments will be reduced substantially. If you want to splurge, build 600 square feet of unfinished space. As long as you reduce the finished area to 1,200 square feet, you'll still be saving a lot of money.

It's not only cheaper, but also more convenient, to store a bicycle in unfinished, unheated space rather than in an oversize bedroom closet.

Chapter 11

Sweat Investments

No book about affordable housing would be complete without some discussion of sweat investments. If you want the best house you can get at the lowest price, plan to put some of your own time and energy into the project.

A sweat investment doesn't necessarily involve physical labor. Not everybody is able or willing to climb rafters or operate a recipro-saw. Sweat can be invested, with high payback, by taking on management responsibilities and paperwork for the building project. If you are also able to do some of the construction work, so much the better. The physical labor can be a pleasant diversion if your regular job is in an office.

Sweat is like money, in that most people have a limited amount to invest. A foolish investment (e.g., doing something you lack the time or competence to do) can have a disastrous result. A wise investment can produce returns that will continue to roll in for the rest of your life.

With a few months of hard work, you may be able to obtain a dream house for as little as half the price a developer would charge for the same house. For example, a house that would otherwise cost $80,000 (not counting the price of the lot) may be built for as little as $40,000. The saving will not always be that great. It depends on the amount of time and energy you are willing and able to invest. But with extensive owner involvement, half price is a realistic goal.

The payback on a sweat investment compounds because each dollar saved can reduce the mortgage principal by a dollar. Suppose your mortgage is at 10 percent interest, with a bank charge of two points, paid back over 30 years. If a sweat investment reduces that mortgage by $40,000, the saving over the life of the mortgage will be $127,232. Do you get that much for a few months' work at your regular job? If not, read on.

Working on Your Own Title Search

Let's start at the beginning. When you buy real estate, you need a title search to confirm that the person selling the property is the rightful owner.

133

If you get a bank loan, the bank will require a title search that is signed by a lawyer. Where I live, most lawyers charge $75 per hour or more for this service.

Many lawyers are willing to allow you to do legwork for them. If you do the research and photocopy the appropriate deeds, you can greatly reduce the legal fees.

As a side benefit, researching a title can be interesting. Old deeds can provide fascinating information about the history of the place where you have decided to live.

Saving on Brokers' Fees

Real estate brokers typically receive 6 percent of the price of any transaction. If you buy a finished house for, say, $100,000, about $6,000 will go to the broker.

Brokers' fees are paid only for the real estate that you purchase through a broker. If you buy a building lot or a run-down house, the broker will receive a commission only on the price you paid.

Suppose you were to buy a building lot for $20,000, then build a house on it that's worth $80,000. You would have what amounts to a $100,000 house. However, the broker would receive a commission of only $1,200—or 6 percent of $20,000. That's a saving of $4,800 compared to the commission that would have been paid if you had bought a finished $100,000 house through a broker.

In most instances, the seller, not the buyer, writes the check to the broker. But the commission must be added to the price in order for the seller to get the desired return. If all other factors are equal, any structure you build should automatically cost 6 percent less than the same structure purchased through a broker.

The same principle applies to any improvement you make after you own the property. If you buy a structure for $20,000, and remodel it thoroughly so that its value increases to $100,000, the real estate commission will only be paid on the initial $20,000 purchase price.

Applying for Your Own Permits

When real estate developers apply for building permits, they hire expensive lawyers and consultants. They have a large burden of proof because their developments will have a large impact on the community. A developer must show that the impact will be (a) as minimal or (b) as beneficial as possible.

Often, in addition to the regular permit fees, developers must pay impact fees or donate land to a community in exchange for the right to develop. The fees and exactions help to provide the new or

134

expanded schools, fire stations, roads, and parks that will be needed because of the development.

In California, the average cost of these fees and exactions, as of this writing, is about $18,000 for each new housing unit built by a developer. It's less in most other states, but other states are working hard to catch up.

If you buy a house from a developer, the $18,000—or whatever the total of fees may be—will be passed on to you with a substantial markup. The cost of the lawyers and consultants who negotiated the deal will also be included in the price. So will the interest on the loan the developer took out to pay the impact fees and the lawyers. Even the fee to the real estate broker will be bumped up. The broker's fee is a percentage of the base sale price, which is raised by the impact fees. By the time the process has run its course, $18,000 in fees can add $30,000 or more to the price of a house.

By making the applications yourself, you can often save large amounts of money. You're one person. The zoning administrator and the members of the planning board are your peers. You're not personally going to have a huge impact on the community. Your kids, all by themselves, aren't going to force the community to expand the capacity of its schools. You aren't going to require a new superhighway or fire station. You just want a place to live.

> *You have significant advantages over the big developers.*

Also, the costs of building permits and some of the other miscellaneous fees are often based on the estimated cost of the construction project. Because you can build less expensively than a developer can, these fees will be lower for you.

In short, you have significant advantages over the big developers. Don't feel guilty about that—they're big guys who can take care of themselves.

Designing Your House

If you hire an architect to design your house, the fee is usually about 10 percent of the anticipated price of the house, and sometimes more than that. If it costs $90,000 to build the house, involvement by an architect is likely to raise the price to at least $99,000.

Detailed plans are useful. In many locations, you'll need them for your dealings with the zoning administrator and the building inspector. A good set of plans provides the information needed for pricing of materials and obtaining competitive bids from sub-contractors. When a work crew arrives, the plans should describe clearly the work that is expected.

If you've never designed a house before, it is usually safest to begin with a set of standard plans. There are thousands of standard plans to choose from. The law of averages says that one of those sets of plans comes reasonably close to the design you want. It will cost, at the very most, a few hundred dollars, compared to the thousands you would have paid to an architect or designer.

You will probably want changes in the standard design, but that's an easy job compared to designing from scratch. Don't hesitate to sketch simple changes yourself. You don't need expert help to design changes like extra insulation, a different type of siding, or a simple carport.

Many of the low-tax ideas in this book will require alterations of standard plans. For example, you might want to eliminate some of the built-in cupboards and counters called for by the plans, and substitute a pantry. If the plans call for a basement, you might want to substitute a slab. In some instances, changes like that require additional modifications. For example, if the design has pipes and wires going through the basement, but you substitute a slab, new routes will be needed for the pipes and wires.

Most of those changes are a function of common sense. However, if you begin to feel overwhelmed by the complexities, it's not unreasonable to call an expert and ask for help.

Sketch the changes first, then find a professional who will consult with you at an hourly rate. The hourly fee will be high, but nowhere near what the same person would have charged, under contract, to design the whole house.

Being Your Own General Contractor

In most new houses, a quarter to a third of the price goes to the general contractor, depending on whose estimates you choose to believe. By being your own contractor you may be able to build a $90,000 house for $60,000. I consider that to be a conservative estimate, as self-contractors are able to take advantage of additional savings. More on that later.

Contracting is hard work. Most general contractors earn their pay. They have to line up workers and subcontractors for every aspect of the job. They have to schedule the work carefully. Problems can arise with scheduling and availability of subcontractors. The general contractor gets paid for headaches as well as time.

136

There are different levels of self-contracting. At the minimum, self-contracting requires hiring subcontractors for all the tasks, seeing that the work is done as agreed, and ordering delivery of materials that are not supplied by the subcontractors.

The greatest financial return can be achieved by rolling up your sleeves and actively managing the construction process, then contributing your own labor when appropriate. That's a big commitment, but it can be exciting, enjoyable, and financially rewarding.

You have a financial advantage over general contractors: you don't have overhead expenses. The quarter or third of the price of the house that they charge is not pure profit. General contractors have to pay people to answer their phones and to handle their bookkeeping. Many have offices to support. They pay for insurance, bonding, and business taxes. They must pay their workers during periods when there isn't much work to do. Their rates must make up for expensive errors that occurred on other projects. Since you aren't carrying that baggage, the time you spend as your own contractor can be more cost efficient.

Scheduling headache: I had to run out and rent this generator for a recent project, because the carpenters showed up before the electric company did.

You also have another advantage over general contractors: *this is your house.* It's a source of excitement. Each good decision means a better place to live, or less money from your paycheck, or both. To the contractor, your house is just another job. You may have to work as hard, but you'll get more enjoyment and satisfaction from the work.

Of the people I've met who have self-contracted, several have compared it to the decision to become a parent. The amount of work was greater than expected, but there were no regrets.

If you have one trusted general carpenter working with you from start to finish, that person will be able to give you valuable advice on your contracting decisions. In fairness, you should ask for advice only during the hours when the carpenter is being paid. Also, the decisions are yours, so don't blame the carpenter if one of your decisions leads to later problems. Keep in mind that the carpenter is not making the extra profit he or she would be earning in the role of general contractor.

Self-contracting requires management skills. The job may go smoothly every step of the way, but prepare for a turn of events that could require tough decisions. If the guy who runs the backhoe gets sick, you may have to reschedule everybody else. If the electricity isn't hooked up on time, you may have to rent a generator so that the carpenters can run their power tools. If the lumber company delivers the wrong siding, it will be up to you to insist that the problem be corrected. If you have the management skills to handle situations like that without risking a nervous breakdown, you'll get a handsome return for your efforts.

The return can be even larger than the usual one-third of the price of construction if you take advantage of all the opportunities available to you. The next few sections of this chapter discuss some of the possible savings.

Hiring Inexpensive Labor for Some Projects

A contractor usually hires subcontractors who also have overhead expenses and high rates. If you shop around, you may be able to find people who will do some of the jobs at lower prices.

If your Uncle Horace, an all-around do-it-yourselfer, is between jobs when you are building your house, he may be willing to provide valuable labor for less money than a contractor would charge.

Construction workers are often available for moonlighting. A contracting firm may pay $8 per hour to a person who does work that is billed at $15 per hour. By hiring the same person at, say, $10 per hour during evenings and weekends, you may save a bundle.

You can hire unskilled people to do some of the jobs that would otherwise be done by skilled people. For example, highly-paid carpenters usually clean up their job sites at the end of each day. You may be able to find a local kid to help clean up the job site, for a fraction of the price you'd pay the carpenters.

Volunteering Your Own Time

Even if you have no construction skills, you can do some of the jobs that would otherwise be done by expensive professionals.

A carpenter doing what amounts to a one-person project may occasionally need an extra pair of hands. If you can provide that extra pair of hands, you may be able to avoid hiring a second

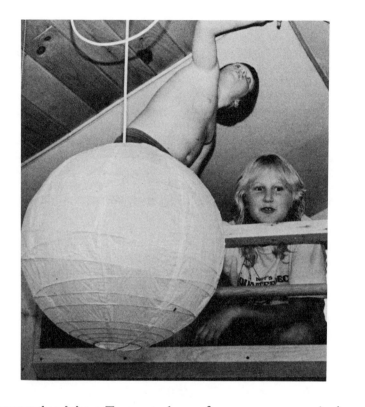

Inexpensive labor: Two members of our crew pause during a recent finishing job. All of our kids enjoy helping out—they do good work at a reasonable price.

carpenter.

A carpenter often has to run to the store for a few more screws or nails, one more 2x4, or another sheet of plywood. If you can take on those gofer jobs, you can make better use of the carpenter's time.

If you're an experienced do-it-yourselfer, you will have many opportunities to save money by doing work yourself. Budget that time carefully. Remember, you're saving bigger money by being your own general contractor. Budgeting your own working time is discussed later in this chapter.

Getting The Best Prices on Materials

General contractors make a profit from materials as well as labor. If you are your own contractor, you can pocket those profits.

Before you start the project, submit materials lists to several lumber companies. Compare the bids, and, if all other factors are equal, choose the lowest bidder. However, if the second (or third) lowest bidder offers better quality, better service, and keeps in stock more of the materials you need, those issues must be taken into consideration.

Regardless of who gets the bid, check the ads run by other lumber companies whenever you need expensive materials. Some lumber stores run "once-in-a-blue-moon sales" every other week. As your own contractor, you can take advantage of those sales. When you do, check the sale prices against the standard prices of your primary supplier. The prices of building supplies run all over the board, so "half price" at one store may be the same as "10 percent off" at another.

It usually makes sense to buy most of your materials from your primary supplier. You presumably chose that supplier because it offers good prices and good service. In the heat of a construction project, it doesn't pay to shop all over town to save a few dollars here or there. When you do save $50 by buying a door from another store, let your primary supplier know about it. The store wants your business, so keep the clerks on their toes by making it clear that you expect the best possible prices from them.

Taking Advantage of Bargains

Used but good materials often become available when you least expect them. If you drive by a renovation project, stop and ask about what's being taken out. It's often possible to obtain bricks, sinks, cabinets, and doors free or cheap. Cleaning off the bricks and stripping 18 coats of paint off the doors may be good tasks for low-cost workers you have lined up for the building project.

Glass and window stores always have cull bins stocked with windows and insulated glass that were cut to the wrong sizes. They may have been a half inch too short or too wide for somebody else's openings. If you haven't cut and framed your openings yet, they may be perfect for your house.

Lumber companies often have plywood with damaged edges. Many other materials may have been returned to the store in slightly damaged condition. The damage may be irrelevant to the function of the material, but the store can't sell it for the full price. Plywood with banged-up edges is no problem if you're putting metal roofing over it. If you're the contractor, you can take advantage of sharply reduced prices for such materials.

Let the people at the lumber store know that you are on the lookout for bargains. Some stores save imperfect but good items for their regular "scavengers." That's easier than displaying the items at reduced prices on the sales floor, so the mark-down is often greater. Once you're known as a scavenger, bargains will appear that you wouldn't otherwise hear about.

Bargain materials often must be bought in advance, when they're available. That's less convenient than having materials delivered to the site just before you need them. However, the extra effort can produce thousands of dollars in savings.

Saving Money with Contractors' Discounts

Contractors get discounts on their purchases from lumber, hardware, paint, and other stores. The discounts range from 2 percent to 40 percent, depending on the store and the volume of business in any given month.

I'll leave the morality to you. Perhaps you'd feel funny about "pretending" to be a contractor when your only construction job is your own house. Yet it's done by a lot of people, and as far as I can tell, most store owners don't seem to mind. Why should they? While you're building your dream house, you'll be buying thousands of dollars worth of materials. The stores that get your business will make substantial profits, even if they discount the prices. If you'd hired a general contractor, the stores would have given discounts to the contractor.

Don't ever lie. That's bad policy and unnecessary. Some states and localities license contractors, so you could get into trouble by overtly claiming that you sell contracting services to consumers. Keep in mind the old expression: "If you walk like a duck, look like a duck, and quack like a duck, then you're a duck." If you look and act like a contractor, the stores will accept you as one.

If your name is Jo Blow, call yourself Jo Blow Construction. You might even spend $2 for a rubber stamp that says "Jo Blow Construction" over your home address. It will look good on top of requests for prices for materials lists.

You might also want a separate checking account. That's handy in any event, as it's the easiest way to keep track of construction expenses for your income tax records. If the checks are in the "three-up" format that many businesses use, you'll look more like a contractor. Maybe the bank will agree to print "Jo Blow Construction Account" on the checks, since it's a special account for your construction project.

Some of the biggest contractors' discounts are on big-ticket items at electrical and plumbing wholesale stores. I've known people who have been able to save huge sums by walking into these stores, acting like plumbers or electricians, and paying with three-up checkbooks.

That, however, is not a task for novices. The clerks in wholesale electrical and plumbing stores don't give advice. If you don't know exactly what you want, or the jargon to use when you ask for it, your credentials may be challenged.

After you complete your dream house, you can either dissolve your contracting operation or keep it up in order to get discounts on future home improvements. Maybe you'll enjoy contracting enough to do some work for friends and neighbors on weekends, and your contractor's discount will continue to come in handy. Keep in mind, however, that if you live in a state or locality with contractor licensing, selling your services without passing the exam could cause trouble.

Doing Some of the Labor Yourself

At the risk of stating the obvious, the cheapest way to build a new house is to do all the work yourself. If you're a reasonably competent do-it-yourselfer and have lots of time, that's not an impossible task. If you do, you'll probably save far more than the 50 percent that was suggested as a goal earlier in this chapter.

Hundreds of books are available to fill in the gaps in your knowledge of construction techniques. Also, people with expertise like to give advice. Don't be shy about asking. If you're not sure how far a 2x8 joist can span, there are lots of people who would be flattered if you asked. The person who answers your question about joists will almost always add unsolicited but potentially valuable advice on other issues.

When I was a young adult in 1971, the only way I could afford a decent house was to build it myself. I did so, with some help and a lot of advice from friends. It wasn't an architectural masterpiece, but it was a good place to live, and I learned skills that have served me well ever since.

It was, however, a consuming job that took a toll on my outside employment and my family life. Since then, I've tried to budget my time carefully, concentrating on the tasks that bring the biggest return for the hours I invest.

Electrical work is an example of a job with a high payback. I drill the holes, string the wires, put up boxes, and hook up outlets. Then I hire an electrician, who handles the tricky parts and inspects my work to make sure it's safe. By doing the easy parts myself, I can save thousands of dollars on an extensive wiring job.

My wife is good at plumbing and masonry. She concentrates on those jobs, minimizing the work that is done by expensive plumbers and masons.

Both my wife and I can tape drywall, but professional tapers do it faster and better. It's useful to have the skill, because we sometimes have a small project at a time when the professionals are booked up for the next three months. However, we hire professionals for drywall jobs whenever it is practical to do so.

Your skills and work preferences are undoubtedly different from ours, so assess them realistically and concentrate your labor on the jobs that will save the most money.

As a rule, the hours you spend handling your own contracting will bring a bigger return than the hours you spend at physical labor. The big money is in finding the right people for each job, getting competitive bids, finding the least expensive materials, being available for judgment calls, scheduling everything, insisting that each job is done as agreed, and getting the bills paid on time.

If you're working so hard at pounding nails that you lose track of the sequence for scheduling subcontractors, you can make an error that can cost thousands of dollars. It would be better to hire somebody else to pound the nails.

Contract Prices and Hourly Prices

There are two ways to pay carpenters and other tradespeople: a contract price or an hourly price. Contract prices are most common.

Consumers like contracts because they eliminate some of the uncertainty. If the contract is well written, it will describe in detail what is to be done and when. If unanticipated problems arise, the consumer should not pay extra to resolve them. Payment of the final installment shouldn't be required until the job is done to the consumer's satisfaction.

Tradespeople like contracts, too, because the extra risks they take on usually result in substantial extra profits. If they do a job quickly and efficiently, they will earn more per hour with a contract than with an hourly price. A tradesperson with an hourly price of $17.50 may get $30 to $40 per hour in a contract job.

Therefore, when you're managing a project yourself, you can often save large amounts of money by hiring people at hourly prices. By doing so, you will take on some risks. For example, if you paid the drywall taper only for the hours worked, extra payment may be needed if the taper has to return later to repair popped nails.

143

However, the total price, including the cost of the return trip, will almost always be lower than a contract price.

Not all tradespeople are willing to work for an hourly price. A good worker who is willing to work for an hourly price may reduce your costs substantially even if the hourly price is high.

Union Rules

Union rules may affect the division of labor in some localities. One union subcontractor may be unable to do a small, simple part of the project without the services of another union subcontractor. Respect that. The person probably understands how arbitrary the situation is, but wants to follow the rules to protect working conditions in the long term.

In a case like that, perhaps there would be a problem if Uncle Horace, who doesn't belong to the appropriate union, did the job. However, you, as the homeowner, may be able to do it. The difference is that you are a do-it-yourselfer working on your own house, whereas Uncle Horace is getting paid.

That kind of nitpicking is unlikely to occur. A union worker may categorize Horace as a do-it-yourselfer too, since he's a relative helping the homeowner. Most workers bend arbitrary rules to get a project done quickly and professionally. Just remember that some decisions—occasionally including union rules—are important to people's careers even if they seem out of place in your project. Any differences of opinion that arise should be resolved as amicably and creatively as possible.

Subcontractors *vs.* Employees

The people you pay to help build your dream house are subcontractors, not employees. Those who work by the hour are paid an hourly price, not a wage.

The distinction is technical but important. If your payments were wages, the person would be an employee. That would make you responsible for withholding taxes. You'd also have to provide for Social Security, workers' compensation, sick leave, unemployment benefits, vacations, holidays, and perhaps health insurance.

If you had a contracting business, you might have to classify some of the people who work regularly for you as employees. There is never a need to take on that additional paperwork when you are paying people to help build your own house.

Suggestions for Efficient Use of Labor

In most situations, the following steps will help to reduce labor costs by using labor efficiently, without taking on undue risks.

1. Hire one general carpenter, possibly two, at a good hourly price to work on the project from start to finish. The carpenter must be competent, trustworthy, and dependable.

2. Also hire less-skilled labor at lower hourly prices. Your kids, your Uncle Horace who's between jobs, neighborhood teenagers, and moonlighting construction workers may do work for less money than a contractor would charge.

3. You, and your lower-cost workers, should concentrate on specific tasks that you can handle from start to finish. That way, your carpenter won't feel responsible if your work isn't quite up to his or her professional standards.

4. Hire out complex jobs at contract prices. A foundation contractor, for example, has his or her own crew, and his or her own preferred subcontractors. Watch over the work, since most subcontractors are less likely to take shortcuts if the owner is there. However, don't get in their way.

5. For jobs that are less complex, like roofing or drywall, pay an hourly price to a competent person if you can. The best deals are often with skilled moonlighters.

6. If you're not familiar with the quality of a person's work, it's safest to begin with a small piece of work at a contract price. If the work is done well, offer an hourly price for additional work.

7. Do everything possible to make conditions pleasant for everybody at the job site. Provide soda or juice for people who are working up a sweat. If they like to have a beer after work, buy the six-pack. The music on the boom box should be chosen by the workers. If your general carpenter likes Haydn, your mason likes Tammy Wynette, and your drywall taper prefers Freezer Burn, try to schedule their work on separate days. Save your Bulgarian polka tape until after hours.

8. Prepare to be tough. If someone you hired has a drinking problem or is incompetent, it's up to you to confront, and perhaps fire, the person. That's hard, particularly if the person is your Uncle Horace. However, a nonproductive worker can destroy your construction budget and the quality of your dream house.

9. Assuming that your general carpenter is doing good work, treat him or her particularly well. This is the one professional upon whom you must absolutely depend, and with whom you must absolutely get along. Don't expect free advice after hours. Don't blame the carpenter if you made a bad decision. If the carpenter doesn't get along with a subcontractor, side with the carpenter

whenever possible. If the carpenter needs an occasional day off or a day's pay in advance, do what you can to help.

Additional Benefits of Controlling Your Project

In addition to financial savings, running the job yourself will usually produce a better house.

For a contractor working at a set price, the incentive is to get the job done as quickly and easily as possible. The person may be as honest as the day is long, but will constantly face temptations to take shortcuts. To illustrate, here are three examples of incidents that occurred during construction of our dream house.

• Our design called for insulation outside of all the below-grade concrete. Our subcontractor tried to backfill around the foundation without properly insulating the footings. My wife stopped the operation and insisted that it be done right. If my wife hadn't been there at that critical moment, we would have lost energy efficiency without knowing why.

• A young moonlighter we hired to help with the roof told us that our shingles were inferior. The contractor he worked for had ordered the same shingles for a condominium project, and had noticed the defects, but put them up rather than delaying the project. The condominium owners may have to replace their roofs in five years, but thanks to the warning, we were able to exchange our shingles for better ones.

• The stressed-skin panels we put up to insulate our walls came from a company 400 miles away. After delivery, we noticed that they weren't quite square and that the edges were tapered. We complained. The company's salesman said, "You're obviously not a real contractor. Contractors put this stuff up, cover it over, and the customer never knows the difference." That's a verbatim quote. Since this was our house, we fought to rectify the problem and eventually did.

In each of the above incidents, it would have been tempting for a contractor to cover up the problem. The project would have stayed on schedule and the unsuspecting homeowner wouldn't have known the difference. However, the house wouldn't have been as energy-efficient, and the roof wouldn't have lasted as long.

Even the most scrupulously honest contractor must make frequent judgment calls. If materials at the site aren't perfect, do you use them or hold up the project by sending them back? If complications arise in a particular procedure, do you spend the extra time to do it right or take a shortcut?

Questions like that arise constantly in any construction project. Sometimes the quicker, easier solution is justified. For a contractor, the natural preference is to keep the project on schedule. Most home-owners prefer to err on the side of doing the job right. By supervising the project, you will improve the odds that the job will be done right.

> *In addition to finan-cial savings, running the job yourself will usually produce a bet-ter house.*

Preparing for the Job

You don't have to be a skilled builder to manage construction of your dream house, but you should understand the general principles of construction. Even if you are working from a standard set of plans, it is important to be familiar with each of the major components of the house you want built.

If judgment calls are made along the way, you should be able to discuss the issues intelligently with the professionals who are working for you. If you save money by hiring unskilled labor for some jobs, you'll have to supervise those parts of the work yourself.

Before you start, read a book on self-contracting. There are several: the most popular is *Be Your Own House Contractor* by Carl Heldman ($8.95, Garden Way/Storey Communications, Inc., Pownal, Vermont 05261). Heldman covers issues that are not discussed in this book, such as applying for loans and preparing estimates of the cost of your building project.

Hundreds of books cover the basics of house construction. Check with your librarian. Any good book on self-contracting will provide a knowledge base, but the more you read, the better prepared you'll be.

Every book you read will offer insights that are different from those in this book. I've tried to concentrate on ideas that are different from the conventional wisdom. But you should also learn as much as you can about the conventional wisdom—if you opt for it, I won't feel insulted.

Property Taxes on Sweat Investments

Not all of the information and suggestions in this chapter will help to reduce your property tax bill. Even though you may have saved a lot of money by doing some of the work yourself, most assessment systems don't take those savings into account.

That said, sweat investments can often produce substantial tax advantages.

Here's an example. My wife once built a Count Rumford fireplace. She was very proud of it, and most people who saw it expressed admiration. The tax assessor looked at it and mumbled "below average." It took Lisa a moment to realize that the assessor was doing her a favor, not insulting her work.

If the assessor knows that you, a nonprofessional, did some of the work, the assessor may assume that the quality is lower. Even if the work looks great, assessors may err on the side of a person who invested sweat rather than just writing checks to a general contractor.

There is another factor—one that's not written up in most assessment manuals—that works in favor of people who have sweat equity. *The amount that you actually paid for a house can affect the assessment.* This is an informal rule. Most assessment systems have roundabout ways to estimate what you could sell the house for, without directly noting how much you paid for it. Yet in practice, assessors seldom estimate fair market values much higher than what the owners paid, plus inflation.

When you applied for a building permit, you may have estimated correctly that the cost of the structure would be $40,000. The assessors are likely to have that figure in mind and work with their formulas to approximate that valuation.

If a developer had built the same house, the cost might have been estimated at $80,000. In that event, the assessors' incentive would have been to find ways to make their formulas approximate that figure.

When a structure is assessed for significantly more than the amount you paid for it, the actual cost is valuable information to present at a grievance hearing. If it's assessed at $80,000 and you paid only $40,000, document your expenditures at an appeal. Even if the assessors know the full value of your sweat equity, they may feel funny about insisting that the structure is worth twice what you paid for it.

One final tax issue: People who invest their own sweat often build their dream houses in increments rather than all at once. Because their own time and energy are limited, they tend to begin with bare-bones houses, which they improve and add on to over time. As discussed in Chapter 4, incremental building can reduce both mortgage loans and property taxes.

Chapter 12

Manufactured Housing

Until recent years, manufactured housing suffered an image problem. That's changing rapidly. Manufactured housing has grown in popularity to the point where it now accounts for roughly half of all new houses built. That's partly because it's getting harder and harder to tell the difference between a manufactured house and a site-built house.

What Is Manufactured Housing?

In the context of house building, anything that is built off site is "manufactured." Almost every modern house contains at least a few manufactured components. Examples include prehung doors, roof trusses, and factory-made cabinets.

A manufactured house is one for which *most* of the components were built off site. That definition covers several categories of houses. The most common are precut, panelized, and modular houses.

Precut Housing

A precut house is a kit prepared at a factory or, less often, at a lumber company. Kits are particularly useful for specialized construction techniques. For example, most geodesic domes and modern log houses are precut.

Precut kits are also available for ranches, capes, and virtually all other traditional house styles. The factory or lumber company delivers all the components to the site, where they are assembled by either a contractor or a do-it-yourselfer.

A good kit is relatively foolproof. There's little if any sawing to do, and there are usually step-by-step instructions for assembling the pieces.

Panelized Housing

People who love the English language hate the word *panelize*. Unfortunately, it has sneaked into the vocabulary, and nobody has yet found an acceptable substitute.

As the name suggests, a panelized house is assembled from panels. Sometimes only the exterior walls are panelized, but sometimes the technique is used to build an entire house.

Wall panels may be as small as 4x8 feet or as large as an entire wall. They usually provide structural support, insulation, and exterior sheathing. They may also include exterior siding and interior drywall. They may even include all windows and doors.

Unfinished panels are called *open* panels. They allow the flexibility to choose any style of windows, doors, siding, and interior finish you may desire. To finish them, you can make sweat investments or use other cheap sources of labor. You could also hire a contractor for finish work, but that would cost more than factory finishing.

Finished panels—with windows, doors, drywall, and siding already installed—are called *closed* panels. If you use them, the house will go up quickly and the finish work will be less expensive than professionally arranged, on-site finishing.

Most panels have grooves ("chases") to run electrical wiring. Many have wiring and outlet boxes already in place.

Structural Foam Panels

Structural foam sandwich panels are gaining popularity at a rapid pace. They consist of rigid foam sandwiched between two sheets of waferboard. The panels provide structural support, insulation, and nailing surfaces for exterior and interior finish materials. Some come in closed form, with windows, doors, and finish materials already in place.

As of this writing, most structural panels make use of either polyisocyanurate foam or expanded polystyrene. The former material has a much higher R-value per inch, but is also much more expensive and blows holes in the ozone layer of the atmosphere. Tune in to the latest technology, because manufacturers are working hard to develop foams that provide better insulation without threatening the environment.

Regardless of the nominal R-value, structural foam panels tend to be very energy efficient because the insulation is continuous. The nominal R-value of expanded polystyrene is no better than that of fiberglass, but if it is not interrupted by studs, it will provide more effective insulation.

As with other panels, structural foam panels may be small—typically 4x8 feet—or they may be the size of an entire wall. Small panels are sometimes connected to each other with 2x4 studs inserted into grooves. The manufacturers call these studs *splines.* Other small panels have built-in interlocking mechanisms with

Structural foam sandwich panels: The walls for this addition went up in about an hour, with panels made by *Foam Laminates of Vermont.* The project is described in detail in Chapter 15.

hooks, tightened with a hex wrench.

Wall-size panels go up more quickly than do small panels, and there is less chance of any interruption in the insulation. They're also cheaper and less labor-intensive. The only disadvantage of wall-size panels is that a crane is needed for installation.

Structural foam panels have become a material of choice for many builders and homeowners in recent years. Like factory-made windows and trusses, they are manufactured components that are useful in site-built houses as well as houses that fall into the "manufactured" category.

Modular Housing

Modular housing is the type of manufactured housing that is most completely assembled off site. It comes in three-dimensional modules, with three or four exterior walls and a roof in place on delivery.

There are two types of modular housing. The first type consists of old-fashioned mobile homes and their modern descendants. These are commonly referred to in the building industry as *HUD-code houses*, because they are built to the specifications of a national building code devised by the U.S. Department of Housing and Urban Development.

HUD-code houses have axles and wheels. They are delivered to building sites as complete units. A single module may be the entire house, or two modules may be put together to form a ranch-style house. The latter is commonly called a *double-wide*.

The second type of modular housing is *state-code housing*. It is built to meet state and local building codes.

State-code houses come in almost every conceivable style. They can also be modified with special-order features. Customizing is costly, however, so the economies will disappear if you depart too far from standard plans.

Modular housing has evolved considerably in recent years. Older mobile homes were cheaply built and were vulnerable to wear and tear. Newer HUD-code houses are more solid and appreciate in value. Nevertheless, many local zoning ordinances have not yet recognized the improvements, and restrict them to certain parts of town.

State-code houses are often indistinguishable from site-built houses. The quality is sometimes better. They are built under controlled factory conditions, protected from the weather, and are strong enough to survive transportation to the site. Because they meet all state and local building codes, zoning ordinances do not discriminate against them.

High-End Manufactured Houses

It's worth noting, at least in passing, that some manufactured houses are astoundingly expensive. In the Scandinavian countries, and more recently in Japan, manufacture of housing has become a high art form. Houses built abroad can be purchased in the United States, if cost is no object.

Imported houses are inherently expensive. The lumber is usually grown in the U.S. or Canada and shipped overseas, where the components are built and shipped back. Shipping costs may not be a big deal with cuckoo clocks and camcorders, but houses are big, heavy items.

Several firms in North America also produce high-end manufactured housing. Their sales appeal is based on quality, not price. In some affluent suburbs, it has become more prestigious to own a house with a good brand name than one built on site.

Tax Breaks for HUD-Code Houses

In many states, laws and assessment procedures have not kept pace with the increase in quality of much of the manufactured housing now on the market. Some state legislatures are still questioning whether "mobile and manufactured homes" should be classified as real estate or personal property.

Several states exempt HUD-code houses from the real estate tax under certain conditions. The statutory language varies, but in those states there is generally no real estate tax if:

1. The house is on land that is not owned by the homeowner—for example, if it is in a mobile home park, and/or

2. The house is not affixed to the land with a permanent foundation.

In the following ten states, HUD-code houses that meet those criteria are not assessed in the same way as other houses:

Arizona	Michigan
District of Columbia	Mississippi
Illinois	Nevada
Iowa	North Dakota
Massachusetts	West Virginia

HUD-code houses that are not listed as real estate in those states may be subject to other taxation. For example, localities in Arizona tax them as personal property. In DC, they are taxed by the Motor Vehicle Bureau. Illinois counties have a "privilege tax." Michigan's taxing jurisdictions have a straight tax of $3 per month. In general, the alternative taxes in these states are lower than the tax on real estate of comparable value.

Several other states not listed above tax HUD-code houses as personal property, but the tax bills are about the same as for real estate of comparable value.

Real Estate Assessments of HUD-Code Houses

When HUD-code houses are assessed as real estate (or as personal property) they are usually assigned a "blue-book" value by the assessor. The blue book is a standard guide, comparable to the guides that determine values of used cars. The market value is listed according to the make, model, and year of the house.

In general, HUD-code houses built before 1981 decline in value every year, whereas more recent models appreciate. After the blue-book value is assigned, the assessment is adjusted to reflect the condition, and any improvements such as porches or storage sheds.

The adjusted blue-book value is the theoretical fair market value of the house. Depending on where you live, the assessed value will be either the same as market value or a percentage of that amount. If you own the land that a HUD-code house sits on, the land will, of course, be assessed in the same manner as any other building lot.

The "blue-book" system is widespread because it simplifies the job of the assessor. However, some assessment systems, including the nationally recognized *Marshall Valuation Service*, assess HUD-code houses with the same methods used for other real estate.

Assessments of Other Manufactured Houses

Many assessors and assessment systems have not yet recognized the improvements in quality of factory-made housing. A manufactured house may get a lower assessment than a site-built house, even if the costs are identical.

While assessors automatically categorize HUD-code houses as manufactured, they may not notice that a house is state code, panelized, or precut. If you have a manufactured house, be sure to mention that to the assessor.

Many assessors assume that the parts of a house that are difficult to see—the thickness of the drywall, the quality of the subflooring, etc.—are of cheaper quality in a manufactured house than in a site-built house. That assumption may or may not be true, but if you have a manufactured house you might as well take advantage of the bias of the assessor.

Frozen Dinners

I'm hungry, so let's digress for a moment and talk about frozen dinners.

Frozen dinners are produced in efficient factories. The recipes and procedures are standardized. The people who do most of the work are not high-priced master chefs; they have specific jobs that they learn to do well. The ingredients are bought in large quantities at discount prices.

When you buy a frozen dinner at the supermarket, the price is substantially higher than what you'd pay for the raw ingredients. You'd save money by buying the ingredients and cooking them yourself, if you don't place a high dollar value on your own time. If you have a source of cheap labor—a kid who's willing to make dinner for a dollar, for example—you'll still save money by choosing raw ingredients.

However, if you don't do your own cooking and don't have a source of cheap labor, the frozen dinner may be a good investment. It's less expensive than hiring a master chef to make all the arrangements for your meals. The saving comes because of your own involvement. You bought the dinner, brought it home, popped it in the microwave, and cleaned up after dinner. The part of the job you weren't willing to do—preparation of the ingredients—was done for you under efficient factory conditions.

The advantages of manufactured housing are identical to the advantages of frozen dinners.

Manufactured housing is produced in efficient factories. The plans and the procedures are standardized. The people who do most of the work are not highly-paid master carpenters; they have specific jobs that they learn to do well. The materials are bought in large quantities and used in ways that minimize waste. Since the work is done inside, bad weather doesn't slow it down.

You can't possibly achieve that level of efficiency at a building site. Hiring a contractor to build at your site is like hiring a master chef to make arrangements to have your meals prepared by a staff of food service personnel in your kitchen.

Since we all need to eat regularly, most of us learn basic cooking skills, and many people become very good at cooking. (Personally, I make very good creamed peas on toast, but that's the subject for another book.) Building a dream house might be a once-in-a-lifetime event, so many people do not learn basic building skills. For that reason, it is more common to hire contractors than to hire master chefs. There's nothing wrong with that. Many people hire master chefs for once-in-a-lifetime occasions, like catering of wedding receptions. It is, however, very expensive.

If the convenience of manufactured housing makes it possible for you to make all the arrangements yourself, manufactured housing will save you money.

If the convenience of manufactured housing makes it possible for you to make all the arrangements for your building project yourself, manufactured housing will reduce your costs substantially.

How to Pocket the Savings

Some developers and contractors put up manufactured houses and then sell them for the same prices as site-built houses. That's a good business practice. Don't blame the contractor for not passing the savings along to you. Housing prices are market-driven, and if the houses are just as good, there's no reason to sell them at a lower price.

As a home buyer, you'll save money by buying a manufactured house only if you make the arrangements yourself. Buying a manufactured house from a developer is like hiring a master chef to pop your frozen dinner into the microwave.

Let's suppose that you want a ranch-style house. It will be built on land that you own, rather than rented land. It must be completely finished and ready to move into as quickly as possible. You lack the time or ability to do any of the construction work yourself or to supervise low-cost labor.

In that scenario, a double-wide modular house will almost certainly be your best buy. By buying it directly from the factory, you'll get it faster, cheaper, and more precisely built than if you had hired a local contractor to site-build a similar ranch. Double-wides have replaced 1950s ranches as the symbols of relatively-affordable "instant" housing.

To pocket the savings, you must do a few things yourself. In effect, you must be your own contractor. Your jobs might include hiring a subcontractor to build a foundation; arranging for electric and gas hookups; and arranging for water and sewer hookups or hiring subcontractors to put in a well and septic tank. If you need landscaping, you'll have to find a subcontractor or work on it yourself.

Those tasks aren't always easy, but they're within the capabilities of most people who are planning their dream houses. Making arrangements for a modular house is much easier than supervising carpenters to build a house on site.

That advantage exists, to some extent, with all forms of manufactured housing. The largest reduction in cost can be achieved if you abide by the following principles:

1. Use standard plans with as few modifications as possible. Modifications can offset the efficiencies of manufactured housing.

2. Make as many of the arrangements yourself as possible. For example, if you need a crane, you will usually save money by hiring

the crane operator yourself rather than paying a middleman to make the arrangements.

3. If you want a "ready-to-move-into" house, have as many of the finish materials installed at the factory as possible. The factory can do the finish work less expensively than can a contractor at the site.

4. However, you can do the finish work less expensively than the factory can—if you do some of it yourself or if you have another source of low-cost labor.

5. If there is more than one module, cluster all the plumbing into one "wet" module (see Chapter 8).

When Manufactured Housing Doesn't Make Sense . . . and When it Does

Factory construction is not cheap. Despite the efficiencies, manufacturers have to pay for their overhead and make a profit.

If you've carved out several months of your time to self-contract and contribute your own labor, manufactured housing will provide fewer opportunities to make good use of that time. If Uncle Horace is between jobs, manufactured housing will provide fewer opportunities to take advantage of his low-cost labor.

Because manufactured housing is standardized, you may not be able to take advantage of materials that become available at bargain prices. The beautiful paneled doors, available for free from the remodeling project next door, will probably not fit into the manufactured house plans. Neither will the half-price windows in the cull bin of the glass company, nor the half-price plywood with slightly banged-up edges at the lumber company. There will be no contractors' discounts, unless you can convince the housing manufacturer that you are a contractor.

If you need an "instant house," a double-wide will be cheaper than a site-built ranch. If you are willing to make a substantial sweat investment, the ranch will be cheaper.

With more complex housing styles, there is less price spread between manufactured and site construction. Yet as a rule, the least expensive way to obtain a new, ready-to-move-into house with minimal involvement is to choose a manufactured house and make at least some of the arrangements for it yourself.

The standardized plans of most manufactured houses leave little flexibility to add features that you want, or to subtract features that aren't worth the price or the tax assessment. A HUD-code house, for example, would probably be assessed at the same blue-book value even if you were able to omit the cabinetry and add a pantry.

Even if you build on site and make a significant sweat investment, some manufactured components will make sense. Structural foam panels, for example, may provide better and cheaper exterior walls than conventional stud framing. Pre-hung doors can save enough time to be well worth the extra price. The less low-cost labor you have available, the greater the savings will be from choosing manufactured items.

Peroration

There was a time when the term *manufactured* was a euphemism for low quality. That's changed, but so has the price. At this writing (1989), the prices of new and late-model HUD-code houses advertised in my local newspaper average about $40,000. That doesn't count the cost of the building lot, the foundation, development costs, or accommodations for water and sewer. Those costs can be avoided in a mobile home park, but you'll pay high monthly rent for the space.

With owner involvement, it's still possible to put up an extremely nice site-built house for less than $40,000, if you already have a lot to put it on. The popular notion that manufactured housing is inherently cheap needs to be put to rest. Other alternatives are, in many situations, much more affordable.

My personal preference is for site building with some manufactured components. That way I can put up whatever I want without any superfluous "added extras." However, manufactured housing is an option to consider, and is the choice of increasing numbers of people who build dream houses with limited budgets.

Chapter 13

Remodeling

Turning a run-down house into a dream house can be far less expensive than building a new structure. That's particularly true if you already own the house, or if you can find one with a cheap purchase price.

Most of the ideas discussed throughout this book apply to remodeling as well as building from scratch. However, there are enough differences to merit a brief look at some of the issues specifically from the viewpoint of a remodeler.

Tax Benefits of Remodeling

A run-down older house has probably been assessed at a very low level for many years. Fixing it up will raise the assessment. However, bureaucracy being what it is, the assessment records may still reflect "substandard" features for many years after they have been upgraded.

By contrast, the assessment of a new house may list all features as new, and in excellent condition, for years after they have begun to deteriorate.

The tax benefits of remodeling often seem random and unpredictable, but it is worthwhile to make a conscious effort to take advantage of them. The objective is to avoid tripping the levers that lead to new assessments. There are two principal levers to watch out for.

1. Exterior improvements. Assessment officials in many communities routinely tour neighborhoods and note the improvements made to the outsides of houses. If you re-side a house, for example, the work will be noticed and the entire house may be reassessed. Also, when town-wide or county-wide reassessments are done every few years, all exterior work will be noted even if the interior isn't inspected.

2. Building permits. In most communities, building inspectors and zoning administrators share information with property tax assessors. If you obtain a permit for a $10,000 kitchen-remodeling job, it's reasonable to assume that the tax assessor will raise the fair market value assessment by $10,000. (The tax assessment, of course, will reflect either the fair market value or a percentage thereof.)

How can you avoid tripping those levers?

Before planning a remodeling project, learn what the permit requirements are in your community. Just call the planning or zoning office and ask. Better yet, drop by the office—there may be a printed handout explaining the requirements in detail. This is information you need anyway to avoid violating the law, but once you have it you can use it to your advantage.

> *Avoid tripping the levers that lead to new assessments: exterior improvements and building permits.*

The requirements vary greatly from place to place. Some towns and counties require a permit only if you change the exterior perimeter of the house. Other communities require a permit if the improvements exceed a certain dollar value.

Once you are familiar with the permit requirements, schedule your remodeling project in a way that will not attract inspectors and assessors to your house any more often than necessary. One example of how this can be done is provided by my friend Helga.

Helga's Example

Helga lives in a city that requires a permit for any improvement that costs more than $500. Helga's house was quite run down when she bought it ten years ago, but she has fixed it up beautifully.

By scheduling the work carefully, Helga has managed to keep her tax assessment at a modest level.

When she bought the house, she determined that one improvement she wanted—new siding and windows—would inherently trigger a new assessment. Therefore, she tackled that project first.

When Helga finished the siding and windows, the assessor paid a visit and inspected the entire house. At that point, the interior was still run down. The new assessment reflected the cost of good siding and windows on a deteriorated house.

No additional exterior improvements were needed. Since that time, Helga has been making interior improvements in small increments. Each increment has cost less than $500, so she has not needed another permit. By her count, she has completed 73 incremental improvements, covering nearly every square inch of the interior.

Helga happens to be a competent do-it-yourselfer, so she is able to spend less than $500 for an improvement that might cost $1,500 if a contractor did it. The cut-off for permits in her city reflects actual expenditures, not the amount or quality of work done.

Helga keeps meticulous records to be sure that each project remains under $500. One of her improvements was refinishing the kitchen cabinets. She had spent $490, and ran out of polyurethane before she could finish the final cabinet. A new can would cost $23, so she left the final cabinet unfinished.

Fortunately, the next project she tackled (about a week later) also needed polyurethane. It didn't need a whole can, so she was able to use the leftovers on the cabinet without exceeding the $500 limit.

Another time, Helga retiled one of her bathrooms and replaced the combination tub-shower. It would have been tempting to schedule those two jobs together as a bathroom renovation. Helga, however, scheduled them as two distinctly separate projects. That way, neither project exceeded $500 and she didn't need a permit.

If Helga had fixed up the inside first, the tax assessor would have upgraded the assessment of the kitchen, baths, and other interior features when he checked the siding and windows. Because of her careful scheduling, the interior improvements have been tax-free.

Sooner or later, the assessors will come by. A new inspection may occur when there is a city-wide reassessment, or if Helga ever needs a permit for a future project.

But even if the assessors were to come tomorrow, Helga figures that she's saved $9,423.67 in property taxes over the last ten years by not tripping the reassessment levers. (As I mentioned before, she keeps meticulous records.)

As an added benefit, Helga has a lower mortgage than she would have needed if all the work had been done at once. With a project of that scale, she would have needed professional help and a very large loan with an interest rate of at least 10 percent. Incremental remodeling allows her to do the work when she has the time, energy, and money to do it.

Reusing Existing Components

In remodeling, the largest initial saving can be achieved by keeping intact, or reusing, existing components of the house.

When you look at a crumbling interior, it's human nature to sigh and say "Burn the house down and start over." That's usually (not always) a bad idea. Almost any house, even one that has been condemned by the Health Department, has components that can be saved as integral parts of your dream house.

Inspect the house thoroughly, and get expert advice if you need it. If this is your dream house, you're going to want to get rid of components that are inherently dangerous, inconvenient, or ugly. But there may be gems in the old structure that are hard to recognize because of their unattractive settings.

The next few short sections discuss some of the expensive components that are often replaced during remodeling jobs. Huge savings are possible if these components can be upgraded rather than torn out.

Crumbling Plaster Walls

Older houses that are in serious need of remodeling often have crumbling plaster walls. Should you repair the plaster, or rip it all down and replace it with drywall?

Replastering large sections of walls is expensive. However, as a rule of thumb, it is less expensive to repair up to half the plaster than to replace all the plaster with drywall.

Wainscotting is a far less expensive solution in many instances. Often, only the lower parts of the plaster walls are crumbling. Those are the parts that get kicked, banged against, and dripped on. You can save money by making minor repairs on the upper part and wainscotting the lower part.

If some of the plaster is buckling and falling off, you may have to remove parts of it to prevent it from pushing out the wainscotting material. However, any portions that can be held in place initially by the wainscotting will remain protected.

Ideally, the wainscotting material should be attractive boards that you ripped out of another part of the house. If such boards don't exist, there are low-cost alternatives. The cheapest, though not the prettiest, is fake-wood paneling.

Another economical wainscotting material is drywall, glued over the lower portion of the plaster. If you use 4x12-foot drywall, hardly any taping will be needed. Attach simple molding to the top. Paint the drywall, then wallpaper the upper part of the wall to mask any defects in the plaster. If you plan this carefully, it will look like the work of an interior designer, rather than a cheap way to fix up an old wall.

If drywall wainscotting doesn't appeal to you, and if you don't have recycled hardwood boards, consider wainscotting with 1x3 or 1x4 pine boards. New boards are not cheap. However, if you put them up yourself the expense will be far less than the cost of hiring a contractor to replace the entire wall surface.

If the electrical system needs upgrading, wainscotting will make the job easier. Just dig out enough plaster from the lower half of the

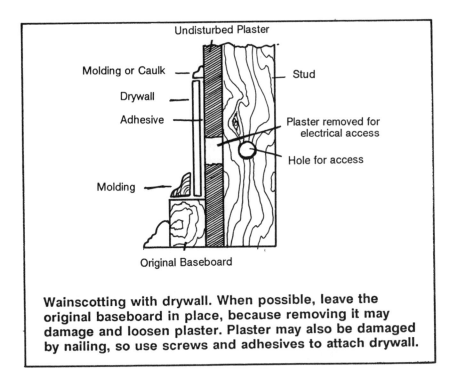

Wainscotting with drywall. When possible, leave the original baseboard in place, because removing it may damage and loosen plaster. Plaster may also be damaged by nailing, so use screws and adhesives to attach drywall.

wall to run new wiring, then wainscot over it. Before doing this you might want to check local codes, because some codes require that wiring be placed deeper into the wall cavity.

When plaster is uneven but not falling down, you can often cover the sins with wallpaper. Look for thick, textured wallpaper—the kind that needs paste. In wallpaper stores, you can often find discontinued rolls of this type of wallpaper for half of the nominal price or less. The thinner and more expensive self-adhesive wallpapers are useless for this purpose.

If the walls are marginal, try two layers of paper. The first layer should be horizontal and the second vertical. The horizontal layer can be truly ugly—the cheapest design you can find on sale. Wallpaper stores always have some designs in stock that they can't even give away. This is an ideal use of them. The outer layer, of course, should be either innocuous or attractive.

In the 1950s, many people used fake-wood paneling to cover crumbling plaster walls. If you pull down the paneling, the plaster will come with it. As long as the wall is still solid, you can cover the paneling with wallpaper. Sizing compound or a special primer may be needed to dull the surface so that the paper will stick. If the paneling has deep grooves, you may need to use two layers, horizontal and vertical, as described above. Test a small section to see if it works. Another alternative that has sometimes produced good results is to fill the grooves with joint compound.

Plumbing and Electricity

Older houses tend to have fewer outlets than newer houses do, so you may want to add new circuits. If your house has no grounded outlets, adding new circuits is a particularly good idea.

If the old nongrounded circuits are in good condition, it may not be worth the expense to replace them. Just be sure that you have grounded circuits for any appliances, tools, computers, etc., that have three-pronged plugs.

Old knob-and-tube wiring has an antique appearance, but it may be fine for outlets that do not require grounding. This type of wiring was discontinued because of the expense, not for safety reasons.

Unless there are empty slots in the service panel, adding new circuits will require you to either replace the panel or add a sub-panel. If the panel is an old-fashioned fuse box, consider replacing it. A breaker box is more convenient and arguably safer.

Corroded iron plumbing pipes may need replacement. More important, if your plumbing system has lead pipes, get rid of them. Lead leaching from supply pipes can cause brain damage. Lead drain pipes can leach toxins into surrounding soils.

The plumbing fixtures in many older houses lack proper venting. Is it worth the expense to upgrade all plumbing to the standards of modern codes? Trust your nose. If you can smell sewer gas, the venting is deficient and needs upgrading. Sewer gas is dangerous, but it's not odorless. If you don't smell it, you don't have it, and the venting is fine regardless of whether it meets the requirements of modern codes. Enjoy the low tax assessment you'll get as a result of substandard plumbing.

My wife, who is knowledgeable about plumbing, says that when money is tight and plumbing decisions must be made, you should consult with a plumber over age 50. Older plumbers, she says, know how to seal cracked toilet bowls with oatmeal and stop leaks in drain pipes with roofing tar.

But when health and safety are at stake, spend what you have to spend. From a property tax standpoint, assessment sheets don't contain boxes to check the quantity or quality of health and safety. Eliminating lead pipes and substandard electrical connections could save your life, without any increase in your tax burden.

Kitchens and Baths

The suggestions in Chapter 8 apply to remodeling as well as building from scratch. However, since kitchens and baths are often the costliest parts of a remodeling project, they deserve brief mention here.

Most remodelers will tell you that as a rule of thumb, old kitchens usually need updating but old bathrooms usually do not.

The art of cooking has evolved rapidly in recent decades. Older kitchens were designed for family members who were willing to spend eight hours a day preparing meals.

Just don't go overboard in remodeling the kitchen. An older kitchen may have some wonderful features; a pantry, for example. Keep the good stuff and build on it. Convenience need not be costly.

There has been little change over the years in the things that people do in bathrooms. You may want repairs and cosmetic improvements, because old baths have often suffered from decay, rot, and other effects of moisture. You may also want a larger water heater, because young people today take longer showers than their parents and grandparents did. But think long and hard before deciding to move the fixtures around or to replace them with modern, less-sturdy fixtures.

Hidden Treasures

One of the joys of remodeling is discovering features that previous remodelers covered up. A recent remodeling project in my area made local news—dilapidated siding was removed from a small house, and underneath it was a historically-significant log cabin.

I've never found anything that's drawn the attention of historians, but in almost every major remodeling project, there are interesting and useful features waiting to be uncovered.

In one project I ripped out three layers of ratty carpet. It was an unpleasant job; the carpets had endured six generations of ill-mannered dogs and cats and several babies. The house was a 1950s ranch, so I expected to find plywood subflooring underneath the carpets.

To my surprise, I found oak flooring. I rented a floor sander for a day (about $40), then mopped on three layers of polyurethane. I've since been told that many people in the 1950s protected their beautiful floors with ugly carpets, to keep them in good shape for later enjoyment by people like us. I don't often get nostalgic about the 1950s, but that was a nice gesture.

165

An acquaintance recently ripped off a layer of sagging ceiling tiles and a layer of damaged drywall, only to find an attractive tin ceiling underneath. Ceilings like that today are fashionable, and extremely expensive.

These were hidden treasures. Refinishing them cost far less than applying cheap carpeting or ceiling drywall. Be on the lookout for items like that, and keep your remodeling plans flexible enough so that you can make use of them.

Treasures with Hidden Costs

Unfortunately, some of the most charming features of older houses can get in the way of affordable remodeling.

Architecturally interesting features are a delight to look at, and are an important part of our cultural heritage. I love to tour beautifully restored old houses and admire the ornate cornices, the pillars, the pilasters, the corbels, and even the wooden gutters. Unfortunately, features like that in a run-down house usually need restoration, not remodeling.

Restoration is inherently expensive. It is done by skilled craftspersons who charge high hourly prices. The artists who created beautiful old wooden gutters worked for 20¢ per hour, but the artists who restore them work for $50 per hour.

When affordability is a concern, it's almost always best to start with a house that does not have architecturally significant features.

Taking Advantage of Recent Improvements

When you buy an older house, the last owner may have made desperate efforts to improve some components before giving up and deciding to sell.

For example, significant partial improvements may have been made to the electrical or plumbing systems before the rotted sills left the previous owner in a state of total frustration and depression.

You may want to make additional electrical or plumbing improvements, but salvage the good stuff. Adding to wiring and plumbing will be a lot cheaper than replacing everything.

Perhaps some sections of the sills and subflooring were also recently replaced. Perhaps in one room, the crumbling plaster was replaced with drywall, and insulated in the process. Take advantage of those improvements and avoid tearing them out along with the substandard components.

Insulation

One of the biggest drawbacks of most older houses is poor insulation. Since it's hidden, insulation does not usually cause significant increases in property tax assessments. If you dump a few bags of cellulose into the attic, or hire a contractor to blow insulation into the walls, the chances are slight that the assessor will even notice. These improvements can increase comfort and reduce heating bills by hundreds of dollars per year without increasing assessments.

If you're tearing down the plaster and lath anyway, you'd be crazy not to insulate between the studs before installing new drywall. If you're tearing down old siding, rigid foam should go up before you install the new siding. The cost will be incidental to the cost of the remodeling project. The payback in reduced heating (and/or cooling) bills may come before you've lived in the house for a year.

Most older houses have uninsulated basements. That is often the largest single source of heat loss. In retrofitting foundation insulation, it's almost impossible to meet the standards you'd insist on with a new structure. You can't insulate underneath an existing slab, for example. However, digging a trench around the foundation and applying rigid foam insulation (e.g., extruded polystyrene) will make a big difference. The best results come if the insulation extends below the frost line. Where I live, the frost line is four feet below the ground surface. Lesser depths suffice in warmer climates.

Whatever you do, *don't* insulate the entire inside of an old basement wall if you live in a cold climate. Concrete absorbs moisture, even under the best of conditions. If the inside is insulated, the moisture freezes. The concrete cracks, heaves, and causes lots of terrible problems. You can often reduce heat loss by insulating the upper portion—perhaps even the upper half—of the inside of a basement wall without inviting damage. But get advice from a local expert before trying even that modest step. It is always better, and safer, to insulate concrete on the outside.

Insulation works best if it is consistent throughout the house. Consistency is easy to achieve when you build from scratch, but almost impossible in most remodeling projects. Even if you can't insulate evenly throughout the structure, it is useful to add insulation wherever it is convenient to do so.

Do-It-Yourself Demolition

A common sweat investment in remodeling is do-it-yourself demolition. Even if you have no construction experience, you may be able to save a large amount of money by tearing out old plaster, carpets, ceilings, walls, and roofing before the carpenters begin their work.

Demolition can be fun, particularly for those of us who spend much of our lives sitting at desks. A couple of days with a sledge hammer and pry bar can release all the tensions and hostilities that have built up for the last year. Professional remodelers do that kind of thing regularly, so they enjoy it less and charge a high price for it.

Before you start, be sure that you have a good understanding of what is to be torn down and what must remain intact. Once you start demolishing things, it's easy to get carried away. Pulling down a post that supports the roof can be disastrous.

Also, don't neglect safety precautions. Depending on the nature of the job, you may need a dust mask, goggles, gloves, steel-toed boots, and a hard hat. If you're knocking down a wall, make sure there are no live electrical wires running through it. Stand back and assess the progress frequently, to be sure that a big beam is not about to fall on your head.

If you're tearing down something that looks like it might contain friable asbestos, don't touch it. Asbestos must be removed by highly trained people with specialized equipment.

Making Use of What is There

The most successful remodeling projects make creative use of what is already there. Look at the existing features, even the ugly ones, and figure out what you can do with them to make them useful and attractive. Tearing things out—although fun—should be a last-resort choice.

A friend remodeled an old brick warehouse to serve as his apartment plus offices for rental income. He stripped off all the interior wall finishes, leaving the exposed brick, which was extremely attractive. Then he insulated the brick on the outside and applied wood and stucco sidings.

The appearance of the building is stunning. What's more, the brick provides thermal mass, so simple systems can be used to heat the apartment and offices. My friend heats his part of the building in winter by building an occasional fire in a wood stove. An unattractive old building that had outlived its original use has become a beautiful, useful, practical structure.

That was a spectacularly successful remodeling project. Yet a step-by-step description of how he did it probably wouldn't help you, because your project isn't likely to be an identical brick warehouse. The only transferrable lesson is that it's important to look at what you have. Then use common sense and creativity to make the best use of it.

Designing Your Project

Every existing house is different. Therefore, the rules of thumb for new construction aren't always applicable when you remodel.

As an obvious example, the advantages of cube-like designs, discussed in Chapter 5, are irrelevant to a remodeler. If the existing house isn't a cube, then it isn't a cube.

Before you begin a remodeling job, stare at the house for a very long time. Acquaint yourself with every feature and every square foot of space. What can be salvaged, and what needs to be torn out? What changes can be made to make better use of space? What are the problems, and what is the most cost-effective way to overcome them? If you spend lots of time brainstorming at the site, you'll come up with design ideas that are better and cheaper than those that first come to mind.

Suppose, as an example, that the house is a "pink trailer" that you purchased cheaply because the upstairs ceilings were less than six feet high. How can you raise the ceilings?

There are standardized solutions to problems like that. A book, or a professional contractor, might tell you that the way to create more headroom in an upper story is to build a cathedral ceiling with lots of dormers.

That would work, but it would also be very expensive. In your specific house, there may be ways to create more attractive headroom at less cost.

Look closely at what's there. If there are five layers of thick ceiling material, removing them and putting thin drywall on the ceiling would make a big difference. If the ceiling would still be too low, you could remove the joists and replace them at a higher level for a semi-cathedral effect. Maybe there would still be one location—the top of the stairway, for example—where people would bump their heads. One small dormer may be needed there.

Always start by considering the least-expensive options. If they aren't adequate, consider the options that are progressively more expensive. This review *must* take place on site. The general rules of thumb were developed for other houses that are not exactly like yours. The best, most cost-effective designs are the ones created specifically for your house.

Even if you have never designed a project before, you are in a better position than anyone else to make at least rough sketches of what needs to be done. Expensive professionals can't possibly spend as much time as you can examining the details of the old structure that will become your dream house. They also know less about your needs and tastes than you do. If you need professional help to check your ideas, hire a designer—or the carpenter who will do the work—to help with the details.

Resources

There are hundreds of good books with helpful information about designs, materials, and techniques used in remodeling. Check your library or bookstore—I'm reluctant to single out specific books because there are so many.

One book is worth mentioning, however, because it has a wealth of information that is not readily available anywhere else. That is the *Cost Cuts Manual*, published by the Rehab Work Group. It was prepared for use by non-profit organizations that rehabilitate affordable housing, but it can serve as a bible for anybody who wants to remodel a house at the lowest possible cost. The manual compares costs of materials and labor and offers practical advice for almost every aspect of residential remodeling. Best of all, it's written in plain English. Although the manual focuses on remodeling, the information is also useful for those who are building from scratch.

The manual carries a hefty price tag ($45), and unfortunately it is not available from book stores or libraries. Borrow a copy from a local nonprofit organization if you can. Otherwise, you can order it from the Rehab Work Group, P.O. Box 1490, Alexandria, VA 22313.

Chapter 14

Case Study One:
Building From Scratch

A few years ago, my wife and I became weary of moving from place to place and decided to build a dream house. This was our first attempt to build with a low-tax strategy.

It's a great house. We expect to live in it for the rest of our lives. If we had bought a house that we liked as well from a developer, the initial and continuing costs would have been at least twice as high.

Our dream house is not a perfect model of a low-tax house. We made some mistakes, and we learned from them. We also chose several features that were more costly than necessary, because of the needs and tastes of members of our family.

Your dream house will undoubtedly be very different from ours because it will reflect your own dreams. However, you will be weighing many of the same practical issues, so retelling our story may provide some useful insights.

Site Selection

We weren't looking for the cheapest possible lot. We had specific criteria for the location of our dream house:

1. We wanted a rural site within commuting distance of the metropolitan area that provides our employment and cultural activities.

2. Because growth was occurring rapidly in our county, we wanted a large enough building site to protect our immediate surroundings from future development.

3. We preferred a lot that had access to water—a lake, a brook, or a pond site.

Because we had a limited budget, we were prepared for disappointment, or at least compromise. To our delight, after searching for several months, we found a site that met our criteria, with some added bonuses.

The Lot

The site we found was ten acres—much larger than we were ready to settle for. It included a modest amount of frontage on a pleasant lake. It even had a cottage. The cottage was rustic but usable. We could live in it while building the dream house. It now serves as a home office and writers' retreat. There were also good neighbors. Good neighbors add to the quality of life without adding to the tax assessment.

The price was $25,000. In our area at the time, that price was

The lake: Significantly, the site won a strong endorsement from our kids.

just slightly more than we would have paid for a typical building lot—measured in feet rather than acres, with no lake frontage or cottage.

Why was the price so reasonable? There were some "pink trailer" characteristics that had scared away other potential purchasers who were looking for lakefront property.

• The acreage was not private. Other families had deeded access over it to get to their cottages.

• The amount of lake frontage was small, and several other families had deeded rights to share use of it.

• The deed was messy, so the title search was time consuming. (It was also expensive, but the extra cost was incidental to the cost of purchasing the real estate.) Other people had put deposits on the land. When their lawyers said "This is a messy deed," they got their deposits back.

• The land was ledgy. Therefore a basement would be impossible, and the septic system would require a mound.

To us, those disadvantages were not important. They made it possible for us to buy a large lot with deluxe features at a price we could afford.

House Design

We have a larger-than-average family, and each family member has at least an occasional need for privacy. We also hate to throw things away, so we need storage space.

Therefore, we planned a five-bedroom house with 2,000 square feet of living space and over 1,000 square feet of unfinished space.

We opted for a long, narrow, two-story design. That's more expensive per square foot than a cubical design, but has two advantages. The long, narrow shape allows more privacy for individual family members, and makes it possible to take maximum advantage of passive solar gain.

The house is a simple rectangle with many south-facing windows on the first story. We added one extra protrusion—a sun space on the south wall. We knew that would add to the tax assessment, but it was a feature we wanted.

We attached a two-story garage to the north side of the house. That provides extra protection from the north winds and ample storage space. (On the off-chance that my tax lister is reading this, I should note that for assessment purposes, the house is actually a story and a half, and the garage is a story and a quarter.)

We put shed roofs on both the house and the attached garage. The appearance from the outside is roughly similar to that of a gable roof covering the entire structure. The double-shed design allowed us to install clerestory windows at the highest part of the house for summer ventilation. Also, shed roofs cost less and are assessed at a lower level than gable roofs.

Energy Efficiency

The two cheapest sources of heat in our region are wood and sunshine. Those aren't the cheapest sources in inner cities, where

173

wood is delivered from distant locations, and multi-unit houses are shaded by skyscrapers. Where we live, sunshine and wood are plentiful. Unfortunately, they are not always convenient. We wanted cheap heat, but did not want to sacrifice comfort or convenience.

Therefore, we chose building materials that are high in thermal

Framing: On the first story, we used posts and beams to supplement the three concrete exterior walls. On the second story, we used conventional stud framing.

mass. The first floor is a thick (eight-inch) insulated slab. Three of the exterior first-story walls and one strategically-located interior wall are constructed of concrete. The thermal mass allows us to make good use of the erratic heat from a south-facing window-wall and a wood stove that is not tended on a regular basis.

Poured concrete is not cheap. Therefore, we opted for traditional wood-frame construction on the second story.

We strapped the exterior of the concrete walls and applied stressed-skin foam panels. The panels consist of four-inch-thick polyisocyanurate with waferboard laminated to the outside, providing a nailing surface for siding. We later filled in the space between the strapping with a cementitious foam insulation called *Air-Krete*. (That's a trade name, but to the best of my knowledge, there is no generic name for this excellent product.)

We insulated the upstairs walls with fiberglass plus five inches of rigid foam. The ceiling insulation consists of 18 inches of fiberglass plus two inches of rigid foam.

We added a solar collector for domestic water heating. Since the solar collector works best in the summer, we also installed a loop through our wood cook stove to help heat water in winter.

The house is easy to heat. We haven't yet gotten around to taking

Sweat investments: Although the concrete work was contracted out, family members pitched in and helped whenever possible, cutting the bill considerably.

full advantage of the energy-saving potential. For example, we haven't hung insulated curtains on all the windows, so much of the solar gain we pick up during the day radiates back out through the windows at night.

Even so, we conveniently heat the house with about three cords of wood per year ($255 at 1989 prices). Those three cords also help to cook our food and heat our water. With a little more effort, we could reduce the wood consumption below that modest level.

Property Tax Issues

Besides keeping the design simple and avoiding central heating, we made other design decisions to reduce our property taxes. Those decisions also reduced our initial costs without diminishing the appeal (to us) of our dream house.

In many houses, the most expensive interior region is the kitchen. Our kitchen is cheap. We have only 63 inches of built-in counter

175

Low-cost, low-tax interior: Features shown here include a portable counter, a portable cupboard, hooks for pans, rustic shelves, and the door to the piggy room. The fire pole cost $20 at the junkyard, and is not taxed. Photo by Alden Pellett

space and no other built-in cupboards. The tax assessors, of course, list the kitchen as substandard.

Yet our kitchen is functional and convenient. We have moveable furniture, including an island on wheels, that serves the same function as counters and cupboards. We also have a piggy room just off the kitchen. The piggy room serves as a pantry, wine cellar, and root cellar. It also holds our refrigerator and freezer, which are economical to operate because the piggy room stays cool most of the year. Piggy rooms are described in more detail in Chapter 8, but it's worth repeating here that they're a lot cheaper—and more useful—than the extensive cabinetry that is typical of modern houses.

Finishing

We also reduced our costs and assessment by minimizing interior finish. The floor of the first story is dyed concrete. It's attractive, permanent, and cost a fraction of what we would have spent on a carpet. It also provides thermal mass for solar gain.

The upstairs floor is softwood. That, too, is cheaper than carpeting and lasts a lot longer. On both floors we have attractive throw rugs, but since they're not attached to the house, they're not taxed.

The concrete walls are skimmed over with joint compound. They look like plaster walls. The second-story walls are finished with drywall. The finish trim consists of simple pine boards. They're cheap, look good, and get a low assessment.

Our first story includes some posts and beams. Post-and-beam construction can be expensive if the notching is done by artists. Posts and beams with simple notching are inexpensive and aesthetically attractive in a rough way.

We continued the rough motif with shelves and any other interior structures that were attached to the house. The decor looks intentional—as if a designer decided to give this house a rustic look. However, tax assessors, if they consult their manuals, can tell that it didn't cost much.

Errors

We avoided building things into any part of the house. We even avoided closets. In retrospect, that wasn't a grand idea. I've since learned that simple closets don't add much to tax assessments. Our original idea was to build portable wardrobes (or perhaps *armoires*) in lieu of closets, but we haven't gotten around to that yet, so all the bedrooms look cluttered.

We took several other steps that haven't particularly paid off. For example, one wall on the second story is less than six feet high. We planned it that way so that the house would be listed as a story and a half, rather than two stories.

I later learned that if assessors can see that a building functions as a two-story structure, they don't like to reduce the assessment to one-and-a-half stories. They simply bump up the "design" factor to offset the arbitrary reduction. The low wall didn't reduce construction costs, and we now know that it didn't reduce our tax assessment, either. We might as well have constructed two stories.

Telling an assessor that you're trying to hold down taxes is like challenging somebody to a duel.

One big indulgence at the time of construction was to mold a big hole in the slab for a hot tub. I'm not sure what we were thinking

177

about at the time. We don't even like hot tubs. However, thanks to our impulsive behavior, we have a big hole in the slab. It's in the sun space, so one of these days we'll fill it with soil and plant an indoor garden.

We've also made a-point of telling everyone we know, including assessors, about our low-tax strategy. I wouldn't advise others to do that. Tax assessors have a lot of discretion. Telling an assessor that you're trying to hold down your taxes is like challenging somebody to a duel. If the assessor gets the impression that you're trying to "beat the system," the incentive is to raise assessments wherever possible. In my case, I was planning to write this book, so it seemed important to run ideas past everybody I met, including tax assessors. Your assessment will probably be lower if you point out the "deficits" to the assessor without mentioning that your house is better for the lack of high-tax features.

Variations from Principles

The hot tub hole was not the only exception we made to the low-tax principles we'd started with. Most of the others were better thought out. Since this was our dream house, it seemed worth paying extra for some features.

I've already mentioned the sun space. We knew it would add corners to the structure and raise the "design factor" of our assessment, but we wanted a sun space.

We built in a dishwasher. We tried a portable one, but hated it. We also installed a built-in vacuum cleaner. We rationalize that it saves us more money in bag costs than it adds to our tax burden.

For siding we chose vertical shiplap, applied with the rough side out and coated with dark transparent stain. The tax manuals in our state give that a low rating, justifiably, because it is inexpensive. However, it looks beautiful, so it gets a higher tax assessment than it should have. We could have sided the house with textured plywood or rolled asphalt for about the same price. That would have reduced our taxes. However, on our dream house, we're willing to pay a little extra in taxes to please the tourists who drive by.

Those were splurges, but without them this would not be our dream house. We made realistic projections of the initial and continuing costs, and decided that they were worth the price. We didn't just put them in because a builder convinced us that they are features of any quality house.

The finished house: The south side (upper photo) is designed to take advantage of solar gain. An unheated garage and a woodshed are attached to the north side (lower photo). Overlooking the garage roof are clerestory windows for summer ventilation.   Photos by Alden Pellett

The Bottom Line

The house cost us about $40,000 to build. The land cost $25,000. But is the assessment $65,000? Unfortunately, no. The total assessment came in at $130,000, and after two levels of appeal it was lowered to $103,000.

The assessment of the structure is within the range of what we spent, a very low range for the features that we enjoy. However, the assessment of the building lot was raised, inexplicably, to a level far more that double the price we paid for it.

Unfortunately, there are no comparable properties—no similar parcels with similar liabilities—in our town. Therefore, we have no convenient way to prove that we are being treated unfairly.

I'm working on that. Perhaps, in the next edition of this book, I'll be able to add a chapter on how to appeal tax assessments of properties without comparables.

Meanwhile, the steps we took to hold down the assessment of the structure were successful. It's a great house, bought at a modest cost, and the taxes on the house itself are modest. If we had added items that are standard in many new houses—central heat, kitchen cabinets, and carpets, for example—the total assessment could have jumped to $200,000 or more. Yet those additional features would do nothing to increase our enjoyment of our dream house.

Other building projects we've pursued since then have been more successful from a cost-tax perspective. We've learned from our mistakes, and, more significantly, have not encountered the problems with land valuation that occurred with our dream house.

Yet we're pleased with our house. Our low-tax strategy made it possible to live in the house we wanted, at a price we can afford, despite the aberration in assessment of the land that it sits on.

Chapter 15

Case Study Two: Remodeling

My wife and I recently completed an extensive remodeling project. We used a low-tax strategy to create an attractive, comfortable house at a modest price. Although we rent the house to others, the procedures we followed were no different than if it had been our own dream house.

Selection of Property

Our criteria in selecting the property were specific and simple. It had to be cheap. The location had to be within a reasonable distance of our own house. The structure had to be one that could be remodeled into a genuinely good place to live, at minimal expense.

In recent years, we've used those same criteria to acquire and renovate several houses in rural, urban, and suburban locations. The house we found this time is in a small town.

It was a tiny house on a half-acre lot overlooking a beautiful river. The price was $16,000. In our county, that's less than the average price of a raw building lot with no structure and no river.

As you may have guessed, the property had some "pink trailer" characteristics. Many other people had looked at it and, despite the affordable price, decided it wasn't what they had in mind.

The house had less than 500 square feet of interior living space. It was owner-built, and some of the construction techniques were nonstandard. The house had been vacant for a while, so its appearance was beginning to deteriorate.

The owner-builder was a delightful older gentleman. He had built with the needs of his own family in mind, rather than the hypothetical needs of future occupants. None of his family members happened to be physically tall, so he hadn't wasted money on high ceilings and doorways.

The ceilings were no higher than six feet from the floor, and in some parts of the house they were lower. The front entry door, which led into an enclosed porch-mudroom, was less than five feet

The view: Other than the low price, the biggest attraction of the property was the river that flows behind the house. It's always beautiful and changes daily—this snapshot was taken after a rainstorm.

high.

That entry door was the first feature of the house noticed by most potential purchasers. I suspect that many of them did not look beyond that door, despite the beautiful location and low price of the property.

Reusing and Upgrading What was There

Remodeling took place in two stages: upgrading the original house, then adding a new wing.

Remodeling a house is almost inherently less expensive than building from scratch. Since this lot and house cost less than most raw building lots, we had a spectacular opportunity to keep it affordable.

Much of the site work was already in place. There was an electrical hookup and an adequate driveway. The well and septic tank needed upgrading, but that was far less expensive than starting from scratch.

The town did not require a permit for interior remodeling. Therefore, we were able to get right to work on that part of the job without struggling through any red tape.

The structure was solid. It contained many features that were in decent condition, or at least salvageable.

The plumbing and electricity needed to be expanded upon, but for the most part, what was there was usable. Much of the existing wiring had already been upgraded in recent years.

The siding needed repairs but was basically sound. The roofing wasn't in great shape, but could be inexpensively repaired rather than immediately replaced. A new roof will be needed in a couple of years, but we'll be better able to afford it then. Most of the windows were in good condition, although we decided to add more windows in strategic locations for light and view.

Much of the interior wall surface was finished with paneling, which we decided to remove rather than repair. The cellulose insulation in the walls was reusable. We covered it with rigid foam to increase the R-value, and put up new drywall.

A small room off the kitchen was well situated to become a pantry. It's not quite a "piggy room," but it eliminates any need for extensive cabinetry. One outstanding feature the house already had was a modest but functional root cellar, accessible through a trap door.

Raising the Ceiling, Opening Up the Living Space

The ceiling, of course, had to be raised. The only reasonable way to do that was to rip off the existing ceiling and replace it with a cathedral ceiling that followed the roof lines.

The new ceiling is attractive, architecturally interesting, and high enough to accommodate a good-sized sleeping loft. We considered adding dormers to increase headroom in the loft, but decided against that, since we were planning to build full-size bedrooms in the addition.

We removed interior partitions wherever possible. Opening up the interior made the house look larger and more comfortable, and allowed better use of space. The dining-living area was still small after it was combined, but far less claustrophobic than the original separate rooms had been.

The open feeling was enhanced by adding windows in three strategic locations. We needed high windows near the peak of the

The new ceiling: For design interest, we covered the part over the sleeping loft with drywall and the rest with pine boards. Some finishing touches were still needed when this photo was taken, but people who had bumped their heads on the old, low ceiling were impressed by the change.

Photo by Alden Pellett

new cathedral ceiling for ventilation and for natural light in the loft. We added windows over the kitchen sink, because we both grew up washing dishes in front of windows. In the living area, we added two large panes of insulated fixed glass to take advantage of the view of the river.

The fixed panes were a good buy from the cull bin of a glass store; they cost only $20 apiece. They were cut with diagonal slants on the top corners, a shape that complemented other shapes in the house. They had been misordered by somebody else, but were perfect in this house. No high-priced architect could have chosen better windows for this location.

The low entry door could not just be replaced with a standard-size door. The wall it was on—the street-side of the mud room—is only slightly over five feet high. However, the end wall of the mud room is high enough for a standard door. That proved to be a better location for a door anyway, because it is adjacent to the parking area. All we had to do was cut a new opening there and install a new (actually a used) door.

The small front door is still there. It gets used when furniture is moved in and out of the house. Long items, like couches and bed frames, can be moved straight through that door and into the house without turning a corner in the mudroom. On those occasions, we are grateful that the extra door is there.

At the risk of belaboring a point, I believe that the small door provided a valuable lesson. To almost everybody who had seen the house before remodeling began, the small door was the most objectionable feature. We all bumped our heads in that doorway at least once, and shouted "This has to go!" or words to that effect. It didn't have to go. It's a good feature of the house, as long as we have another door for everyday use. In remodeling, don't tear anything out until or unless you are certain that there will be no future use for it.

Permits for the Addition

As is true almost everywhere, we needed a permit to build an addition. Because of the layout of the house and lot, we also needed a zoning variance.

The original house was built before zoning, closer to the road than would be allowed today. The lot is a long narrow parcel, sandwiched between the road and the river. It is not deep enough to allow an addition that would meet today's setback requirements.

We planned a narrow addition, attached only to the back four feet of the end-wall of the existing house. That design kept the addition as far from the road as possible.

When we applied for the variance, we didn't hire a lawyer. We did not fret and moan about the ordinance. The ordinance happened to be a good one, and we acknowledged that. If we had a piece of land that we could make reasonable use of within the confines of the ordinance, that's what we would have done. We made it clear that if the neighbors had any concerns, we would accommodate them to the best of our ability. The zoning board understood our position and granted a variance with no hassle at all. I've often heard developers complain about the

If you don't use a fancy lawyer to make unreasonable requests, local governing bodies usually bend over backward to accommodate your legitimate needs.

"unreasonable" permit requirements and actions of local governing bodies. But in my experience, if you don't hire a fancy lawyer to make unreasonable requests, local governing bodies usually bend over backward to accommodate your legitimate needs. The "trick" is to be a good neighbor, and try to meet the honest concerns of people in the neighborhood.

Design of the Addition

Although the design was influenced by setback requirements, the addition turned out to be very attractive.

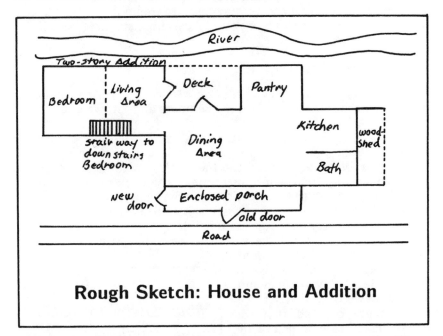

Rough Sketch: House and Addition

Technically, it is a one-story structure with a basement. However, the land slopes toward the river, so the basement has an exposed exterior wall with a view of the river. The basement is one of the most pleasant parts of the house, and functions as a lower story.

The dimensions of the addition are 12x24 feet. It is a simple rectangle, but it adds architectural interest to the house because it jags back from the rest of the house. Aesthetically, it complements the original house in an attractive way.

The upper story is divided into a living room and a small bedroom. The lower level serves as a bedroom and is large enough to deserve the description "master bedroom." The sleeping loft in the older part of the house provides extra sleeping space for overnight guests.

No additional unheated storage space was needed, because the large mudroom and a woodshed in the older part of the house serve that function.

Out of habit, we still refer to the structure as "the little house." However, it now has about 1,100 square feet of well-laid-out finished living space, plus convenient additional room for storage. Compared to the condominiums and multifamily housing units that many modern families endure, it is no longer little.

The Deck

I usually recommend against decks. They're popular features that often serve no useful function. If you have a suburban house with a level yard, the yard is a fine place for lawn chairs and picnic tables. Covering part of the yard with a deck simply adds to the cost and to the tax burden.

However, a deck is useful if it can add quality living space to a house during the warm summer months. It's a lot cheaper than adding enclosed space.

This house had an ideal location for a small deck. It was a pocket of space at the back of the house, overlooking the river, between the new addition and an older, smaller addition.

The bank that goes down to the river is steep. The deck makes it possible to walk out the back door and enjoy the view, without seeing (or being seen from) the road.

It cost about $100 to build, but will add substantially more than that to the tax assessment. Nevertheless, it adds enough to the quality of life in the house to merit the extra expense.

The Lower Story of the Addition

The foundation and basement were built at a busy time in our lives, so we hired a contractor. The contractor handled the excavation, built the forms, and poured the concrete. He covered the concrete walls with rigid foam insulation and backfilled. He's competent and honest, so we didn't feel a need to watch over his work.

Where the outer basement wall was above grade level, we stuccoed over the rigid foam with special mortar mix made especially for that purpose. It's expensive, but reportedly holds up better than ordinary mortar.

187

The concrete floor on the lower level is dyed brick red. It is an attractive, finished floor. Dyeing and polishing added $40 to the cost of pouring the slab, but saved us from the expense of a carpet or other finish materials. The insulated concrete walls provide thermal mass, helping to heat the house comfortably and economically.

The walls were skimmed over with a thick sealing compound. (We used *Thoroseal* brand; I am not aware of a generic name for the product.) That adds some protection from moisture and evens out the walls to create the appearance of plaster. The product is usually used on the outside, where waterproofing is more important. However, the interior application provided additional sealing and smoothed out the imperfections of the concrete. We coated the sealer with textured paint.

The aesthetic results are imperfect because the concrete walls are uneven and bowed in places. In retrospect, we should have worked more closely with the contractor, who had not understood our intention to finish the walls in this manner. Many basement contractors assume that the basement, if finished, will be strapped and drywalled on the inside. However, the imperfections on the walls are not particularly noticeable unless you are looking for them.

Upper Story—Sandwich Panels

For the upper story of the addition we chose a construction technology that was new to us. We were impressed by it. We built the exterior walls with structural foam sandwich panels. As discussed in Chapter 12, these panels consist of rigid foam sandwiched between two layers of waferboard. They are structurally stronger than conventional stud framing. They also provide continuous, efficient insulation.

We happened to be in an ideal position to take advantage of the technology. The panels we used were made by a nearby manufacturer, Foam Laminates of Vermont. The panels, the crane, and the experts were all nearby.

Each panel was the size of an entire exterior wall. The walls went up with a crane, in about an hour. Framing windows and doorways was an easy job—we just cut the openings with a saw. Although a chain saw was recommended, we found that the waferboard dulled the chain quickly. We were able to make more accurate cuts with a circular saw, although that meant sawing from both sides.

We also went to the trouble of scooping out the foam around the window and door openings and imbedding 2x4s for extra support. Many people who use these panels say that extra step is not needed. Because the product was new to us we opted for a conservative approach. Even so, preparation of the openings took less time than it would have taken with conventional stud walls.

Screwing drywall to the interior went quickly because of the continuous waferboard surface. Another option would have been to glue the drywall. We're creatures of habit and accustomed to screws. If you're new to drywall and have the luxury of a continuous surface, gluing may be a better choice, because there would be no screw heads to mud over.

We nailed vertical shiplap to the outside. That's my favorite siding; it's inexpensive, attractive, and easy to apply. It also matched the siding on the older part of the house.

Many manufacturers make sandwich panels in different locations. I'm sure that prices and quality vary greatly. But for this project, the structural panels from Foam Laminates of Vermont were tighter, straighter, better insulated, and easier to finish than the stud walls we would have otherwise built. The price was about what we would have spent for materials alone—never mind labor— for stud walls.

Questions and Concerns About Structural Panels

Whenever a new building material is used, it should be examined critically. Several concerns were raised about our use of structural panels in this project, and they were all resolved to our satisfaction.

• **Effect on the environment:** Some types of rigid foam blow holes in the ozone layer of the atmosphere. However, the panels we chose use expanded (not extruded) polystyrene, which is environmentally safe. It has a lower R-value per inch than does polyisocyanurate, but because the insulation is continuous, the effective R-value is much better than that of an ordinary stud wall with fiberglass insulation.

• **Effect on health:** Another concern we had was that most waferboard contains high concentrations of formaldehyde, a carcinogenic indoor air pollutant. However, the waferboard used for these panels was made with phenolic resins and contains no formaldehyde.

• **Longevity of the product:** While the panels were going up, the phone rang. It was my editor at the *Journal Of Light Construction.* I described what was happening, and how impressed I was by it. He said, "Oh, then you won't want to hear about the article we're preparing on carpenter ants."

I later read the article my editor was talking about, and learned that carpenter ants love to burrow into rigid foam. That's one extra thing to think about, but it is not in itself a reason to avoid rigid foam. After all, carpenter ants got their name from their tendency to burrow into wood, long before rigid foam was invented. Unless your house is built entirely of concrete or metal, your responsibilities as a homeowner will include watching out for these critters, and doing whatever you have to do to keep them away.

Windows and Doors

We selected windows and doors for the addition according to what was available at bargain prices. We put in two attractive casement windows that were on sale at half price at our lumber store because they were missing a side strip. The side strip served no function. After installation, it is impossible to tell whether these windows have side strips or not.

The other windows in the addition are either fixed glass, obtained cheaply from local cull bins, or sliders that were on sale.

A neighbor obtained three interior doors free from a nearby airport remodeling project and offered them to us. They are of commercial quality, and therefore superior to the cheap interior doors we would have otherwise bought for this project. That episode was also a reminder that some of the things that make a house a good place to live in—like having good neighbors—have nothing to do with prices and tax assessments.

There are two entry doors to the addition: one on the exposed side of the basement and one on the deck. Because they are both on the view side of the house, they had to include windows. It took some shopping around, but we were able to obtain good insulated doors with glass at a reasonable price.

Heating

The older part of the house had been heated with a very large, old-fashioned gas heater. It was hooked up to a modern, well-built chimney.

The old heater took up more space than seemed reasonable, and drew its combustion air from inside the house. During the initial remodeling stage we replaced it with a smaller, more modern gas wall furnace. We used the chimney for a wood stove. Since it was a small house, either the wood stove or the wall furnace was more than sufficient to heat it.

When we built the addition we added a second chimney and installed a second wood stove in the lower level. With all the insulated thermal mass there, we figured that it was an ideal location for a stove. We also moved the wall furnace to the lower level. Since heat rises, any single heat source works best at the lowest living space.

Since the house is rented, we did not want to rely too heavily on wood heat. Not all tenants care to fuss with wood stoves, even in a house where that is convenient.

In practice, it is possible to heat the entire house with only the single gas heater. However, because of the long horizontal span of the house, the heat distribution is not ideal. Therefore, we installed a second wall furnace upstairs, closer to the opposite end of the house.

The two stoves and two heaters provide an ideal heating system for the house. The occupants have a choice of low-cost (wood) heat or convenient (gas) heat at any time, to provide any level of heat they want in any part of the house. The comfort level is equivalent to that of zoned central heat, at a tiny fraction of the cost.

The Roof

The gentleman who built the original house knew how to put up a structure that meets basic needs at the lowest possible cost. For example, he had used vertical shiplap for siding long before I learned how cost-effective that material is.

The roof he installed on the original house was metal, with a shallow but adequate pitch. For consistency, we used metal roofing with the same pitch on the addition. It was an excellent choice.

The roof trusses were easy to build and put up because they had to span only 12 feet. My wife built the first truss. Then we hired our teenage son to build the rest, using the first truss as a model. If the span were longer, it would have made sense to order prebuilt Fink trusses from a local manufacturer. It would have also made sense to have them put up while the crane was at the site. However, when the span is only 12 feet, using a crane seems silly.

We chose to include a substantial overhang with soffits and fascias. With cheap labor (including our own) available, these features added practically nothing to the cost and made the structure look a little classier. If we'd hired a general contractor the added cost would have been significant. (The features will, of course, add to the tax assessment.)

The materials cost of the metal roofing was higher than for roll roofing or even asphalt shingles. With better planning, we might have been able to offset that expense by applying the roofing over strapping instead of plywood sheathing. However, the materials cost was offset by low labor costs. Two of us were able to put it up in an afternoon.

The addition: Functionally, it's a two-story structure, and looks like one from the side facing the river. For tax assessment purposes, it's a one-story structure with a basement.

Photo by Alden Pellett

I convinced my wife not to include gutters. I have a strong dislike for gutters, partly because I've spent disproportionate periods of my life cleaning and repairing them. If the lack of gutters results in drainage problems, my wife will have earned the right to say "I told you so." In the meantime, we will have saved a few dollars in property taxes.

Finish Work

We kept the finish work as simple as possible. The interior is an attractive living environment without fancy embellishments.

As noted above, the concrete walls on the lower level were simply skimmed over with thick sealing material, than painted with rough textured paint.

The upstairs drywall is less than perfect. We encountered scheduling problems with professional tapers, so we did much of the work ourselves. The imperfections aren't very noticeable, however, and can be remedied later if we get around to it.

All trim boards are ordinary 1x4 pine stock. They look fine, if you notice them at all. They were primed to seal the knots, then coated with the same off-white paint as the walls.

The kitchen cabinets were also built with pine boards. Some were left as open shelves. Some needed doors, so my wife spent an afternoon making cabinet doors from scrap boards. She connected the boards together with Z braces and attached hinges and knobs.

An alternative we've used in other projects is to purchase louvered shutters to use as cabinet doors. They're more expensive than scrap lumber but far cheaper than manufactured or custom-built cabinet doors.

For quick, precise cutting of trim boards, it's useful to have a table saw at the site. We bought a lightweight one with an aluminum base, on sale for $95. It served our needs better than a heavy-duty professional table saw because we could move it easily to the location where we were working. The labor savings during this one project more than made up for the cost of the saw, and we still have it for future projects. Most finish carpenters also use power miter saws. They're not cheap, but any tool that allows you to do good work yourself rather than hiring high-priced professionals will pay for itself quickly.

Tax Implications

At this writing, the house hasn't yet been reassessed to reflect the work we've done. At least in theory, the assessment should be modest.

The lower level of the addition should be rated as a basement, even though it serves as quality living space. The skimmed-over walls are still concrete, and the dyed floor is still an "unfinished" slab, no matter how attractive those features may be. They were cheap and shouldn't add any more to the assessment than what they cost.

The upstairs floor is softwood, a relatively inexpensive material. There is a carpet remnant in the smaller bedroom, but since it's cheap I won't worry unduly about the taxes on it.

Some of the bargain windows and doors will add more to the assessment than what we paid for them. That's life. They look just

The kitchen: In this view from the dining area, you can see some of the features that make the kitchen convenient, at extremely low cost. I like the rustic decor, but if you don't, it's not mandatory in a "low-tax" kitchen.

as good as expensive windows and doors.

The kitchen is small, simple, and basic. Functionally, it provides everything a cook might want in a kitchen. In designing it, we had a lot of informal help from a friend who happens to be a gourmet chef. But it costs no more to put things in convenient places than to put them in inconvenient places. The kitchen was cheap to build, and contains no features that would trip any levers to make the tax assessment any higher than what we paid for it.

The bathroom is also simple and basic. It's a convenient, pleasant place to do the things that people do in bathrooms. Yet since it didn't cost much money, the assessment should be low.

From a tax standpoint, the imperfections on the basement and upstairs walls should help. I don't recommend imperfections, but these aren't particularly noticeable unless you're looking for them. Aunt Minnie, to whom we may want to show off the house, wouldn't notice them. The tax assessor, who has a legal duty to record quality of workmanship, will. At least we hope he or she will.

For tax purposes, it might have been better to build the addition first, then fix up the original house. Since the work on the original house didn't require a permit, it would not have triggered an automatic reassessment. The addition did trigger a reassessment, which will reflect the work we did on the original house as well as the addition.

The bottom line is that we have an extremely pleasant house in an attractive location, built and remodeled for a fraction of what we

194

could have otherwise spent for an "average" house in our county. What's more, all costs of owning the house—including property taxes and heating—should remain at bargain-basement levels for many years to come.

Chapter 16

Home Businesses, Burial Plots, and Other Unique Tax Issues

The general principles of property taxation covered throughout this book apply to most homeowners. If you have a home business, run a farm, or own specific types of property, other issues can become important.

Unique Tax Provisions

In all jurisdictions there are specific statutory provisions that affect the tax bills of people in certain situations. In Alabama, you'll get an exemption for tobacco leaves if you store them in hogsheads. In Kentucky, a certified alcohol production facility in your basement will produce a tax break. In Oregon, there may be tax benefits if you raise bi-valve mollusks.

Some exemptions are more narrowly defined in practice than they appear in statutes. Property used as rest rooms by soldiers is exempt in Delaware, and facilities for "idiotic men" are exempt in New Jersey. Yet use of your bathroom by a relative who's in the service—or the behavior of your husband on Super Bowl Sunday—won't qualify you for a tax break. There's a body of case law that

> *In Oregon, there may be tax breaks if you raise bi-valve mollusks.*

prevents frivolous use of legislative provisions even when the wording is sloppy or insensitive.

Nevertheless, it's worthwhile to explore some of the unique features of your local or statewide system, to see whether any of them may affect you. Section 2 lists many of the unique exemptions that exist in individual states.

Your Low-Tax Dream House

Burial Plots

Virtually every state has some kind of exemption for public cemeteries. The exemption usually—not always—extends to all burial plots.

If you live in a rural area, perhaps there is an old burial ground on your property. Perhaps you have designated burial plots on your land for your own family. Can you get a tax exemption?

When asking for an exemption, be sure that your request is reasonable. Scattering Aunt Minnie's cremains on the badminton court isn't likely to win an exemption for the badminton court. The area should be marked off and serve exclusively as a burial ground.

My wife, who wrote the book *Caring For Your Own Dead* (Upper Access Publishers, Hinesburg, Vermont), says most people who choose home burial do so for reasons other than property tax reduction. Yet the exemption seems worth mentioning here, because it may not be noticed unless you bring it to the attention of the assessor.

Fallout Shelters

Many—not all—states have exemptions for fallout shelters. Most limit the exemption to a certain number of dollars of valuation multiplied by the number of people the shelter can accommodate.

Not all shelters are reserved exclusively for worst-case scenarios. If yours contains a ping-pong table, will the assessor list it as a recreation room or as a fallout shelter? That may be a judgment call. Be sure that the assessor knows it's a fallout shelter. Put up Civil Defense signs, post rules, and make the room look like it exists more for survival than for ping-pong.

Travel Trailers as Guest Rooms

Printed on the envelope of my car registration is the statement: "Trailers Are Motor Vehicles." That's not true of course. What the Motor Vehicle Department meant to say is that you must register travel trailers for road use in the same manner as motor vehicles.

Where I live, "motor vehicles" (including those without motors) are not subject to property taxation. If a travel trailer is still on its wheels and not permanently attached to utilities or a foundation, localities don't tax it.

What if you have a travel trailer in your yard that serves as living space? Maybe it's a guest bedroom. Maybe it's a retreat when you need to get away from the kids, or when the kids need to get away from you. An older travel trailer may provide low-cost living space if you don't go to the expense of registering it for road use.

That idea may not appeal to everybody, but if you live in a jurisdiction where it would result in tax benefits, it may be worth thinking about.

Nonstandard Items

If some features of your house are atypical, assessors may ignore them. For example, our house has a fire pole. It didn't cost much ($20 at the junkyard) but it does add to the quality of life, particularly for our children and their friends.

The manual used by our assessors says nothing about fire poles. They usually exist only in fire stations, which are not taxed. Therefore, our pole is a feature that adds nothing to our assessment.

We also have a hanging bed. An argument could be made that the bed is "built in" since it's attached to the ceiling with ropes. However, hanging beds are so rare that the assessors overlook ours.

Facilities for the Handicapped

Architectural features needed for accessibility by handicapped persons are usually exempt from property taxation. Such items tend to be expensive. Be sure that your assessor knows that they are necessary.

If a member of your family is wheelchair-bound, for example, making all parts of the house accessible will be among your highest priorities in building or remodeling. Those improvements might look very classy to an assessor who is unfamiliar with them. Check your assessment to be sure that they do not add to your tax burden.

Assessments at Use Value

If you own a 300-acre farm near a booming metropolis, it may be worth millions of dollars—to a condominium developer. As a farmer, you don't make as much money as developers do. If the land were assessed at its value for development, you couldn't afford the taxes.

Fortunately, in most states your farm can be assessed according to its use value, rather than its potential market value. This assessment approximates the amount of money you could expect to receive if you sold the property to another farmer, rather than to a developer.

Use assessment systems tend to be statewide, because most states reimburse localities for cost of providing the tax break. In some states, the tax break is considered an incentive for farming, so it is available only to "working" farmers. In other states, it is considered an incentive to keep land open, so it is available to owners of forest land, wetlands, or any other substantial parcels of open space.

In most locations, you will have to sign up for this type of special assessment. In exchange for the tax break, you'll usually have to agree to keep the land open for a certain number of years. If you sell the land to a developer, you'll have to pay a penalty—perhaps all the tax savings you received over the years.

If you don't plan to subdivide your land, assessment at use value can reduce your tax burden to a fraction of what it would be with market-value assessment.

Another variation of use-value assessment is often available to people who live in areas zoned for commercial use. Commercially zoned property is usually more expensive than residentially-zoned property. However, if you use it as a residence, you receive no benefit from the zoning. Therefore, it is often possible to have your house assessed at its use value: what it is worth as a house, rather than what it would be worth if you sold it to a commercial establishment.

Property Taxes for Businesses

While the focus of this book is on dream houses, I assume that some readers have, or plan to start up, businesses of their own.

Many of the low-tax principles for residences also apply to businesses. For example, the simpler the design, the lower the initial cost will be, and the lower the taxes will *usually* be, regardless of whether you have a business or a residence.

If your business is located in a commercially zoned area, you'll pay extra for that. The value of the location will be reflected in the tax assessment, perhaps disproportionately.

Also, in many places, there are substantial differences between assessments of businesses and assessment of residences. The most common examples are the "income approach" and taxation of business personal property.

Income Approach To Business Assessment
Residential valuations are determined by the market approach, the cost approach, or both (See chapter 2). Business property is sometimes (not always) valued by the income approach.

The income approach values property according to the amount of income it produces. The more money you make the higher your assessment will be. The assumption is that the market value of a business is influenced more by its profitability than by the quality of the real estate.

If your assessment is based exclusively on the income approach, the only way to reduce your tax bill will be to earn less money. In that case, adding a few features to make life more pleasant at the workplace won't raise your taxes. However, in most instances, income is considered in combination with cost and market calculations.

For a struggling new business, the income approach can sometimes provide much-needed tax relief. If you're not making much money, and you find out that the assessors use the income approach for the successful businesses in town, make sure they also use it for your business.

Personal Business Property

In many states, localities tax business personal property even though "household furniture and personal effects" are exempt. If you live in such a state, moveable items used for business may be taxed to the same extent as built-in items.

A carpet or a counter will be taxed as real estate, while a rug or a table may be taxed as personal property. The ultimate effect on the tax bill may or may not be the same.

It's an issue worth exploring in detail. In some jurisdictions the tax rate for personal property is higher than the rate for real estate. In other jurisdictions it is lower. Even if the tax is at a higher rate, the assessed value of personal property may depreciate, while the assessed value of real estate may appreciate. While designing your business space, plan to keep your pocket calculator handy.

There may be other reasons for choosing moveable equipment. For example, moveable items can be depreciated more quickly on your federal income tax forms. You can also move them around if you want to rearrange your business space. Avoiding built-ins is often a good policy even if it does not provide the same property tax benefit in a business as in a house.

A few jurisdictions also have property taxes on business inventories. This is less common than in the past. Inventory taxes are a nightmare to administer, so many localities have repealed them. Where these taxes exist, there is an obvious incentive to hold "inventory sales" to reduce the stock on the assessment date.

Home Businesses

Most people with home businesses depreciate some of their belongings on their income tax returns. They sometimes depreciate rooms in their houses as "home office" space. By doing so they reduce their income taxes, but sometimes unwittingly raise their property taxes.

Suppose, for example, that your home occupation is mending clothes.

When you fill out your income tax form, you can probably depreciate your sewing machine. You may also be able to depreciate the table that the machine is on and the chair next to it. The desk nearby may also be depreciable, because you do your billing and keep track of your business records there. If the whole room is used for your sewing business, it might possibly qualify for a home office deduction.

> *By depreciating belongings on your income tax form, you may raise your property taxes.*

Perhaps some of this property is also used, now and then, for nonbusiness activities. The distinction between business and household property can seem arbitrary. When you fill out income tax forms, the incentive is to call it business property.

For property tax purposes, however, you're often better off if you call it household personal property.

Any item listed as business property is subject to property taxation in many localities. Also, many jurisdictions have special tax breaks for owner-occupied houses. These include homestead exemptions, property tax relief programs, and lower tax rates for residences than for other property. These tax breaks are for residences only, and can be jeopardized if part of the house is a business.

You can't have it both ways. If you tell the IRS that your property is for business use, you can't honestly tell your local assessor that it's for household use. Conversely, if you don't claim an income tax break for an item, you can use your income tax forms to demonstrate to the local assessor that the item is not business property. The best possible way to avoid paying business property taxes on something is to show that you didn't claim a federal income tax deduction for it.

In practice, in most jurisdictions assessors ignore tiny home businesses. It's not worth their time to fuss with business property worth a few hundred dollars or less.

If your home business grows from a small sideline to a full-time occupation, with increasingly expensive equipment and additional space in your house, it's worthwhile to become familiar with the business property tax provisions in your locality. Without proper planning, the property tax bill can come as a shock.

Rental Property

It is not unusual for homeowners to become landlords sooner or later. If you obtain a dream house when you're young, perhaps you'll have extra space to rent out once the kids grow up and leave home. Or, if you're like me, you may have so much fun building and remodeling your own dream house that you'll want to continue making sweat investments in rental property.

With care and personal involvement, the returns on this kind of investment can be tremendous. If you can hold down costs to provide good housing at affordable rents, you'll do well by doing good.

Depending on where you live, some of the cautions about business property can apply to rental property. For example, homestead exemptions usually are not granted for rental property. Homestead tax relief, however, may be granted to your tenants. The relief will be based on the assumption that a certain percentage of the rent that they pay goes toward the property taxes you pay. If that is the case, make sure that your tenants know about the tax relief that is available.

Some jurisdictions tax rental property as "business property," at a higher rate than residential property.

Towns and counties that tax business inventory often extend the tax to furniture and appliances that the landlord provides in rental units.

Rental property is sometimes assessed by the income approach. That means the assessment is based on the amount you charge for rent, rather than the physical characteristics of the real estate.

These issues should all be considered when you make an investment in rental real estate. For example, suppose your property is in a jurisdiction with an inventory tax and an income approach to assessment of rental properties. If the tenant supplies the furnishings and appliances, you can avoid the inventory tax as well as the cost of the furnishings. You can pass those savings along to your tenant in the form of lower rent. With lower rent, the income-based tax assessment of the real estate will be reduced.

The tax provisions vary greatly depending on where you live. The only general advice I can give is that if you are weighing becoming a landlord, check out the local tax system for rental units ahead of time. In almost all localities, rental property carries tax burdens that are different from those of owner-occupied residences.

Fluff

A low-tax strategy should consider all aspects of your lifestyle. Many of the general principles in other chapters of this book apply to families who live in houses, work somewhere else, and have dogs named Fluff. Your equation may change if you have a licensed distillery in your basement, a burial ground in the back yard, a travel trailer for guests, and a dog that bites the assessor.

Section Two

Residential
Property Tax Summaries

Introduction to Section Two:

How to Use
the Information
Listed for Your State

This section consists of short summaries of the property tax systems within each state. The state-by-state format was chosen because property tax systems are governed by statewide constitutions, laws, regulations, precedents, and traditions. If you live in, say, Colorado, the general information listed for that state should hold true regardless of where you live in Colorado.

Keep in mind, however, that property taxes are not always as uniform statewide in practice as in theory. The systems are administered by counties, townships, cities, villages, school districts, and other local assessing units. There are tens of thousands of assessing units, each of which has its own idiosyncracies.

The information listed for your state should help to steer you in the right direction, but I encourage you to do your own additional research within your locality.

Doing Local Research

The information needed for local research should be available from your local assessment office. Many jurisdictions have handouts with general information and answers to frequently asked questions. They may have photocopies of relevant statutes and ordinances. The most detailed information will be found in the manual used by the assessors. If it is not on public display, ask if you can borrow a copy for a couple of days and photocopy a few pages.

If possible, schedule a time to talk informally with a local assessor or assessment official. This should come after you've read the accessible material, so that you can make efficient use of the person's time. Ask specific questions about the tax implications of items you may wish to include in your dream house. An informal conversation is the best way to learn about local quirks—the policies that can affect your assessment but are not written down anywhere.

Let me give you an example of a common local quirk. In most assessment systems, permanent landscaping improvements like stone walls or hedges should add to the valuation. Yet many local assessors have an informal policy of ignoring such improvements. Why? "We just don't like to penalize people for improving the appearance of a neighborhood," one assessor commented when I asked.

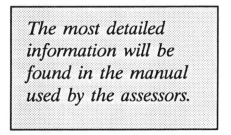

The most detailed information will be found in the manual used by the assessors.

Here's another example. In my state, solar collectors are exempt *if* local people so vote at a Town Meeting. The electorate in my town hasn't gotten around to so voting. Therefore, in theory, solar collectors are assessed for taxation. However, in practice, they are not. The local assessors don't list them, because they feel that solar collectors should not be taxed. Even if a new assessor were to disagree, changing the policy would be a lot of work. If one collector were taxed, the assessors would have to list all the collectors in town. To anybody considering adding solar collectors, that's a significant bit of information. Yet it's not written down anywhere (until now).

The people who assess your property probably have similar informal policies that can have tax implications for your dream house. Property tax assessment systems are never as well organized in practice as they appear to be on paper. Decisions are often made to keep the system as simple as possible. For example, when sheds are listed, the guidelines for distinguishing between a shed that is real estate and one that is personal property may be complex and vague. In any given community, a decision might be made to simplify matters by listing sheds on foundations as real estate and all other sheds as personal property. Knowing how the distinction is made may affect your decision on whether to build your shed on a foundation or not.

Repeating for emphasis, local idiosyncracies like that are usually not written down anywhere. They're not secret conspiracies; local assessment officials are usually willing to discuss them freely. But the only way to find out about them is to ask.

The Summaries

In gathering the information for each state, I made every effort to assure that it would be accurate and current as of early 1989. The amount of available information varies somewhat from state to state.

Some of the people I interviewed simply answered my questions, while others volunteered additional information that was worthy of inclusion. For the sake of consistency, I have broken down the information into the following specific categories.

What is taxed: In some states, only real estate is taxed. Localities in other states tax additional categories of property. A typical example would be "tangible personal property unless expressly exempt." This first paragraph of each state summary explains, in capsule form, the types of property that are taxed.

Exemptions for personal property: States that provide for a personal property tax usually exempt household goods and personal effects. States that provide only for taxation of real estate use a variety of standards to determine what is, or is not, real estate. In each state summary, I've tried to indicate how local assessors distinguish between taxed real estate and untaxed personal property.

Homestead exemption or other tax relief: A homestead is a house occupied by the owner, plus the land the house sits on, up to a specified maximum. Typically, no more than two acres of land will be listed as part of a homestead. In some states a certain amount of the value of a homestead, ranging from $5,000 to $75,000, is exempt from taxation.

In some states the tax rate on a homestead, or on a certain amount of the value of a homestead, is lower than for all other categories of property.

Some states offer homestead exemptions to certain classifications of citizens, such as veterans, disabled veterans, other disabled persons, or elderly homeowners. In a few states, the categories are pretty exclusive: "mothers of double-amputee Civil War veterans," for example. Sometimes these exemptions are allowed only if household income and/or assets are below a certain amount.

Some states provide property tax relief instead of exemptions. Usually that means you have to pay the full amount of the tax, but part of it is refunded when you file your state income tax return.

Another type of tax relief available to elderly homeowners in some states is "deferral." This means that taxes can be deferred until the owner dies or sells the house. At that time, all back taxes must be paid, usually with interest. If you plan to leave your house to your grown children when you die, it may be better to ask them to help pay the property taxes than to defer the taxes. More often than not, houses with deferred taxes are sold at tax sales before the heirs can come up with the money to bring the payments up to date.

Unique exemptions: This is a catch-all category. Some of the unique exemptions are significant. For example, if state statutes exempt solar collectors, low-income housing, residential improvements up to a certain amount, or fallout shelters, I've tried to list those exemptions.

I've also included exemptions that seemed interesting, regardless of whether they affect many people. If you want to know which states exempt implements of husbandry, eleemosynary theatres, temporary structures to shade ginseng plants, or structures that contain animal waste other than chicken manure, you'll find the information in this section.

Tax burden for residential real estate: This section is a little essay on how property is assessed. Any statewide limitations on taxation are noted.

Where the information was accessible, I also included an estimate of range of average property tax bills in your state for a residence with an actual market value of $100,000. If you browse through, you'll find that the bills vary from less than $300 to more than $8,000.

These comparisons need to be put into perspective to account for local conditions. Several of the people I interviewed noted that in some places you can buy a mansion for $100,000, while in other places that's the price of a substandard outhouse. Since none of them suggested a better basis for comparison, I included the information and will trust the reader to supply the perspective.

Dates of assessment and payment: Property is usually assessed according to its value as of a certain date. If you make an improvement before that date, you'll pay taxes on it this year. If you make an improvement a day later, you won't be taxed until next year. The magic dates for assessment are included in this section. So are the dates when tax bills come due.

Assessing officials: These are the people who are responsible for the initial assessments of your property. They are usually the best people to contact if you have questions about local assessment practices or if you wish to straighten out an error in your assessment.

Appeals: The squeaky wheel gets the grease. Assessors sometimes err on the high side, knowing that if they make a mistake in that direction the taxpayer will have a chance to correct it. Appealing a faulty assessment is a fundamental right. Take advantage of it. The paragraph under this heading lists the levels of appeal available in your state.

Assessments based on: Many states publish their own assessment manuals, which explain in detail each judgment call that should be made in assessing your house. Manuals show how to calculate the extra assessment you'll get by choosing cedar clapboards instead of pine, or by adding five more feet of kitchen counter. Manuals are not generally easy to read, but if you want the details of how your house is assessed, the information is there.

In states that do not publish their own assessment manuals, local assessors generally are able to use any nationally recognized system. The most common is the *Marshall Valuation Service* manual. It is often called "Marshall and Swift," the name of the Los Angeles-based publisher that developed this assessment system.

Manuals are not always easily accessible. For example, New York State is preparing a new eight-volume manual, and there is no statutory requirement that it be displayed anywhere for public perusal. Members of the public do have a right to photocopy pages, at a cost of 25¢ per page. If I lived in New York, I'd raise a stink about that.

Nevertheless, in most localities any genuinely interested citizen can usually find a way to obtain access to the manual. Local officials usually cooperate fully with people who want to do honest research, rather than just fretting and moaning about taxes.

Many assessments are based on computer programs. The most widely used systems, including "Marshall and Swift," can be used either with manual calculations or with computer software. Don't feel intimidated: you don't have to be a computer expert to check the accuracy of the data entered into the computer or the information on the printout.

Source of statewide tax information: Information regarding your state came from a variety of sources, including my own research in the law library. However, in every state I found at least one knowledgeable high-level official who was willing to work with me to help assure that the information is accurate and useful. If the person was publicity-shy, I've listed only the office where he or she works. I've listed the names of those who were willing to go public, because they deserve credit. These officials were eager to be sure that taxpayers have accurate information. They are conscientious public servants.

211

If the information about your state proves useful to you, please drop a card in the mail to thank the person or office listed here. Tax assessing is a thankless job; the people who try to help the public to understand how the system works deserve an occasional note of gratitude.

ALABAMA

What is taxed: Both real estate and personal property, unless expressly exempt.

Exemptions for personal property include: Family portraits and certain items of personal property owned by individuals for personal use in the house. In practice, the exemption is broader than it appears in the statutes. Household items that are not attached to the structure or land are not assessed for property taxation.

Homestead exemption or other tax relief: For those under age 65, up to $4,000 of the assessed value of a homestead is exempt from the state tax, and up to $2,000 is exempt from the county tax. For those who are age 65 or older, or who are disabled, the exemption rises to $5,000 if taxable income is under $12,000, or the entire value of the residence if taxable income is under $7,500.

Unique exemptions: Artesian wells are not taxed, if leased to a municipality. Other exemptions include nuclear fuel assemblies and byproducts if they are used or useful in producing electricity, and tobacco leaves stored in hogsheads.

Tax burden for residential real estate: Tax rates for real estate in Alabama are among the lowest in the nation. The annual tax bill on a residence with an actual market value of $100,000 ranges from $275 to $300, depending on where you live in Alabama.

Dates of assessment and payment: Assessment occurs annually, between October 1 and the third Monday in January, to determine values as of October 1. Taxes are payable October 1, based on assessment as of October 1 of the preceding year.

Assessing officials: Responsibility for initial assessments lies with the county tax assessor, or with city assessors in cities with independent tax systems.

Appeals: Assessments can be reviewed, revised, and equalized by county boards of equalization. Appeals of the decisions of County Boards are made to the Circuit Court of the county where the taxpayer's property is located.

Assessments based on: A statewide assessment manual. A computer program is used for most assessments.

Source of statewide tax information: James K. Green, chief, Alabama *Ad Valorem* Tax Division.

ALASKA

What is taxed: Real estate and personal property, unless expressly exempt.

Exemptions for personal property include: Household furniture and personal effects of members of a household. Other exemptions include money on deposit, and one motor vehicle per household owned by a resident age 65 or older. In practice, household items that are not attached to the structure or land are not assessed for property taxation.

Homestead exemption or other tax relief: If you are over age 65, or a disabled veteran, or a widow or widower of a qualified person and over age 60, the first $150,000 of assessed value of your homestead is exempt.

Unique exemptions: Two percent of the value of a structure with an approved fire protection system is exempt.

Other unique issues: While in many states, energy conservation features such as extra insulation or solar collectors add little to the tax assessment, that's not true in Alaska. Assessors here reason that these features add considerably to the market value of a residence.

Tax burden for residential real estate: The maximum rate that can be imposed by municipalities is 3 percent of assessed value. Farmland may be assessed only on its value as farmland. In practice, the annual tax bill for a residence with actual market value of $100,000 ranges between $800 and $1,500, depending on where you live in Alaska.

Date of assessment: Values are set annually, as of January 1 of each assessment year.

Assessing officials: The municipal assessor of each community is responsible for initial assessments.

Appeals: Appeals may be made to the local board of equalization within 30 days after notice of an assessment is mailed. The Board's decision may be appealed to the Superior Court.

Assessments based on: 100 percent of market value. There is no statewide manual. Computer programs are used for most assessments.

Source of statewide tax information: Office of the State Assessor.

ARIZONA

What is taxed: Real estate and personal property, unless expressly exempt.

Exemptions for personal property include: All household property owned by the user and not used for commercial purposes. In practice, household items that are not attached to the structure or land are not assessed for property taxation.

Homestead exemption or other tax relief: There is an exemption for veterans, on a sliding scale, if the owner-occupied residence is assessed at less than $7,800. Assessed value is 10 percent of full cash value, so the exemption may apply if the homestead's actual value is up to $78,000. For disabled veterans, the amount of the exemption increases, based on the percent of disability. A similar exemption is available to widows, widowers, and the disabled, if caps on income are not exceeded.

Tax burden for residential real estate: Arizona's assessment system is complicated. However, it results in relatively modest taxation of owner-occupied homes. If there is no homestead exemption, the annual tax bill on a house with an actual market value of $100,000 ranges from about $750 to $1,000, depending on where you live in Arizona.

In the late 1970s, Arizona adopted a tax limitation package roughly similar to California's Proposition 13. It has since been modified with catch-up provisions to allow adequate funding of essential services. The resulting system is best explained in several steps.

1. There are two sets of numbers used as a basis for assessment: *full cash value* and *limited value*. Full cash value, in theory, is similar to actual market value. The limited value has limits on the amount of increase each year, so when actual values rise rapidly, the limited value lags behind. In any year, the limited value may be increased by the greater of (a) 10 percent or (b) 25 percent of the difference between last year's limited value and the present full cash value. Limited value may not exceed full cash value.

2. The limited value is used for calculating the "primary" property tax, which generally includes all taxes levied by elected officials. Full cash value is used to calculate the "secondary" tax, to cover items like bond issues, budget overrides, and special assessments.

215

Your Low-Tax Dream House

3. Different categories of property are assessed at different percentages of the limited or full cash value. The assessment for an owner-occupied home is 10 percent. For rental residential property, the assessment is 15 percent.

4. The maximum "primary" property tax bill cannot exceed 1 percent of the limited value of the property. The amount levied by any county, city, town, or community college district may not exceed a 2 percent increase from the amount levied in the preceding year.

Dates of assessment and payment: Property is valued on November 30, according to its value and ownership as of the following January 1. Real estate taxes are paid in two equal payments. The first is payable October 1, and becomes delinquent November 1. The second is payable March 1, and becomes delinquent May 1.

Assessing officials: The responsibility for initial assessments lies with the county assessor, an elected official, under the supervision of the Department of Revenue.

Appeals: Appeals must be initially made to the county assessor. The second stage of appeal is to the county Board of Supervisors, sitting as the Board of Equalization. The Board's decisions may be appealed to the state Board of Tax Appeals or the county superior court.

Assessments based on: Full cash value, determined by a market approach to assessment, and limited value, described above. Procedures are described in manuals that are published by the state and prescribed for use by all assessors. Computer programs are used for most assessments. The state has a central computer service used under contract by some counties, while other counties have their own programs, which must be consistent with the state program.

Source of statewide tax information: Arizona Department of Revenue, Division of Property Valuation and Equalization.

ARKANSAS

What is taxed: Real estate and personal property, unless expressly exempt.

Exemptions for personal property include: Arkansas is one of the few states without a statutory or constitutional exemption for household furniture and personal effects. Legislative attempts to enact such an exemption have failed. In theory, the socks in your laundry basket are taxable.

Personal property in Arkansas is self-assessed, which may offer some protection against unfair valuations. Nevertheless, inequities in personal property taxation are reportedly the most common complaints when grievances are filed in Arkansas.

Homestead exemption or other tax relief: Up to 100 percent of the value of a homestead may be exempt for disabled veterans and their families, or the families of those who died or are missing while within the scope of military duties.

Unique exemptions: Capital invested in textile mills may be exempt for a period up to for seven years.

Tax burden for residential real estate: Property is initially appraised at true market value, or in the case of personal property, its usual selling price. Then it's placed on the tax record at 20 percent of that value. Property used solely as a residence by the owner is assessed only on its value as a residence. Agricultural land (including timber and pasture land) values are based on soil productivity. The annual tax bill for a residence with an actual market value of $100,000 ranges from $410 to $1,300, depending on where you live in Arkansas. The tax bill for household personal property is in addition to that amount.

Dates of assessment and payment: Real estate is assessed on its value as of January 1. Annual assessment takes place between the first Monday in January and July 1. Taxpayers self-assess personal property for value between January 1 and April 10. However, personal property acquired between April 10 and June 30 is taxable for the current year, and must be assessed by June 30. Returns of taxable property are filed with the county assessor. Taxes are all payable between the third Monday in February and October 10. Real property taxes may be paid in installments—¼ by the third Monday in April, ¼ by the third Monday in July, and ½ by October 10. Personal property taxes must be paid on or before October 10.

Assessing officials: The initial assessment is made under the direction of the county assessor.

Appeals: Assessments can be equalized by the county equalization board, which may initiate the action or which may act on an appeal by the property owner. The decisions of the board may be appealed to the county court. The Public Service Commission must equalize assessments between districts, cities, townships, and counties. Decisions of the Public Service Commission may be appealed to the circuit court.

Assessments based on: Three separate statewide manuals covering assessment of real estate, personal property, and business personal property. A computer program is used for most assessments.

Source of statewide tax information: The Arkansas Assessment Coordination Division.

CALIFORNIA

What is taxed: Real estate and personal property, unless expressly exempt. Floating homes are assessed as real estate. A mobile home is taxed as a vehicle if purchased before 1980, but as real estate if purchased new since 1980. However, older mobile homes can be switched to a real estate classification on request of the owner, or if the vehicle license fee becomes delinquent.

Exemptions for personal property include: Household furnishings, personal effects and pets not held or used in connection with a trade, profession, or business. In practice, household items that are not attached to the structure or land are not assessed for taxation.

Homestead exemption or other tax relief: A homeowner's exemption is allowed for the first $7,000 of the full value of the owner's primary residence.

Limited exemptions are also available for servicemen, veterans, and their families. Property tax relief is available to those who are elderly, blind, or disabled, and whose incomes meet specific guidelines.

Unique exemptions: Fruit and nut trees are exempt. So are parking lots used by persons attending religious services.

Tax burden for residential real estate: Thanks to Proposition 13, valuation is as much a function of when you bought the property as what it's worth.

The base value is the assessed value as of 1975-76. Property may be reassessed only after new construction, transfer, or sale after the 1975 assessment. In that event, the new assessment becomes the base. The taxable base value may increase by the rate of inflation or by 2 percent in any year, whichever is less.

The maximum amount of tax on real property cannot exceed 1 percent of the full cash value of the property, but that limit may be exceeded to pay for outstanding debt service.

A residence with an actual market value of $100,000 would be taxed no higher than $575, and probably considerably less, if you bought it before 1975. The tax would be about $1,100 if you bought it last year.

Dates of assessment and payment: Property is generally assessed according to its value as of March 1, or whenever there is new construction or a change of ownership. This is another unique feature of California law. If, for example, you build an addition that is completed on April 1, you will get a supplemental tax bill. In effect, the March 1 lien date will be moved to April 1, for that year only. In short, despite the March 1 valuation date, you won't save money in California by building on March 2 as opposed to February 28.

Assessments are made between March and July. Tax payments on real estate are due in two installments: the first is due November 1 and delinquent December 10; the second is due February 1 and delinquent April 10.

Assessing officials: County assessors are responsible for initial assessment of all properties.

Appeals: An appeal may be made to an assessment appeals board appointed by the county Board of Supervisors. In a few of the smaller counties, an appeal is made to the Board of Supervisors, acting as a local Board of Equalization. No further appeal is allowed unless fraud or other lawbreaking is alleged.

Assessments based on: Market value as of the date the property is acquired or newly constructed. To assist county assessors in appraising property, the state prepares a series of manuals. Computer programs are not used for most assessments.

Source of statewide tax information: California Department of Property Taxes, State Board of Equalization.

COLORADO

What is taxed: Real estate and tangible personal property, unless expressly exempt.

Exemptions for personal property include: Personal effects and household furnishings not used for production of income.

In Colorado, the distinction between taxable real estate and nontaxable household goods is not always based on whether an item is physically attached to the house or land. For example, carpets are exempt, even though they are attached to the house. However, built-in appliances are taxable, while free-standing appliances are not. Wood-burning stoves, swimming pools (including above-ground pools), and storage sheds (including those not on a foundation) are generally assessed. If you have questions about assessment of a particular item, you should contact the county assessor.

Homestead exemption and other tax relief: Colorado statutes refer to a "homestead exemption," but it does not affect property taxes. The exemption exists to protect homeowners from certain types of creditors.

Senior citizens and disabled homeowners may apply for an income tax credit/refund when they file an income tax form with the Colorado Department of Revenue. Senior citizens may also apply for property tax deferral through the county treasurer's office. Both programs have eligibility requirements.

Unique exemptions: Any increase in land value due to timber planting is exempt until the timber matures for economic use.

Tax burden for residential real estate: Assessments are a percentage of actual value, or, for agricultural lands, a percentage of their value based on productive capacity.

Residential real estate is currently assessed at 16 percent of actual value. All other taxable property, including vacant residential land, is assessed at 29 percent of actual value. These percentages are adjusted to assure that the total aggregate tax burden on residential real estate does not increase in proportion to the tax burden on other taxable property.

I was unable to obtain a reliable estimate of the range of annual tax bills for a Colorado residence with an actual market value of $100,000.

Dates of assessment and payment: Real estate is assessed according to its value as of January 1. Property is appraised every two years, until 1993 when assessors will revalue property annually. Taxes are payable on January 1 of the year following assessment, and become delinquent the following August 1. There is no penalty if payment is made in two installments, in February and July, or paid in full by the end of April.

Assessing officials: County assessors are responsible for valuing all property within their jurisdictions except for public utilities, which are valued by the state property tax administrator.

Appeals: The initial protest must be made to the county assessor. Then, an appeal may be made to the Board of County Commissioners, sitting as the County Board of Equalization. An appeal of the county board's decision can then be filed with either the state board of assessment appeals (BAA), the district court, or as a third option, the taxpayer may request binding arbitration. A decision by either BAA or the district court may be appealed to the court of appeals, then to the Colorado Supreme Court.

Assessments based on: Cost and market approaches, using data from an 18-month period prior to the assessment date. Statewide manuals, referred to as *A.R.L., Volumes Three through Five*, are available to assessors for use in determining cost-approach values. Computer programs are used for assessments in most counties, and vary from county to county.

Source of statewide tax information: Colorado Division of Property Taxation.

CONNECTICUT

What is taxed: Real estate and tangible personal property, unless expressly exempt.

Exemptions for personal property include: Fuel and provisions for use of the family, household furniture, private libraries, musical instruments (including radios and televisions), watches and jewelry, and personal wearing apparel. In practice, household items that are not attached to the structure or land are not assessed for property taxation.

Homestead exemption or other tax relief: Limited exemptions are available to blind persons and to war veterans. Reductions in taxes are available to the elderly and disabled if income guidelines are met.

Unique exemptions: Boats and vessels, all livestock, business inventories, farm produce and machinery, carriages, wagons, and bicycles are exempt.

Tax burden for residential real estate: Each municipality assesses at a uniform percentage of fair market value, currently 70 percent. Reduced assessment levels are available for qualified farms, forest land, and open spaces. The tax bill on a house with an actual market value of $100,000 ranges from about $1,000 to $4,000, depending on where you live in Connecticut.

Dates of assessment and payment: Real estate is assessed according to its value as of October 1. Returns on personal property must be filed with the municipal assessors by November 1. In general, tax payments are due July 1 and must be paid by August 1. In most locations, taxes may be paid in multiple installments: most commonly two installments, but sometimes three or four.

Assessing officials: Municipal assessors are responsible for initial assessment.

Appeals: The first appeal is to the local Board of Tax Review. Decisions of local boards may be appealed either to the superior court or to the state Appeals Board for Property Valuation.

Assessments based on: A percentage of fair market value. Connecticut has no statewide assessment manual, and computer programs are not in widespread use for assessment.

Source of statewide tax information: Frederick M. Chmura, assessment and equalization manager, Connecticut Office of Policy and Management.

DELAWARE

What is taxed: All real estate, unless expressly exempt.

Exemptions for personal property include: All personal property is exempt. In practice, household items that are not attached to the structure or land are not assessed for taxation.

Homestead exemption or other tax relief: Up to $5,000 of the assessed value of the homestead of a person age 65 or older is exempt if income guidelines are met. Municipalities are empowered to enact exemptions for all residents over age 65.

Unique exemptions: Property used for soldiers' rest rooms is exempt in Delaware. So is the first $10,000 of property used as a college fraternity. If you own a motion picture studio, it may be exempt from taxation for 15 years. Commercial forest plantations are allowed a 30-year exemption.

Tax burden for residential real estate: Property is required by law to be assessed at true value. The value of land actively used for agriculture, forestry, or horticulture is assessed according to its value for that use. Mobile homes are considered to be real estate, and reassessed every five years, based on their value outlined in a national appraisal guide. The county tax rate cannot exceed half of 1 percent of the assessed valuation in Kent and Sussex Counties. In New Castle County the tax rate is based on the amount needed for both the operating budget and the capital budget.

There is no statewide office that coordinates assessments in Delaware, and we were unable to obtain a reliable estimate of the statewide range of annual tax bills for a residence with an actual market value of $100,000. However, in New Castle County, the average tax bill for such a residence is about $900.

Dates of assessment and payment: Delaware statutes do not appear to specify a particular date at which valuation is set. Taxes are due May 1 in Sussex County, June 1 in Kent County, and July 1 in New Castle County. In the city of Wilmington, taxes are due in July and August.

Assessing officials: In New Castle and Sussex Counties, responsibility for initial assessments lies with the Department of Finance. In Kent County and in the City of Wilmington, local Boards of Assessment have the responsibility.

Appeals: The local Board of Assessment is required to give taxpayers ten days notice of any increase in assessment or new assessment. An initial appeal may be made to the local board. If you are dissatisfied with the board's decision, you may appeal it within 30 days to the superior court of the county where the property is located. There is no state agency for equalization of assessments.

Assessments based on: True value, which is generally interpreted as equivalent to market value. There is no statewide manual. Computer programs are used for many assessments.

Source of statewide tax information: Francis Lally, supervisor, Assessment Division, New Castle County. (Because there is no statewide office in Delaware, persons interested in obtaining additional information should contact the offices for the county where they own property.)

DISTRICT OF COLUMBIA

What is taxed: Real estate, and tangible personal property used in a trade or business, whether or not for profit, unless expressly exempt.

Exemptions for personal property include: All personal property that is not used in a trade or business. In practice, household items that are not attached to the structure or land are not assessed for taxation.

Homestead exemption and other tax relief: The first $22,000 of assessed value of a Class 1 residence is exempt. To qualify as Class 1, the residence must be owner-occupied and contain no more than five dwelling units. You must apply for this classification. If no application is filed, the District will automatically classify your property as Class 2 (more than five units and/or not occupied by the owner), and you will not receive the homestead exemption.

In addition, the District has a Senior Citizen Homestead Tax Relief Program. If you are over age 65 and meet the income guidelines of the program, your tax bill can be cut in half.

Unique exemptions: Rental property may be exempt if rented to low-or-moderate income persons who receive assistance under specified federal programs.

Tax burden for residential real estate: Tax rates are set annually by the mayor and City Council. Different rates are set for different classes of property, in a system which generally favors residential owners.

For Fiscal 1989, Class 1 property (occupied by the owner and with five or fewer units) is taxed at $1.22 per $100 of assessed value. By comparison, the rates for other types of real property are as follows: larger apartment buildings, $1.54; hotels and motels, $1.82; other real estate, $2.03; and taxable personal property (used in a trade or business), $3.10.

If you own a Class 1 house valued at $100,000, and qualify for the Senior Citizen Relief Program, your total tax bill will be $475.80. If you do not qualify for the relief program, your tax bill on the same house will be double that amount. If you own a $100,000 Class 2 building, your tax bill will be $1,540.

Dates of assessment and payment: Assessments reflect the value of real estate as of January 1. Payments are in two installments, due September 15 and March 31. Personal property, when taxable, is valued as of July 1, and taxpayers who are liable must file returns during July. Payment is due when the return is filed.

Assessing officials: The mayor is technically responsible for all assessments of real property. But since the mayor has a lot of other things to do, the job is delegated to assessors in the Office of Real Property Taxes, Department of Finance and Revenue.

Appeals: Initial grievances may be made to the assessor, who may make adjustments in case of error, or in case of recent damage to the property. Appeals may be taken to the Board of Equalization and Review, then to the superior court of the District of Columbia.

Assessments based on: Fair market value, under methods described in detail in the District's *Real Property Assessment Manual.* Computer programs are used to a limited extent, for some phases of the assessment process.

Source of tax information: Assessment Division, D.C. Department of Finance and Revenue.

FLORIDA

What is taxed: Under Florida law, all property must be assessed, whether it is taxable or not. Property is taxable unless expressly exempt. Intangible personal property—like stocks, bonds, and interests in time-share condos—is taxed in Florida, although the first $20,000 in intangible property owned by any resident is exempt.

Exemptions for personal property include: Household goods and personal effects, unless they are used for commercial purposes. Therefore, household items that are not attached to the structure or land are not assessed for property taxation. Other personal property exemptions include mobile homes and motor vehicles if they are subject to a license tax. There are numerous exemptions in the tax on intangible property, including money, municipal bonds, and most mortgages.

Homestead exemption or other tax relief: The first $25,000 in assessed value of the homestead of a Florida resident is exempt. Additional exemptions are available to elderly, blind, and disabled persons, raising the total exemption to a maximum of $26,500 of the assessed value of a homestead. Persons qualifying for the homestead exemption may defer portions of their taxes that exceed a percentage of their income. The homestead of a totally disabled veteran (or his/her surviving spouse, until or unless the spouse remarries) is totally exempt.

Unique exemptions: Devices that use renewable energy sources are exempt in Florida.

Tax burden for residential real estate: Tax rates vary greatly from county to county. The annual tax bill on a residence with actual market value of $100,000 ranges from about $1,000 to $2,000, depending on where you live in Florida.

Dates of assessment and payment: Taxes are assessed as of January 1 annually, except that construction work in progress is considered to have no value until it is substantially completed. After receipt of a tax notice, payment is due November 1, or as soon afterward as the assessment roll is in the hands of the tax collector. Payments become delinquent the next April 1, or 60 days after mailing of the tax notice, whichever comes later. There is a 4 percent early-payment discount for payments in November, 3 percent in December, 2 percent in January, and 1 percent in February.

Assessing officials: The county property appraiser is responsible for initial assessments.

Appeals: Appeals may be made to the Property Appraisal Adjustment Board, then to the circuit court. Every two years the assessment rolls of each county are to be reviewed in depth by the Division of *Ad Valorem* Tax.

Assessments based on: There is no statewide manual, but most counties use the Marshall and Swift *Residential Cost Handbook* or similar guides. Computer programs are used in some of the larger counties.

Source of statewide tax information: Glenda Lumpkin, revenue economist, Florida *Ad Valorem* Tax Division.

GEORGIA

What is taxed: All real estate and personal property, including intangible property, unless expressly exempt. Mobile homes are considered tangible personal property, and placed in a separate class, taxed similarly to motor vehicles. In practice, however, they are taxed at about the same level as real estate.

Exemptions for personal property include: Personal clothing and effects, household furniture, furnishings, equipment, appliances, and other personal property used within the home if not held for sale or rental. Other exemptions include tools and implements of trade of manual laborers, and all domestic animals up to $300 in actual value. A separate but overlapping exemption exists for tangible personal property (except motor vehicles, trailers, and mobile homes) whose value does not exceed $500.

In practice, household items that are not attached to the structure or land are not generally assessed for taxation. For some of the borderline items, no firm statewide policy has been established. For example, whether or not an above-ground pool is taxed is likely to depend on the appearance of the pool. Whether or not a satellite dish is taxed is likely to depend on the opinions of your local assessor.

Homestead exemption or other tax relief: The first $38,000 of the assessed value of the homestead of a disabled veteran is exempt. The first $4,000 of the assessed value of the homestead of a person age 65 or older is exempt, if net income meets specific guidelines. Also, a person age 62 or older who meets income guidelines may be exempt from school taxes for the first $10,000 of assessed value, and may defer taxes on the first $50,000 of assessed value of the homestead.

In interpreting the above exemptions, note that assessed value is 40 percent of actual market value. Therefore, a $10,000 exemption, for example, would eliminate taxation of the first $25,000 of the market value of a residence.

Unique exemptions: Farm products that are held in storage by the original producer for less than a year are exempt. So are statues and books that are displayed in public hallways and not offered for sale. Georgia also has a significant "free port" exemption designed to attract new business; it varies from county to county.

Tax burden for residential real estate: Assessments for residential real estate are 40 percent of fair market value. In most counties, the school tax is limited to 20 mills (2¢) for each dollar of assessed value.

The annual tax bill for a residence with an actual market value of $100,000 ranges from about $800 to $2,000, depending on where you live in Georgia. The average tax bill for such a residence is about $1,200. These figures may be lower for those who qualify for homestead exemptions.

Dates of assessment and payment: Assessments reflect the value of real estate as of January 1. Returns must be filed with the tax commissioner or tax receiver between January 1 and April 1, or during shorter specified periods in some counties.

Taxes are due by December 20 in some counties, and by November 15 in others. A few counties have two installments, which become due September 1 and December 20.

Assessing officials: Responsibility for initial assessments lies with the county Board of Tax Assessors.

Appeals: Appeals may be made first to the assessors themselves, then to the county Board of Equalization, then to the superior court of the county where the property is located, then to the state Supreme Court.

In Georgia, almost all assessments occur from the exterior of the structure only. Also, assessments are heavily influenced by actual sales prices. If a house down the street that looks like yours on the outside is sold, your assessment is likely to be directly affected by that sale. If your house doesn't have all the interior features that exist in the other house, prepare to document that at a grievance hearing.

Assessments based on: Fair market value. The state does not issue a manual for assessors to use in appraising individual residential properties, but assessors are trained and certified by the state.

Source of statewide tax information: Georgia Department of Revenue, Property Tax Division.

HAWAII

What is taxed: Real estate only. Hawaii's definition of real estate includes land, houses and all other structures, fences, and any improvements that are essential to the utility of the real estate or that cannot be removed without substantial damage.

Exemptions for personal property include: Personal property is not taxed. However, given Hawaii's precise definition of real property, it's important to be sure that exempt furniture is not only moveable, but small enough to fit through the doorway. In practice, most household items that are not attached to the structure or land are not assessed for property taxation.

Homestead exemption or other tax relief: Hawaii allows a homestead exemption of the first $20,000 of assessed valuation. The exemption increases to $40,000 when the owner-occupant reaches age 60, and $50,000 at age 70. Additional exemptions are available to those who are blind, disabled, or who suffer from Hansen's disease. All property owned and occupied by a totally disabled veteran is exempt.

Unique exemptions: Growing crops and tree-farm properties are exempt. When improvements are required because of an urban redevelopment, rehabilitation, or conservation program, they will not increase the value for tax purposes for seven years.

Tax burden for residential real estate: The rates are fixed by each county government. The tax bill for a residence with an actual market value of $100,000 will vary from about $500 to $900, depending on where you live in Hawaii.

Dates of assessment and payment: Property is assessed on its value as of January 1. Taxes are due in two installments, payable by August 20 and the following February 20.

Assessing officials: Property is assessed by the local assessor for each assessment district.

Appeals: The assessment may be appealed to either a board of review or to the Tax Appeal Court. Decisions of the Tax Appeal Court may be appealed to the state Supreme Court.

Assessments based on: The cost method (replacement cost less depreciation, if any) is used for most assessments. A market approach—using direct comparisons of sales prices—is used in some cases, especially in valuation of residential condominiums. The basic reference used statewide is the *CLT (Cole Layer Trumble) Manual.* Assessments are computerized, using the CLT Computer Program. Data are maintained by the Real Property Assessment Division of each county.

Source of statewide tax information: Edwin J. Ferreira, administrator, Real Property Assessment, State of Hawaii.

IDAHO

What is taxed: Real estate and all personal property, unless expressly exempt.

Exemptions for personal property include: Household goods, furniture, furnishings, wearing apparel, and personal effects held for exclusive use of the taxpayer and family, not for sale or commercial use. Also exempt are registered motor vehicles and recreational vehicles, with the exception of house trailers. In practice, household items that are not attached to the structure or land are not assessed for taxation.

Homestead exemption or other tax relief: A sizeable homeowner's exemption is available for owner-occupied structures. The exemption is for the structure only, not the land it sits on. Half the value of an owner-occupied structure, up to a maximum of $50,000, is exempt.

In addition, tax reductions are available, if income guidelines are met, to the following categories of persons: fatherless children under age 18, persons age 65 or older, widows or widowers, blind or disabled persons, and former prisoners of war.

Unique exemptions: Agricultural crops (excluding standing timber), trees that bear fruits and nuts, and grape vines are exempt. So are nonpatented mining claims, and nonprofit telephone systems with no more than 25 subscribers.

Tax burden for residential real estate: Tax rates tend to be higher in urban areas than in rural areas. For a residence with an actual market value of $100,000, the tax bill in an urban area would range from $1,053 to $2,823, with a statewide average bill of $1,785. In rural areas, the tax bill for a residence with the same market value would range from $730 to $1637, with a statewide average of $1,214.

Dates of assessment and payment: Taxes are based on assessment as of January 1, and payable in two installments: December 20 and the following June 20. Assessments must be performed between January 1 and the fourth Monday in June. Each year, at least 20 percent of properties are to be assessed, so each property is assessed at least once every five years. The results of each year's appraisals are used as an index to revise the valuations of all properties that were not appraised in that year.

Note: If a new house is built and occupied after January 1, a fee is charged in lieu of the prorated tax for the portion of the year that it was occupied. Therefore, there may be no tax advantages to delaying construction until after the assessment date.

Assessing officials: Property is assessed under the supervision of the county assessor, an elected official.

Appeals: Valuations are equalized by the Board of County Commissioners, which serves as a Board of Equalization from the fourth Monday in June through the second Monday in July, and from the fourth Monday in November through the first Monday in December. Decisions of that board may be appealed to the Board of Tax Appeals or to the District Court.

Assessments based on: Market value. The Idaho Department of Revenue and Taxation provides guidelines to assessors with procedures to compare properties to determine market value. A statewide manual is published by the State Tax Commission. Computer programs are generally not used for assessments.

Source of statewide tax information: Clyde J. Morgan, Jr., Idaho property tax administrator.

ILLINOIS

What is taxed: Real estate only. In Illinois, mobile homes that are not on permanent foundations are not considered to be real estate, but in lieu of property taxes, they are subject to a use tax and a privilege tax, based on the age and square footage of the structure.

Exemptions for personal property include: Illinois repealed its personal property tax in 1978. In general, household items that are not attached to the structure or land are not assessed for property taxation. However, borderline items such as wood stoves and above-ground swimming pools are generally assessed as part of the real estate.

Homestead exemption and other tax relief: Up to $3,500 of any increase in the assessed value of a homestead since 1977 is exempt. (That's $10,500 in actual market value.)

Persons age 65 or older may claim an additional $2,000 exemption of assessed value ($6,000 of actual value) and may receive additional property tax relief if household income is less than $14,000. Similar relief is available to disabled persons meeting the same income standards.

If residents age 65 or older live in a mobile home to which they hold title, the privilege tax is reduced to 80 percent of the tax that would otherwise be due.

Unique exemptions: When new improvements are made to an existing residential structure, the first $30,000 of the actual value of the improvements is exempt from taxation for a four-year period. There is an eight-year exemption of the increased value when a historic building is restored or rehabilitated.

Tax burden for residential real estate: Residential real estate is generally assessed at one-third of its actual value. The tax bill for a house with an actual market value of $100,000 ranges from $1,376 to $4,200, depending on where you live in Illinois. There are special, lower valuation systems for farmland and for structures equipped with solar energy heating or cooling systems.

The privilege tax on mobile homes ranges from 15¢ per square foot for a new mobile home to 7½¢ per square foot on a mobile home that is 15 or more years old. That's a low rate compared to taxation on real estate in Illinois, so if you have a mobile home, it may be worthwhile to avoid putting it onto a permanent foundation.

Dates of assessment and payment: Property is assessed according to its value as of January 1, and the tax on that assessment is payable the following year. In general, each individual property is reassessed every four years.

In counties with fewer than a million inhabitants, property taxes are payable in two installments that become delinquent June 1 and September 1. In counties with more than a million inhabitants, installments become delinquent March 1 and August 1. If tax bills are not mailed 30 days before the delinquent date, the delinquent date is extended.

Assessing officials: In most instances, the township assessor is responsible for initial assessments.

Appeals: The supervisor of assessments has the power to change or equalize assessments. Appeals may be made to the local board of review. In some smaller counties, the board of review is the same as the Board of County Commissioners. Otherwise, it is a separate panel. In Cook County, appeals are taken to the county Board of Appeals.

In Cook County, no further levels of appeal have been provided in state law. If your house is in another county, a state Property Tax Appeal Board will hear complaints that are not settled at the Board of Review level. Payment of taxes under protest is generally unsuccessful unless fraud can be proven.

Assessments based on: The *Illinois Real Property Appraisal Manual*, issued by the Department of Revenue, is used in 101 out of 102 counties. The exception is Cook County, where assessors use cost schedules and guidelines taken from other sources. Computer programs are not widely used for assessments in Illinois.

Source of statewide tax information: Assessment Administration Division, Illinois Department of Revenue.

INDIANA

What is taxed: Real estate and tangible personal property, unless expressly exempt. There is a separate tax for intangible personal property.

Exemptions for personal property include: Most personal property, although items such as boats, motor homes, mobile homes, and trailers are subject to property taxation. Automobiles and small trucks are subject to an excise tax in lieu of property tax. Household items that are not attached to the structure or land are generally not assessed for property taxation.

Homestead exemption or other tax relief: A homestead credit is allowed for 4 percent of tax liability on a primary residence and surrounding land, up to one acre. The amount of the credit may be increased if sufficient funds are available, or at the option of a county that has adopted its own income tax.

A deduction of $1,000 is allowed from the assessed value of a residence if the property is mortgaged or is being purchased under contract.

In addition, the state funds a credit against all property tax liability, including taxes on residences. The basic credit amount is

20 percent. However, this percentage is affected by the amount of municipal debt and other factors in any particular location.

Other deductions, which are contingent on income and/or property value limitations, are available to blind and disabled persons, certain disabled veterans, and persons age 65 or older.

Unique exemptions: Rehabilitated residential property may qualify for a deduction in property taxes for a five-year period if specific guidelines are met. Solar, geothermal, and hydroelectric heating and cooling systems are exempt.

Other unique issues: In Indiana, appliances are not assessed for taxation, even if they are built in. Therefore, if your heart is set on a built-in refrigerator, this is a good place to live. Also, no land-scaping improvements—even permanent improvements like a stone wall or rock garden—are taxed.

Tax burden for residential real estate: The amount of annual growth in property tax levies is limited by law. The effective limitation is on the levy, not the rate. Although the annual growth is generally limited to 5 percent, exceptions for certain items such as municipal debt cause the actual growth to vary, depending on the location.

Judging by the wording of the statutes, it would appear that the tax bill on a residence with an actual market value of $100,000 should not exceed $2,000 in incorporated cities and towns, or $1,250 in unincorporated areas. However, there are so many exceptions that these technical limits don't necessarily apply, in practice, in any locality.

Dates of assessment and payment: The statutory dates for assessment are January 15 for mobile homes and March 1 for all other property. Personal property is subject to annual assessment (based on returns filed by taxpayers), while each parcel of real estate is reassessed once every eight years. Taxes are payable in two equal installments which are due May 10 and November 10. However, if the tax bill is less than $25, counties may require payment in full by May 10.

Assessing officials: Residential property is assessed by township assessors.

Appeals: Assessment decisions by the township assessor are subject to review by a county Board of Review. The board is made up of the county assessor, county auditor, county treasurer, and two taxpayers appointed by the county Board of Commissioners. Its

Your Low-Tax Dream House

decisions may be appealed to the state Board of Tax Commissioners, then to the tax court.

Assessments based on: Assessments are set at a uniform rate of one third of the "true tax value" of real property. True tax value is established under rules and guidelines adopted by the state Board of Tax Commissioners. True tax value seems to approximate replacement cost minus depreciation; by law it does not have to equal fair market value. The principal guide for valuation is the *Indiana Real Property Assessment Manual.* Computer programs are widely used; approximately ten different programs are in use in various parts of the state.

Source of statewide tax information: The office of the Indiana State Board of Tax Commissioners.

IOWA

What is taxed: Real estate, unless expressly exempt.

Exemptions for personal property include: The personal property tax was repealed as of the 1987 tax year. In general, household items that are not attached to the structure or land are not assessed for property taxation.

Homestead exemption or other tax relief: A homestead tax credit is available to all homeowners. The credit is equal to the actual tax levy on the first $4,850 of the actual value of the residence. The minimum tax reduction resulting from the credit is $62.50.

Disabled veterans may receive a credit of the full amount of taxes on a homestead, if annual household income does not exceed $10,000. If the veteran dies, the credit may be continued for his or her unremarried spouse and/or minor children.

An additional homestead credit, based on household income, is available to persons age 65 or older. If the eligible person dies, the credit may remain in effect for a spouse age 55 or older. This credit is on a sliding scale based on income, ranging from 25 percent to 100 percent of the taxes due on the homestead.

Unique exemptions: Normal and necessary repairs do not increase the taxable value of a building if the repairs do not exceed $2,500 per year. Solar energy systems will not increase a property's taxable value for five years. Other exemptions include coal held for the production of methane gas, wildlife habitats, and forest and fruit tree reservations.

Tax burden for residential real estate: The tax bill on a residence with an actual market value of $100,000 varies from approximately $1,850 to $2,250, depending on where you live in Iowa. Reduced assessments are applied to agricultural lands and structures, according to a formula based on productivity.

Dates of assessment and payment: Property is assessed every two years to reflect its value as of January 1. Assessments are to be completed by April 15. Payment may generally be made to the county treasurer's office in two installments, which become delinquent on October 1 and the following April 1.

Assessing officials: Initial assessments of residential property are made by the county or city assessor.

Appeals: Assessments are equalized by the county Board of Review. Adjustments are made to the assessments of classes of property by the Department of Revenue and Finance. Decisions by the Board of Review may be appealed to the district court in the county where the board sits, then to the state Supreme Court.

Assessments based on: Residential property is assessed at market value, but then adjusted so that taxable value is a percentage of that amount. The adjustment formula is established by the Iowa Department of Revenue and Finance to limit, on a statewide basis, increases in residential property taxes resulting from revaluation. The Department of Revenue and Finance provides each assessor with a copy of the *Iowa Real Property Appraisal Manual*. Computer programs are not widely used for assessments in Iowa.

Source of statewide tax information: Donald E. Reed, supervisor, Appraisal Section, Local Government Services Section, Property Tax Division, Iowa Department of Revenue.

KANSAS

What is taxed: Real estate and personal property, unless expressly exempt. Mobile homes used as dwellings are assessed in the same manner as realty.

Exemptions for personal property include: Household goods and personal effects not used to produce income. Kansas also has a separate exemption for wearing apparel. In practice, household items that are not attached to the structure or land are generally not assessed for taxation.

Homestead exemption or other tax relief: Property tax refunds, adjusted according to income, are available to persons who are disabled, age 55 or older, or who have minor dependent children in their households. The same refunds are available to renters, based on the presumption that 15 percent of their rent goes toward property taxes.

Unique exemptions: Young horses, cattle, mules, asses, sheep, hogs, and goats are exempt. (In practice, no livestock are taxed.) Another exemption applies to antique aircraft used for recreational or display purposes.

Tax burden for residential real estate: Beginning in 1989, the Classification Amendment to the Kansas Constitution takes effect, providing different assessment rates for several subclasses of real estate and personal property.

Under the new system, residential real estate is assessed for taxation at 12 percent of fair market value. Agricultural real estate is assessed at 30 percent of use value. Vacant land is assessed at 12 percent of fair market value, and all other real estate at 30 percent of fair market value.

Mobile homes are classified as tangible personal property, but, like residential real estate, assessed at 12 percent of fair market value. Other types of taxable personal property (including minerals, public utilities, and motor vehicles) are assessed at 30 percent.

This new system is being put into effect at this writing, so there is no objective way to judge its impact on residential tax burdens. Under the old system, the statewide average tax bill for a residence with an actual market value of $100,000 was approximately $1,200, with sizeable variations depending on where you live in Kansas.

Dates of assessment and payment: Property is assessed according to its value as of January 1. Payments are due November 1, but may be paid in two installments, which become delinquent after December 20 and the following June 20.

Assessing officials: County appraisers are responsible for initial assessments.

Appeals: The county Board of Equalization equalizes and revises assessments of both real and personal property. The Board's decisions may be appealed to the state Board of Equalization.

Assessments based on: A classification formula called for by Article II, Section I of the Kansas Constitution. Computer programs are being used to implement the new system.

Source of statewide tax information: Kansas Department of Revenue, Division of Property Valuation.

KENTUCKY

What is taxed: All real estate and personal property, including intangibles, unless expressly exempt. All mobile homes are considered to be real estate.

Exemptions for personal property include: Household goods of a person used in his or her home. This means that household items that are not attached to the structure or land are not assessed for property taxation.

Homestead exemption or other tax relief: Real property owned and maintained by a person age 65 or older, or who is disabled, is exempt except for special assessments, up to a particular value that is adjusted for inflation. The exempt value as of 1989-90 is $18,400.

Unique exemptions: Certified alcohol production facilities are exempt from all local taxation. However, they are subject to a state property tax of a tenth of a cent per $100 of valuation.

Other unique tax issues: Interior features have relatively little effect on residential assessments in Kentucky, because interiors are rarely inspected. Also, local governments may impose moratoriums on property assessments or reassessments to encourage repair, rehabilitation, or restoration of structures within their jurisdictions.

Tax burden for residential real estate: All property is to be assessed at its fair cash value. On application, agricultural and horticultural lands may be assessed on their agricultural or horticultural value. The annual tax bill for a residence with an actual market value of $100,000 ranges from $600 to $1,200, depending on where you live in Kentucky.

Dates of assessment and payment: Real estate and tangible personal property are assessed by counties according to their value as of January 1. The assessment date for first and second-class cities is July 1. The date for third-class cities is set by city ordinance, and the date for fourth, fifth and sixth-class cities is January 1.

State, county and district taxes are due on September 15 and delinquent on the following January 1. The due and delinquency dates for cities and towns are as follows: first class, due January 1, delinquent May 1; second class, set by local ordinance; third class, due June 1, delinquent October 1; fourth class, due July 1, delinquent August 1; fifth and sixth class, set by local ordinance. Cities may provide discounts for early payment.

Assessing officials: County assessments are made by the property valuation administrator. Cities and towns, which are divided into six classes, have city assessors to evaluate property subject to their taxing authority, or may adopt the county assessments.

Appeals: For county assessments, appeals may be made to the county Board of Assessment Appeals. For assessments made in cities classified in the first, second, fifth, and sixth categories, appeals may be made to the city Board of Equalization. For assessments made in third and fourth-class cities, appeals may be made to the City Board of Supervisors. Further appeals may be taken to the courts. In practice, relatively few assessments are appealed in Kentucky.

Assessments based on: Fair cash value, which is roughly equivalent to fair market value. A statewide manual for assessment of properties is under development early in 1989. Computer programs are not routinely used for assessments.

Source of statewide tax information: James F. Coffman, commissioner of property taxation for Kentucky.

LOUISIANA

What is taxed: All real estate and personal property, unless expressly exempt.

Exemptions for personal property include: Personal property used in the home, or on loan in a public place. In practice, household items that are not attached to the structure or land are not assessed for taxation.

Homestead exemption or other tax relief: The first $7,500 in assessed valuation of a homestead, including up to 160 contiguous acres, is exempt. Assessed valuation of a residence is only 10 percent of actual value, so in practice, the first $75,000 in actual value of a homestead is exempt. However, the exemption does not apply to some municipal taxes.

Unique exemptions: Agricultural products owned by the producer, agricultural machinery, and farm structures except for the principal residence are exempt. So is equipment attached to any owner-occupied residential building or swimming pool as part of a solar energy system, and any Mardi Gras property used for nonprofit purposes.

Tax burden for residential real estate: Residential property and land are assessed at 10 percent of fair market value. Qualified farm, horticultural, marsh, and timber land are assessed at 10 percent of use value. Improvements made to qualified commercial structures in a downtown, historic, or economic development district will be assessed for five years on the basis of the property's assessed value in the year prior to the year the work was begun.

Thanks to the substantial homestead exemption, the property tax burden for homeowners in Louisiana is among the lightest, if not the lightest, in the nation. The annual tax bill for a residence with an actual market value of $100,000 ranges from about $100 to $400, depending on where you live in Louisiana.

Dates of assessment and payment: Property is assessed according to its value as of January 1, except in Orleans Parish, where valuations are as of August 1. Each parcel of real property is assessed at least once every four years, and personal property is assessed annually. Each taxpayer is required to file a return listing taxable personal property with the parish assessor by April 1, except that in the Parish of Orleans, the return is filed with the Board of Assessors within 20 days after the form for the return is delivered to the taxpayer.

Taxes must be paid by December 31 each year, except that in Orleans Parish real estate taxes are paid by February 1 and personal property taxes by May 1.

Assessing officials: Responsibility for initial assessments lies with parish assessors.

Appeals: Assessments are subject to review in each parish by the Board of Review. Decisions of the Board of Review may be appealed to the Tax Commission, then to the district court.

Assessments based on: Cost and market value are used for residential assessments. The Marshall Valuation Service *Residential Cost Handbook* serves as a statewide manual. Computer programs are widely used; each assessor's office has its own program.

Source of statewide tax information: Hal B. Macmurdo, coordinator, Louisiana Tax Commission.

MAINE

What is taxed: All real estate and personal property, unless expressly exempt. State and county taxes are levied not against the property owner, but against the city or town.

Exemptions for personal property include: Household furniture, including television sets and musical instruments; wearing apparel; farming utensils; and mechanics' tools. A separate exemption applies to individually owned personal property with a just value of less than $1,000, except items used for industrial or commercial purposes, and vehicles and camp trailers that are not subject to an excise tax.

In practice, most household items that are not attached to the structure or land are not assessed for taxation. However, the policies on this issue are not consistent statewide, as different assessment schedules are used in different municipalities. In some localities, some of the household items not taxed in most other states, including rugs, free-standing appliances, and wood stoves, may be subject to property taxation.

Homestead exemption or other tax relief: Maine has a program that allows tax relief benefits for families with relatively low household incomes. The maximum benefits increase for those who are age 62 or older, blind, or disabled. In addition, there is a limited homestead exemption for aged or disabled veterans and their families.

Unique exemptions: Beehives; up to $10,000 worth of farm machinery used exclusively for production of hay crops, if it is not self-propelled; and radium used for medical purposes are exempt in Maine.

Tax burden for residential real estate: Property is assessed at its just value, except that forested land, farmland, and open-space land may be assessed according to current use value. The annual tax bill on a house with actual market value of $100,000 ranges from $112 to $2,804, depending on where you live in Maine. The average is about $1,370.

Dates of assessment and payment: Assessments are based on the value of property as of April 1. Dates of payment are fixed by each municipality.

Assessing officials: Local assessors are responsible for initial assessments. State and county taxes are equalized among the towns by the Bureau of Taxation.

Appeals: The first appeal is made to the local assessor. The second appeal may be made either to the local Board of Assessment Review or to the county commissioners. Further appeals may be taken to the Superior Court.

Assessments based on: Just value, which is roughly equivalent to fair market value. Although an assessment manual has been published by the state, its use is optional, and many municipalities base their valuations on schedules developed by professional revaluation companies. Computer programs are generally not used for Maine assessments.

Source of statewide tax information: Property Tax Division, Maine Bureau of Taxation.

MARYLAND

What is taxed: Real estate and tangible personal property, unless expressly exempt.

Exemptions for personal property include: Residential personal property that is not used in a business, occupation, or profession. In practice, household items that are not attached to the structure or land are generally not assessed for property taxation.

Homestead exemption or other tax relief: A homestead tax credit is available if the assessment of an owner-occupied residence increases by more than 15 percent per year.

Additional tax credits are available on a sliding scale based on household income. In this scale, if household income is $12,000, for example, the tax limit is $360. If household income is $30,000, the tax limit is $1,920. A credit is issued for any taxes paid above the limit, up to a maximum credit of $1,500. There are several limitations on the tax credit program: for example, you may not receive the credit if your net worth—not counting your residence—exceeds $200,000.

Unique exemptions: Maryland has many specific exemptions and "special assessments," which serve the same function as exemptions. (A special assessment lists the item but gives it no value.) The following are among the items not taxed:

• Changes to a dwelling necessitated by the health or medical condition of a resident, to the extent that these improvements do not exceed 10 percent of the total value of the property.

• Manure banks or other facilities to store animal wastes from agricultural livestock production. The statute appears to exclude

241

poultry manure storage facilities from this tax benefit, but in practice, no such distinction is made by assessors.
  • Property owned by Gunpowder Youth Camps.
  • Radiation fallout shelters.

Unique tax credits: Counties and cities may provide tax credits for a number of items, including the following:
  • Structures that use solar or geothermal energy, or qualifying energy conservation devices for heating or cooling.
  • Restoration of historic structures.
  • An improvement to a cemetery that is used as a dwelling by a cemetery employee.
  • Open space and open areas, tobacco barns, and improvements to provide family or group child day care services.

Other unique issues: In Maryland, the official policy is not to enter the home for assessments, unless invited to do so by the homeowner, or unless the property is being assessed for the first time. The quality of the interior is estimated, based on the quality of the exterior. Therefore, if your interior doesn't look as good as your exterior, make a point of inviting the assessor in. If your interior is fancier than the exterior, don't invite the assessor in.

Also, relatively minor features make little difference in Maryland assessments. Approximately 90 percent of the value of real property is determined by the size and location of the land and buildings.

Tax burden for residential real estate: Real property assessments are at full cash value, which is interpreted to be equivalent to market value. However, farmland, marsh land, woodland, country clubs, and land held for later development are valued at use value. Mobile homes are assessed in the same way as real estate. Deficient wells and septic systems may be assessed at reduced rates.

The annual tax bill for a residence with an actual market value of $100,000 varies from $376 to $2,592, depending on where you live in Maryland.

Dates of assessment and payment: Property is assessed according to its value as of January 1. Real property is physically reassessed (from the outside of the house) once every three years, and the increase in valuation is phased in over three years. Also, building permits, which are reviewed every few months, can trigger a new assessment. Taxes on real estate become due July 1, and may be paid without interest until October 1.

Assessing officials: Assessments are performed by the state Department of Assessments and Taxation, which has 24 offices, in each county and in Baltimore City. Initial assessment responsibility lies with the Supervisor of Assessments in the county where the property is located, or, in Baltimore City, the Department of Assessment.

Appeals: Appeals may be made to the local supervisor of assessments. Further appeals may be made to the Property Assessment Appeal Board with jurisdiction where the property is located, then to the Maryland Tax Court, then to a county circuit court, then to the Court of Special Appeals.

Assessments based on: The Maryland Department of Assessments and Taxation provides a detailed *Procedures Manual* for assessors. A standard analysis of sale properties is made, to determine appropriate depreciation and land value rates for comparable properties.

To a greater extent than in virtually any other state, Maryland assessments are made under a uniform statewide system.

Source of statewide tax information: Henry J. Sikorski, assistant state supervisor, Maryland Department of Assessments and Taxation.

MASSACHUSETTS

What is taxed: Real estate and personal property, unless expressly exempt. Mobile homes in mobile home parks are exempt from property taxation.

Exemptions for personal property include: Household furniture and effects of every person, whether kept in a public warehouse or used in the home. Other personal property exemptions include wearing apparel, farm utensils, cash on hand, tools of a trade, boats, fishing gear and nets used exclusively in commercial fishing to an amount not exceeding a total value of $10,000, and most domestic animals.

In practice, household items that are not attached to the structure or land are not assessed for property taxation.

Homestead exemption or other tax relief: Limited property tax exemptions are available to the elderly and disabled, with special provisions for disabled wartime veterans.

Unique exemptions: Air raid, bomb, or fallout shelters are exempt. So are hydropower facilities built since 1979, and property other than real estate that produces income which is subject to the state income tax.

A 20-year exemption is allowed for solar or wind-powered devices used to heat or supply energy for a taxable property.

Tax burden for residential real estate: All property subject to taxation is appraised at full cash value. Real estate is divided into four classifications: Class I, residential; Class II, open-space land; Class III, commercial; and Class IV, industrial. Different tax rates may apply to each classification.

If you own more than five acres of agricultural or horticultural land, you may apply to have that land valued solely according to its use value. The value of recreational land is determined according to its use, but in no case will it exceed 25 percent of fair cash value.

As a result of a special initiative petition (Proposition 2½), the total taxes on real estate or personal property in a community cannot exceed 2½ percent of its fair cash value. In practice, the annual tax bill on a residence with an actual market value of $100,000 ranges from $474 to $2,500, depending on where you live in Massachusetts.

Dates of assessment and payment: Property is assessed according to its value as of January 1. All residents of the commonwealth are required to file returns listing their taxable personal property by March 1.

Taxes are generally payable in two installments, with payment deadlines of November 1 and May 1. Also, cities and towns may require residents to pay a preliminary tax, not to exceed 50 percent of the tax payable in the preceding year.

Assessing officials: The assessors for each city or town are responsible for initial assessments.

Appeals: Aggrieved persons may apply in writing to the assessors to request abatement. The deadline for this initial grievance is October 1. Further appeals may be made to the county commissioners or to the Appellate Tax Board.

Assessments based on: Fair cash value, interpreted as equivalent to fair market value. There is no single statewide manual or system. Local assessors, often with the advice and assistance of professional revaluation firms, develop and use mass appraisal systems appropriate for the properties in their communities.

The Massachusetts commissioner of revenue has responsibility for establishing minimum standards for assessment performance and for certifying, every three years, whether or not locally assessed values represent full and fair cash value.

Source of statewide tax information: Harry M. Grossman, chief, Property Tax Bureau, Massachusetts Department of Revenue.

MICHIGAN

What is taxed: All real estate and personal property, unless expressly exempt. A mobile home in a licensed mobile home park is not considered real estate, and is subject to a separate tax of $3 per month.

Exemptions for personal property include: All personal property that is owned and used by a householder and not used to produce income. In practice, household items that are not attached to the structure or land are not assessed for property taxation.

Homestead exemption or other tax relief: There is a limited homestead exemption for disabled veterans who have received pecuniary assistance for specially adapted housing. In addition, residents age 65 or older may defer payment of special assessments if household income falls within guideline levels.

There is also an income tax credit for homeowners (and renters) when property taxes on the homestead exceed a percentage—usually 3½ percent—of household income.

Unique exemptions: Normal repairs, replacement, and maintenance are exempt from taxation until the property is sold. These may include substantial improvements such as rewiring, replacement of siding or porches, resurfacing of ceilings and floors, insulation, and replacement of plumbing fixtures or the furnace. Even if these repairs or maintenance add to the value of the house, they are noted separately by the assessor, and do not increase the taxable value of the house until it is sold.

Tax burden for residential real estate: Property is assessed at 50 percent of its true cash value. The total amount of general property taxes imposed for any one year cannot exceed 50 mills for each dollar of assessed valuation. This means that for every $1,000 of value, taxes cannot exceed $50.00. Exceptions to this rule, however, are made for charter rates, authority rates, and debt levies. In practice, the annual tax bill for a house with an actual market value of $100,000 varies from $1,800 to $5,625, depending on where you live in Michigan.

Dates of assessment and payment: Property is assessed according to its value as of December 31. In most cities and townships, taxes are levied on July 1 and December 1. In Detroit, all taxes become due July 15, and may be paid in full, without penalty, by August 31. Other alternatives available to Detroit taxpayers include payment in two equal installments by August 15 and the following January 15, or earlier payments made earlier in accordance with a monthly prepayment plan. In townships, a 1 percent collection fee may be added if late tax payments are made prior to February 15, and 4 percent may be added thereafter.

Assessing officials: The township supervisor, or in cities, the city assessor, is responsible for initial assessments. Assessors must be certified by the state assessors' board.

Appeals: Assessments are reviewed in March by the Board of Review of the township or city. Decisions of the local boards may be appealed to the Tax Tribunal.

Assessments based on: A detailed assessors' manual is published by the state. Cost manuals are also approved by the state. Most local assessors use either the manual or the cost schedules published in the Marshall and Swift *Residential Cost Handbook.*

Source of statewide tax information: State Tax Commission, Michigan Department of Treasury.

MINNESOTA

What is taxed: All real estate and personal property, unless expressly exempt. Manufactured homes are considered to be personal property rather than real estate, but are in effect taxed at about the same rate.

Exemptions for personal property include: All personal property is exempt except manufactured homes, personal property of utilities and pipelines, and a few other miscellaneous items. In practice, household items that are not attached to the structure or land are not assessed for taxation.

Homestead exemption or other tax relief: The first $68,000 in value of a homestead is taxed at a lower rate than is any value above that amount. Tax reductions are available for homesteads located within areas eligible for relief from the Taconite Property Tax Relief Fund. Also, up to $2,000 in tax liability is exempt for homesteads of persons who have received the Congressional Medal of Honor.

Unique exemptions: An exemption is available for certain types of wetlands and prairie land.

Tax burden for residential real estate: Property is valued at market value. Assessments, which are called tax capacities, are a percentage of the market value, depending on classification of the property. Residential real estate that is used as a homestead by its owner is Class 1 property. For the first $68,000 in value, it has a gross tax capacity of 2.17 percent of market value, and a net capacity of 1 percent of market value. The value between $68,000 and $100,000 has a gross capacity of 2.5 percent of market value, and value in excess of that has a gross capacity of 3.3 percent.

The state pays to the taxing districts the difference between the gross and net tax capacity for each property. Agricultural homestead properties are assessed at lower gross and net tax capacities.

In practice, the annual tax bill on a home with an actual market value of $100,000 would range from $1,100 to $2,550, depending on where you live in Minnesota.

Dates of assessment and payment: All property is taxed according to its value and classification as of January 2. Each parcel of real estate is valued at its market value each year and must be appraised or reappraised at least once every four years. Real estate tax bills in excess of $100 may be paid in two equal installments by May 16 and October 16. Personal property taxes for manufactured houses are due on or before August 31.

Assessing officials: Township, village, city, and county assessors are responsible for initial assessments.

Appeals: County assessors examine the local books to determine if there is any omitted property. Appeals may be made to the local Board of Review, which is made up of the town board or the council of a village or city. Further review is made by the county Board of Equalization, made up of the county commissioners and the county auditor. Appeals of non-homestead property where the amount of tax in dispute exceeds $5,000 may be made to the commissioner of revenue.

Appeals of local assessments may be made to the Minnesota Tax Court or District Court, but 50 percent of the tax is paid if it becomes due prior to the court hearing. Decisions by the Regular Division of the Minnesota Tax Court or District Court may be appealed to the state Supreme Court, but such appeals are limited by statute to specific legal issues. All decisions by the Small Claims Division of the Tax Court are final.

Assessments based on: Market value, under procedures described in the *Minnesota Property Tax Administrator's Manual.* Computer programs are not widely used for assessments in Minnesota.

Source of statewide tax information: Thomas E. Nash, senior appraiser, Local Government Services Division, Minnesota Department of Revenue.

Your Low-Tax Dream House

MISSISSIPPI

What is taxed: Real estate and personal property, unless expressly exempt. Mobile homes may be classified either as real estate or as personal property. To be classified as real estate, the mobile home must be on, and anchored to, land owned by the taxpayer, and the wheels and axles must be removed.

Exemptions for personal property include: Household furniture kept for the owner's personal use; all wearing apparel; jewelry to the value of $100; provisions on hand for family use; libraries of all persons; and pictures and works of art not kept or offered for sale as merchandise. In practice, household items that are not attached to the structure or land are not assessed for property taxation.

Homestead exemption or other tax relief: Homeowners are allowed an exemption on the first $5,850 of assessed value ($58,500 of actual value) on assessments for county and school taxes. The exemption reduces taxes by as much as $240. Homeowners who are age 65 or older, or totally disabled, qualify for a total exemption of the first $6,000 of assessed value ($60,000 in actual value) of eligible property. The latter exemption applies to municipal taxes as well as county and school taxes.

Unique exemptions: Municipalities may exempt from taxes (except school district taxes) new structures or improvements within a central business district, for up to seven years. Other exemptions include most farm animals, horse-drawn vehicles, nuclear fuel, and growing nursery stock.

Tax burden for residential real estate: Class I property (single-family, owner-occupied) is assessed at 10 percent of true value. Other categories and assessment percentages are: Class II (real estate other than Class I or IV), 15 percent; Class III (personal property other than motor vehicles and Class IV property), 15 percent; Class IV (public utility property), 30 percent; and Class V (motor vehicles) 30 percent.

Once assessments are equalized according to those percentages, the tax rate is fixed by officials of each county, subject to statutory limits. In practice, the tax bill on residential property with an actual market value of $100,000 ranges from about $500 to $1,000, depending on where you live in Mississippi.

Dates of assessment and payment: Real estate is assessed according to its value on January 1. All county, school, and municipal taxes are due in three installments. One-half of the total tax bill must be paid by February 1, one-quarter by May 1, and one-quarter by

248

August 1. Taxes become delinquent after the due dates. Interest accrues at the rate of 1 percent per month on the total amount due.

Assessing officials: County assessors are responsible for initial assessments. Municipalities must adopt the values established by the county for the property within municipal limits, unless they have specific permission from the state tax commission to adopt other values.

Appeals: Appeals may be made to the county Board of Supervisors, sitting as the Board of Equalization. Municipal authorities have no power to modify or correct an assessment made by the county assessor. The power of the county board is strictly circumscribed. If the taxpayer fails to get a satisfactory resolution from the county board, the only route available for further appeal is the circuit court.

Assessments based on: Constitutionally-mandated percentage of the true value of the property, by its class. A statewide manual is used. Most of the 82 counties use computer programs for assessments. They all make use of a statewide point system, based on the cost method of assessment.

Source of statewide tax information: Richard R. Brown, director, Property Tax Bureau, Mississippi State Tax Commission.

MISSOURI

What is taxed: Real estate and tangible personal property. Mobile homes used as dwelling units are assessed as residential realty.

Exemptions for personal property include: Household goods, furniture, wearing apparel, and articles of personal use, owned and used by a person in his or her home. In practice, household items that are not attached to the structure or land are not assessed for taxation.

Homestead exemption or other tax relief: None.

Unique exemptions: Historic motor vehicles are assessed at a special reduced rate (5 percent of actual value).

Tax burden for residential real estate: Property is valued at its true value, except that the true value of agricultural or horticultural property is its use value. Assessments are set at a percentage of true value, depending on the classification of the property. Residential real estate is assessed at 19 percent of true value; agricultural and horticultural property, 12 percent; other real property, 32 percent;

personal property (with a few exceptions that have different rates), 33.3 percent. The average annual tax bill for a residence with an actual market value of $100,000 is $940.

Dates of assessment and payment: Property is assessed according to its value as of January 1. Taxes become delinquent the following January 1. As a general rule, tax bills must be mailed at least 15 days prior to the delinquent date.

Assessing officials: Assessments are made by local assessors and their deputies.

Appeals: Taxpayers must file their appeals to the county Board of Equalization on or before the second Monday in May for St. Louis City, the third Monday in June for first-class counties, and while the Board is in session for all other counties. Further appeals involving valuation issues must be made to the State Tax Commission, the county circuit court, and the state appeals court or Supreme Court, respectively.

Assessments based on: The percentages of true value, as described above. True value has generally been interpreted as equivalent to market value. There is no statewide manual. Computer programs are used for most assessments in the various counties.

Source of statewide tax information: Missouri State Tax Commission.

MONTANA

What is taxed: All property, unless expressly exempt.

Exemptions for personal property include: All household goods and furniture, including clocks, musical instruments, sewing machines, and wearing apparel. Other specific exemptions listed in statutes include bicycles used for personal transportation, and truck canopy covers or toppers weighing less than 300 pounds and having no accommodations attached. In practice, household items that are not attached to the structure or land are not assessed for taxation.

Homestead exemption or other tax relief: If household income doesn't exceed $10,000 for a single individual or $12,000 for a married couple (a figure indexed to inflation), the first $80,000 in value of a homestead is taxed at a lower rate, adjusted according to income level. A total homestead exemption is offered to veterans who died or became totally disabled in service to the country, and to their surviving, unremarried spouses, if household income does not exceed a specified amount.

Unique exemptions: Investment in a nonfossil energy source is exempt up to $20,000 for a single-family residence, or up to $100,000 for a multi-family residence, for a period of ten years following installation. Other exemptions include unprocessed, perishable fruits and vegetables; clubhouses and buildings belonging to any organization of honorably discharged veterans; half the sales price of coal sold by producers who extract less than 50,000 tons per year; and down-hole equipment for oil and gas wells.

Tax burden for residential real estate: Property is divided into 20 classifications. Residential real estate (including any mobile home used as a residence) is assessed at 3.86 percent of market value. Agricultural land is assessed similarly, but based on the value of the land for agricultural purposes. Improvements to existing buildings may be taxed at a reduced rate for four years following construction, upon approval by the municipality. The annual tax bill for a residence with an actual market value of $100,000 varies from about $1,150 to $1,544, depending on where you live in Montana.

Dates of assessment and payment: Property is assessed on its value as of January 1. Property is revalued on a five-year cycle. The next cycle begins in 1991. Taxes may be made in two installments, due November 30 (or 30 days after the tax notice is postmarked, whichever is later) and the following May 31.

Assessing officials: The Department of Revenue is responsible for initial assessments of taxable property in each county.

Appeals: Appeals may be made to the county Tax Appeal Board. Further appeals may be made to the state Tax Appeal Board, then to the district court.

Assessments based on: A percentage of market value, as described above. Market value is determined according to the Montana appraisal manuals and the Marshall and Swift *Residential Cost Handbook.*

Source of statewide tax information: Montana Property Tax Division.

NEBRASKA

What is taxed: Real estate and tangible personal property, unless expressly exempt.

Exemptions for personal property include: Household goods and personal effects. In practice, household items that are not attached to the structure or land are not assessed for property taxation.

Homestead exemption or other tax relief: All or part of the first $35,000 in value of a homestead may be exempt for veterans with service-connected disabilities. Other persons with specific disabilities described by law, and persons age 65 or older, may be totally exempt from taxation of the first $35,000 in value, if specific income guidelines are met.

Unique exemptions: There is a 15-year exemption for turbine-powered aircraft not used to transport elected officials, and for mainframe computers requiring environmental temperature controls. Nebraska also exempts business equipment used in manufacture or processing of agricultural products, if the taxpayer and tax commissioner have signed an agreement pursuant to the Employment and Investment Growth Act.

Tax burden for residential real estate: All property taxes are local; the state was prohibited from levying a property tax by a constitutional amendment approved by voters in 1966. Residential and commercial properties are assessed according to actual value. Agricultural property is assessed according to its value for agricultural use.

With the exception of school districts, all units of local government have specific limitations on property tax rates. The annual tax bill on a residence with an actual market value of $100,000 varies from about $1,350 to $2,700, depending on where you live in Nebraska.

Dates of assessment and payment: All property is assessed according to its value as of January 1. Real estate taxes may be paid in two equal installments, due as follows: in counties with less than 100,000 population, May 1 and September 1; in larger counties, April 1 and August 1. Personal property taxes are due December 1 and July 1.

Assessing officials: County assessors are responsible for initial assessments.

Appeals: The valuations set by the county assessors may be reviewed and equalized by the county Board of Equalization. The state Board of Equalization equalizes assessments among the counties. Appeals of board decisions may be made to the district court, then to the state Supreme Court.

Assessments based on: Actual value, determined by using the Nebraska Agricultural Land Valuation Manual and the Marshall and Swift *Residential Cost Handbook*. Computer programs are used by approximately 75 percent of the counties.

Source of statewide tax information: Larry D. Worth, property tax administrator, Nebraska Department of Revenue.

NEVADA

What is taxed: All real estate and personal property, unless expressly exempt. Mobile homes may be classified as real estate if permanently affixed to a foundation; otherwise they are classified as personal property.

Exemptions for personal property include: Household goods and furniture. This constitutional exemption has been interpreted to include, without limitation, all personal effects and all appliances that are not attached to the structure or land.

Homestead exemption or other tax relief: Property tax relief is available to residents age 62 or older who have household incomes not over $15,100. An allowance is made against property taxes due. The allowance is based on income, and cannot exceed $500. The relief is available to renters as well as to homeowners.

Disabled veterans may receive an exemption, ranging from the first $5,000 of assessed valuation (if 60 percent disabled) to the first $10,000 (if 100 percent disabled). Property of widows and orphaned children is exempt to the extent of $1,000 of assessed value, and property of totally blind persons is exempt to the extent of $3,000 of assessed value.

In interpreting the above exemptions, it should be noted that each $1,000 in assessed value equals $2,857 in taxable value. "Taxable value" is defined as replacement cost minus depreciation. Therefore, a $5,000 exemption, for example, would mean that the first $14,285 of the "taxable" value of the house is not taxed.

Unique exemptions: Property of noncommercial theaters, and privately owned airports used by the public without charge are exempt. Also, any residence that contains a qualified fallout shelter is exempt to the extent of $1,000 of assessed value ($2,857 of actual taxable value).

Tax burden for residential real estate: Property is assessed at 35 percent of taxable value. Approved agricultural and open-space lands are assessed at 35 percent of their value as agricultural or open-space land.

The state property tax (as of 1988) is 6.46¢ per $100 of assessed value. All property tax levies combined are restricted by the Constitution to $5 per $100 of assessed value, and by law to $3.64 per $100 of assessed value. This means that all property taxes cannot exceed $1.27 per $100 of taxable value of the property.

The average annual tax bill on a residence with an actual value of $100,000 is $845. The maximum for such a residence would be $1,274.

Dates of assessment and payment: Real estate is valued according to its condition as of October 1 of the year preceding the current year. The assessment becomes a lien on the property as of July 1. Property is physically reappraised every five years. Taxes on real estate may be paid in four equal installments, which are due on the first Mondays in August, October, January, and March.

Assessing officials: The county assessor is responsible for initial assessments. Assessments are equalized among counties by the state Board of Equalization.

Appeals: Appeals are made to the county Board of Equalization, then to the state Board of Equalization, then to the courts of local jurisdiction.

Assessments based on: Taxable value, determined by a cost approach. Most counties use computer programs developed by Marshall Valuation Service. The state supplements this system with its own manuals covering personal property and rural real estate costs.

Source of statewide tax information: Division of Assessment Standards, Nevada Department of Taxation.

NEW HAMPSHIRE

What is taxed: Real estate only. By law, mobile homes are considered to be taxable as real estate. (However, a travel trailer "with the capability of traveling immediately" is not considered to be real estate.)

Exemptions for personal property include: Personal property is not taxed. In practice, household items that are not attached to the structure or land are not assessed for property taxation.

Homestead exemption or other tax relief: Veterans receive a standard exemption amounting to $50 off the tax bill. A veteran with a total, service-connected disability, or the surviving spouse of a veteran killed on active duty, may receive $700 off the tax bill. A veteran who is a double amputee or paraplegic may receive a total exemption.

If the municipality so votes, an exemption is available for legally blind persons, amounting to the first $15,000 in assessed value of the homestead. The first $5,000 in valuation is exempt for persons age 68 or older if total household income (not counting Social Security and certain other income sources) is less than $5,000 ($6,000 if married). Municipalities may, if local voters approve, offer one of two larger and less restrictive homestead exemptions for the elderly.

Unique exemptions: With approval of the voters, municipalities may adopt exemptions for wind-powered energy systems, solar heating or cooling systems, or wood heating systems. Fallout shelters are exempt up to a cap of $200 multiplied by the number of persons the shelter is designed to accommodate.

Tax burden for residential real estate: Property is assessed at its full and true value in money, except that open-space land may be assessed at its current use value. If there is a change in use of open-space land, it is subject to a land use change tax amounting to 10 percent of its full and true value.

If a residence is located in an industrial or commercial zone, its owner may apply to have it assessed according to current residential use value. Once the full and true value or the current use value is determined, the figure is adjusted by an Equalization Adjustment Ratio.

As of 1988, the average tax rate was $28.50 for each $1,000 in assessment. The Equalization Ratio was 57 percent, so the average effective tax rate was $16.25 per $1,000 of actual value. In other words, as a statewide average, the annual tax bill for a residence with an actual value of $100,000 would be about $1,625. The bill would range from $258 (Newington) to $4,016 (Stratford), depending on where you live in New Hampshire.

Dates of assessment and payment: Property is assessed according to its value on April 1. Returns must be filed with the Select Board on or before April 15. Taxes become delinquent on December 2. Cities and towns with more than 10,000 population may permit payment in two installments due July 1 and December 1.

Assessing officials: The select board of each town is responsible for initial assessments. The field work is often done by the state Property Appraisal Division in smaller municipalities, and by private revaluation firms in larger municipalities.

Appeals: Appeals may be made initially to the select board. Further appeals may be made either to the Board of Tax and Land Appeals or to the county superior court. A final appeal may be made to the New Hampshire Supreme Court.

Assessments based on: The state Department of Revenue Administration makes available an appraisal manual for assessing officials who want to use it. Private firms, conducting revaluations, usually opt to use their own replacement cost manuals. The state Property Appraisal Division does not use a computer program, but private firms sometimes do.

Source of statewide tax information: Richard M. Young, assistant director, New Hampshire Property Appraisal Division.

NEW JERSEY

What is taxed: Real estate is taxed locally, and business personal property is taxed by the state. A mobile home that is affixed to a permanent foundation, or that is made habitable by being connected to utility systems, is taxed as real estate. However, mobile homes in parks are exempt from the real estate tax.

Exemptions for personal property include: The state tax applies only to business personal property. Locally, the only personal property subject to taxation appears to be property of telephone, telegraph, and messenger companies. In practice, household items that are not attached to the structure or land are not assessed for taxation in New Jersey.

Homestead exemption or other tax relief: A homestead rebate is offered for taxes paid on the first $10,000 of assessed valuation. The rebate is computed by a complex formula, which provides higher rebates in municipalities with higher tax rates. The rebate cannot exceed 50 percent of the net property tax otherwise due.

Senior citizens, totally disabled persons, and surviving spouses are allowed an additional $50 homestead rebate. Additional homestead exemptions are available to veterans with specified service-connected disabilities, and to their widows.

Also, cities in which residential neighborhoods have been declared to be in need of rehabilitation may regard home improvements, in some cases up to $15,000 in value, to be exempt from real estate taxes for five years.

Unique exemptions: Facilities for treatment of feeble-minded or idiotic men are exempt. Other exemptions apply to personal property stored in a public warehouse, the value of fallout shelters erected on residential property, and automatic fire suppression systems.

Tax burden for residential real estate: Assessments are expressed in "taxable value," which, in the case of real estate, must be between 20 percent and 100 percent (in a multiple of 10 percent) of true value. The percentage is established by the Board of Taxation in each county by April 1, and must be uniformly applied to all real estate in the county in the following tax year. The percentage may be changed only after it has been in effect for at least three years.

If the board fails to properly establish the percentage, the level will be set at 50 percent of true value. Owners of five or more acres of land actively used for agriculture or horticulture may apply to have it assessed only on its use value for agriculture or horticulture.

We were unable to obtain a reliable estimate of typical tax bills for properties with an actual market value of $100,000. However, the average assessment in New Jersey is $74,000, and tax bills on properties assessed at that level range from $1,516 to $3,188, depending on where you live in New Jersey.

Dates of assessment and payment: Property is assessed according to its value as of October 1. Tax payments may be made in four installments, which become delinquent after February 1, May 1, August 1, and November 1.

Assessing officials: The assessors of the local taxing districts are responsible for initial assessments. Assessors are appointed, and those who hold the position must hold a state tax assessor certificate.

Appeals: Appeals are made to the county Board of Taxation, which also meets each February 1 to equalize assessments among the taxing districts in the county. Any action by the county board may be reviewed by the Tax Court. Appeals may be made directly to the Tax Court if the assessed value exceeds $750,000.

Assessments based on: New Jersey has a manual called *Real Property Appraisal Manual for New Jersey Assessors*. It is updated each year to reflect changes in cost schedules. Computer programs are generally not used.

Source of statewide tax information: George J. Lorbeck, chief, Assessor Assistant Section, New Jersey Division of Taxation.

NEW MEXICO

What is taxed: Real estate and tangible personal property, unless expressly exempt.

Exemptions for personal property include: Tangible personal property "owned by a person," unless it is held for business purposes, or unless a federal depreciation tax deduction is taken on it. In practice, household items that are not attached to the structure or land are not assessed for property taxation.

Homestead exemption or other tax relief: There is an exemption of $200 for any head of family who resides in New Mexico. An additional $2,000 exemption applies to veterans and/or their surviving spouses.

Unique exemptions: Community ditches and all laterals thereof are exempt. So are private railroad cars that are subject to the gross earnings tax.

Tax burden for residential real estate: The taxable value of property is set at one-third of market value. Maximum tax rates are set by the Department of Finance and Administration.

For 1988, the maximum rates for taxation of residential property are as follows: for county general purposes, $11.85 per $1,000 net taxable value; for school district general operating purposes, 50¢ per $1,000 net taxable value; for municipal general purposes, $7.65 per $1,000 net taxable value. In setting the rates, the department may not set rates that exceed the dollar amount derived by multiplying the growth control factor by the property tax revenue due for the prior year. However, taxes to pay principal and interest on public obligation debts, and taxes for specific purposes approved by the voters, are in addition to the established maximum rates.

In practice, the annual tax bill for a residence with an actual market value of $100,000 ranges from $254 to $1,510, depending on where you live in New Mexico.

Dates of assessment and payment: Property is assessed according to its value on January 1. Taxes are payable in equal installments due on November 10 and the following April 10. However, the Board of County Commissioners may provide for prepayment of taxes on an installment basis, with payments due July 10 and January 10.

Assessing officials: The county assessor is responsible for initial assessments.

Appeals: Petitions of protest may be filed either with the county assessor or with the secretary of the Taxation and Revenue Department. Once a petition is filed, the taxpayer is entitled to a hearing. Further appeals may be made to the Court of Appeals.

Assessments based on: A statewide manual is used for assessment of properties in New Mexico. Computer programs are not generally used.

Source of statewide tax information: Richard L. Martinez, chief, New Mexico Central Assessment Bureau.

NEW YORK

What is taxed: Real estate only. Mobile homes are considered real estate if they are located within an assessing unit for more than 60 days, unless they are unoccupied and for sale.

Exemptions for personal property include: Personal property is not taxed in New York. In general, household items that are not attached to the structure or land are not assessed for taxation.

Homestead exemption or other tax relief: There are limited homestead exemptions for veterans. The maximum amounts are set by the state, but exemption limits can vary as a result of local options. Municipalities may also grant exemptions of up to 50 percent of the valuation of property owned and occupied by low-income persons age 65 or older.

Unique exemptions: Property of dental societies is partially exempt in cities with populations of 175,000 or more. Fallout shelters are exempt, up to a cap of $100 multiplied by the number of persons the shelter is designed to accommodate.

In New York City, a substantial temporary exemption exists for newly constructed or reconstructed one-and-two-family residences. The value of the improvement is 100 percent exempt during construction and for two years after construction. The amount of the exemption declines thereafter, phasing out completely after the eighth year.

Tax burden for residential real estate: By state law, all real estate is to be assessed at a uniform percentage of actual value. With state encouragement, the trend among localities has been toward assessment at 100 percent of market value.

An owner of qualified agricultural land is entitled to agricultural assessment, the level of which is determined annually by the state.

Eligible tracts of forest land are exempt to the extent of 80 percent of assessed value.

The rate is the aggregate of all local levies; there has been no state property tax since 1929. We were unable to obtain an estimate of the range of tax bills for properties in New York with an actual market value of $100,000.

Dates of assessment and payment: In most municipalities, real estate is assessed as of March 1, and valued according to its condition and ownership as of the preceding January 1. Dates of payment vary among counties and municipalities. In New York City, taxes are payable in four equal installments, which become due on July 1, October 1, January 1, and April 1.

Assessing officials: The assessors of each city, town, and village assess real property within their boundaries. In New York City, real estate is assessed by the Real Property Assessment Bureau.

Appeals: In most jurisdictions, assessments are reviewed, and complaints heard, by the local Board of Assessment Review. Owner-occupants of one-, two-, or three-family homes may take a further appeal to a small claims assessment review hearing officer.

Other appeals of the Board of Assessment Review's decisions may be made to the supreme court of the judicial district where the complaint was made.

In New York City, applications to have assessments corrected may be made during the time that the books of annual record of the assessed valuations are open for public inspection, and final determinations are made by the city tax commission. Appeals of the commission's decisions may be made to the courts.

Assessments based on: Specific procedures for assessment are found in rules and regulations promulgated by the state Board of Equalization and Assessment. The state Division of Equalization and Assessment provides assistance to local assessors in following these procedures, including computer programs to help determine the values of properties. The *Local Assessor's Handbook* is the standard guide, and the state is working on a new, eight-volume assessor's manual. A computer program, *The Real Property Information System*, is available but not used by all localities.

Source of statewide tax information: New York State Division of Equalization and Assessment.

NORTH CAROLINA

What is taxed: All real estate and personal property, unless expressly exempt. There is a state tax for intangible personal property, while real and tangible personal property are subject to local taxation.

Exemptions for personal property include: Most non-business personal property, other than cars, boats, and aircraft. In practice, household items that are not attached to the structure or land are not assessed for taxation.

Homestead exemption or other tax relief: The first $34,000 in assessed value of a homestead owned by a qualifying disabled veteran is exempt. The first $12,000 in assessed value of realty owned by a resident age 65 or older, or permanently disabled, and whose disposable income for the previous year was not over $11,000, is exempt.

Unique exemptions: Buildings equipped with solar heating/cooling systems are assessed as if they had conventional heating/cooling systems. Special nuclear materials, held for or in the process of manufacture, are exempt. There is a special exemption for any motor vehicle chassis that is temporarily in North Carolina for the purpose of having a body mounted thereon.

Tax burden for residential real estate: Real estate is to be assessed at its true value in money. Realty designated as historic property is taxed, upon annual application by the owner, at 50 percent of true value. Qualified agricultural, horticultural, and forest land may be taxed according to its present use. The annual tax bill on a residence with an actual value of $100,000 varies from about $350 to $1,500, depending on where you live in North Carolina.

Dates of assessment and payment: Real estate is assessed at least every eight years according to its value on January 1. Taxes are due September 1, but there is no penalty if payments are made by the following January 6. Counties, cities, and towns may establish a schedule of discounts for taxes that are paid early. Taxable personal property is assessed annually.

Assessing officials: All assessments are made under the supervision of the county tax assessor.

Appeals: The county Board of Equalization hears appeals and makes revisions. Further appeals may be made to the Property Tax Commission.

Assessments based on: There is no state manual, and there are no uniform standards for the 100 counties in North Carolina. Most counties contract with mass appraisal firms, which in most cases prepare manuals that are used in reassessments every eight years and for adjustment of the figures in the intervening years. Some counties do their own reassessments in-house, and this appears to be the general trend. Computer programs are used in a minority of assessments now, but the trend is toward computerization.

Source of statewide tax information: James Wagner, property valuation specialist, *Ad Valorem* Tax Division, North Carolina Department of Revenue.

NORTH DAKOTA

What is taxed: All property, unless expressly exempt. Mobile homes are subject to a tax permit in lieu of a property tax.

Exemptions for personal property include: All personal property not required to be assessed by the state Board of Equalization. In practice, that means that virtually all forms of personal property other than railroads and airlines are exempt. Household items that are not attached to the structure or land are not assessed for taxation.

Homestead exemption or other tax relief: Residents age 65 or older, or who are disabled, with annual incomes of $12,000 or less (after deductions for medical expenses) may have their assessments reduced according to a formula based on income. There are additional provisions for exemptions for disabled veterans and for blind residents.

Unique exemptions: Through 1989, there is a three-year exemption on the first $75,000 in value of new single-family houses and condominiums (not counting the land on which they sit). Localities are allowed to grant a 15-year limited exemption to developers of projects in urban renewal areas.

Other exemptions include qualified wetlands, and minerals in the earth which, if removed from the earth, would be subject to gross production or severance taxes.

Tax burden for residential real estate: A "taxable value" is established for all property subject to taxation. First, an "assessed value" is established, at a level of 50 percent of the "true and full value." The taxable value of residential real estate is 9 percent of the assessed value. For agricultural property, the assessed value is 50 percent of the true and full value for agricultural purposes, and the taxable value is 10 percent of that value. After these computations are made, the tax rate is the aggregate of all lawful levies.

In practice, the annual tax bill on a residence with an actual market value of $100,000 ranges from about $1,000 to $2,000, depending on where you live in North Dakota.

Dates of assessment and payment: All real estate is assessed according to its value on February 1. Payments become delinquent on March 1 of the following year, but may be made in two equal installments, which are due March 1 and October 15. If taxes are paid in full by February 15, a discount of 5 percent is allowed.

Assessing officials: Initial assessments are made by local assessors of the district, township, or city.

Appeals: Assessments are equalized by the Board of Equalization of the township or city. An appeal may be made to the local board, or, as an alternative, an application for abatement may be filed with the county auditor. Abatements are subject to final approval by the Board of County Commissioners. Decisions of the county board may be appealed to the district court. Also, assessments are equalized among the counties by the state Board of Equalization.

Assessments based on: The state provides an assessors' manual, which is used in most localities. The manual includes a copy of the statutory code on taxation, guidelines, forms, terminology, and a real estate valuation schedule for residential and commercial property.

The more than 1,200 local assessors are required to attend instruction for 24 hours and successfully complete a statewide standard test to become certified.

Source of statewide tax information: Barry Hasti, supervisor of assessments, North Dakota.

OHIO

What is taxed: Real estate and personal property, unless expressly exempt. Taxable property includes, but is not limited to, property used in business, domestic animals not used in agriculture, ships and boats, and aircraft. A manufactured home that is leased or rented is exempt from property taxes, but is subject to an annual license fee.

Exemptions for personal property include: Household furniture and other household items not used for business. In practice, household items that are not attached to the structure or land are not assessed for taxation.

Homestead exemption or other tax relief: Persons who are age 65 or older, or who are totally disabled, are allowed property tax relief if their incomes fall within guideline levels.

Unique exemptions: Monuments and monumental buildings are exempt. Other specific exemptions exist for prehistoric earthworks; historic buildings and lands; air or noise pollution control facilities; patterns, jigs, dies, and drawings; spirituous liquors held in warehouses; and personal property used in making juice or wine.

Tax burden for residential real estate: All property is appraised at its true value, except that agricultural land may, on application, be appraised at current use value. The assessment is 35 percent of the appraised value. The tax rate is the aggregate of all lawful levies, but an annual computation is made to reduce taxation of real estate by 10 percent.

The annual tax bill on a residence with an actual market value of $100,000 varies from $1,056 to $2,695, depending on where you live in Ohio.

Dates of assessment and payment: Property is appraised every six years, but if a change in value occurs, property may be revalued during any year in the interim. Real estate taxes may be paid in two installments due December 31 and June 20.

Assessing officials: The county auditor, under the supervision of the Department of Taxation, is responsible for initial assessments.

Appeals: Assessments by the county auditor may be appealed to the county Board of Revision. Further appeals may be made to the Board of Tax Appeals, then either to the county Court of Appeals or the state Supreme Court.

Assessments based on: There is no statewide manual. Computer programs are used for most assessments in Ohio.

Source of statewide tax information: David Stone, assistant administrator, Ohio Department of Tax Equalization.

OKLAHOMA

What is taxed: All real estate and tangible personal property, except that which is expressly exempt, or which is relieved from ad valorem taxes because of payments in lieu of taxes. A manufactured home located on land owned by the owner of the home is taxed as real estate. If it is on land owned by others, it is taxed as personal property.

Exemptions for personal property include: Household goods, tools, implements and livestock of every person maintaining a home, *not exceeding $100 in value.* Personal property of veterans or their widows is exempt up to a maximum value of $200. Family portraits are exempt. With those exceptions, household personal property is taxed in Oklahoma. Items physically attached to the house or land are taxed as real estate, and items that are not attached are taxed as personal property. At least in theory, once the cutoff of $100 or $200 in value has been surpassed, even the socks and underwear in your laundry basket are taxed.

Homestead exemption or other tax relief: Homesteads are exempt to the extent of $1,000 of assessed value, plus an additional $1,000 of assessed value if gross income for the preceding year did not exceed $10,000. (In interpreting this, please note that assessed value is a fraction of actual value.)

Unique exemptions: Fallout shelters are exempt. So are property rights attached to, or inherent in, cotton manufactories.

Tax burden for residential real estate: By law, residential property is not to be assessed at more than 35 percent of its fair cash value. As a result of a 1988 order by the State Board of Equalization, all property is to be assessed at a level between 11 and 14 percent of cash value. The state is barred by the Constitution from levying a property tax.

In practice, the annual tax bill for a residence with an actual market value of $100,000 ranges from about $800 to $1,100, depending on where you live in Oklahoma. In addition to that figure, however, personal property taxes must be paid on household furniture and personal effects.

Dates of assessment and payment: Property is assessed according to its value as of January 1. Taxes may be paid in two installments due January 1 and April 1.

Assessing officials: The county assessor is responsible for initial assessments.

Appeals: The county Board of Equalization equalizes, corrects, and adjusts assessments by the county assessor. Appeals of the decision of the county board may be made to the district court, then to the Supreme Court. The state Board of Equalization equalizes assessments among the various counties, and the district attorney, acting on behalf of the taxpaying public of the county, may file a complaint with the state board concerning the assessments.

Assessments based on: A fraction of fair cash value, as described above. Most residential assessments are based on the *Marshall Valuation Service*, published by Marshall and Swift. Computer programs are generally not used.

Source of statewide tax information: Robert L. Hartman, director, Oklahoma *Ad Valorem* Tax Division.

OREGON

What is taxed: Real estate and tangible personal property, unless expressly exempt.

Exemptions for personal property include: All tangible property for the owner's personal use, with the following exceptions: property held for sale or use for business or production of income or investment, personal property required to be registered or licensed, floating homes, and boat houses. In practice, household items that are not attached to the structure or land are not assessed for taxation.

Homestead exemption or other tax relief: State income tax refunds ranging from $36 to a theoretical maximum of $750 are available to offset property taxes on a homestead, with the amount based on household income, if income (with prescribed modifications) is under $17,499. Also, qualified residents age 62 or older may defer homestead property taxes.

There is also an exemption of up to $7,500 of the assessed value of the homestead of a disabled veteran whose income falls below guideline levels. Additional exemptions exist for veterans of the Civil War, the Spanish-American War, the Philippine Insurrection, and the Boxer Rebellion.

Unique exemptions: Solar, geothermal, wind, water, or methane gas energy systems are exempt. Agricultural waste facilities are exempt, if the owner has not elected to take credit for them under income tax provisions. Fallout shelters are exempt, up to a maximum of $1,500 for a single-family unit or $750 per family for a multi-family shelter. Other exempt items include racks, trays, and in-water structures to raise bi-valve mollusks; and beverage containers having a refund value.

Tax burden for residential real estate: Property is valued at 100 percent of true cash value. Land within a farm zone used exclusively for farming is assessed according to its value for farm use. There is no statewide property tax. The annual tax bill on a residence with an actual market value of $100,000 ranges from about $1,800 to $2,800, depending on where you live in Oregon.

Dates of assessment and payment: Property is assessed according to its value as of 1 a.m. January 1. Each property is to be reappraised at least once every six years. Generally, taxes are payable in three installments, due November 15, February 15, and May 15. A discount of 2 percent is allowed if two-thirds of the tax bill is paid by November 15. A discount of 3 percent is allowed if the full bill is paid by November 15.

Assessing officials: Initial assessments are made by a certified appraiser, under the direction of the county assessor.

Appeals: Appeals may be heard, and corrections made, by the county Board of Equalization. Further appeals may be made to the Department of Revenue, then to the Oregon Tax Court, then to the state Supreme Court.

Assessments based on: The state issues several manuals, including an *Appraisal Methods Manual* and a *Ratio Study Manual*. Computer programs are used in about half of the tax jurisdictions.

Source of statewide tax information: Assessment Standards and Equalization Division, Oregon Department of Revenue.

PENNSYLVANIA

What is taxed: All real estate, unless expressly exempt. There are separate taxes for intangible personal property, corporate loans, and capital stock.

Exemptions for personal property include: Household personal property is not subject to taxation. In practice, household items that are not attached to the structure or land are not assessed for property taxation.

Homestead exemption or other tax relief: Property tax rebates, adjusted according to household income (up to a maximum income of $15,000) are available to persons age 65 or over, widows and widowers age 50 or over, and permanently disabled persons age 18 or over. There is a homestead exemption for veterans who are severely disabled as a result of military duty.

Unique exemptions: New residential buildings are not taxed until they are occupied, or conveyed to a purchaser, or until one year from the first day of the fourteenth month after the building permit was issued. Local taxing authorities may temporarily exempt the value of new residential construction or improvements in a deteriorating area.

Tax burden for residential real estate: By statute, assessors are required to value property according to actual (market) value. The assessed value is then adjusted downward, to make it consistent with the assessed value of other, similar property. The statewide average assessed value is 25 percent of market value. The percentage ranges from 10 percent of market value in Elk County to 74.3 percent in Beaver County.

Land and structures are valued separately, and in some jurisdictions are taxed at different rates. (In Pittsburgh and Scranton, buildings are taxed at only half the rate of land.) Qualified farm or forest land, on application of the owner, may be assessed on its value for farm or forest use. With the exception of Philadelphia, the county, city, and school taxes are administered separately in each taxing jurisdiction.

There are statutory tax rate limitations for the various classes of counties, cities, townships, and school districts. However, these limitations apply to taxes for "general purposes" only, and may be exceeded when real estate taxes are enacted for "special purposes." Also, the limitations do not apply in the cities of Philadelphia, Pittsburgh, and Scranton, or in the Philadelphia School District, or in jurisdictions that have adopted home rule charters.

Because of the diversity in property taxation statewide, we were unable to obtain an estimate of the range of annual tax bills for residences with an actual market value of $100,000 in Pennsylvania.

Dates of assessment and payment: In first-class counties, assessments must be completed by the third Monday in September; in second-class counties, by the first Monday in September. There is no date prescribed for third-class counties. In counties classified fourth through eighth, assessments must be submitted to the Board of Assessment on or before August 1.

Statutes do not appear to specify a date as of which the property is valued. Property is subject to assessment for all purposes once every three years, with a system for revision of each assessment in the intervening years. Tax payment schedules are different in each class of county or city. In some instances there are discounts for early payment.

County classifications, based on population, are as follows as of this writing: First Class, Philadelphia; Second Class, Allegheny; Second Class A, Montgomery and Delaware; Third Class, Bucks, Westmoreland, Lancaster, Luzerne, Chester, York, Berks, Erie, Lehigh, Dauphin, Lackawanna, and Northampton. All other counties fall into classes four through eight, and are treated the same by statute for property taxation purposes.

Assessing officials: In first-class counties, the Board of Revision divides the city or county into districts and assigns assessors to each district. In second-class counties, the Board of Property Assessment, Appeals, and Review is authorized to divide the county into three districts, and make triennial assessments in one district each year. In third-class counties, the Board of Assessment Appeals divides the county into districts and appoints an assessor for each district. In all other counties, assessments are made by the chief assessor appointed by the Board of Assessment Appeals.

In general, taxes levied by cities, townships, boroughs, and school districts are based on county assessments.

Appeals: Appeals may be made to the Board of Assessment Appeals. Specific deadlines for appeals vary according to the class of county or city. Further appeals may be taken to Court of Common Pleas.

Assessments based on: Percentages of market value, as explained above. There is no statewide manual.

Source of statewide tax information: Pennsylvania Department of Community Affairs. (There is no statewide office that coordinates or equalizes property taxation in Pennsylvania.)

RHODE ISLAND

What is taxed: Real estate and personal property, unless expressly exempt.

Exemptions for personal property include: Household furniture and family stores, including clothing, bedding, and other such household tangible personal property. In practice, household items that are not attached to the structure or land are not assessed for taxation.

Homestead exemption or other tax relief: There is a $10,000 homestead exemption for the president and professors of Brown University. Property of veterans is exempt to the extent of $1,000, or $2,000 if the veteran served in any of several foreign conflicts. Additional exemptions of up to $10,000 are available to disabled veterans. Property of parents of a son or daughter who died in combat is exempt to the extent of $3,000.

Blind persons qualify for an exemption of $6,000, which may be increased to $18,000 by towns or cities. Also, municipalities may freeze the valuation of real estate held by persons who are disabled, or by low-income persons age 65 or over.

Unique exemptions: Fallout shelters are exempt to the extent of $1,500. Other exemptions apply to precious metal bullion, and to personal property used for recycling or treatment of hazardous waste.

Tax burden for residential real estate: Property is assessed at 100 percent of fair cash value, or a uniform percentage thereof, to be determined by the assessors of each town or city. Solar, wind, and cogeneration energy systems are assessed at a level no higher than what the assessment would have been for a conventional energy system that would otherwise be needed for the building. Designated farmland, forest land, and open-space land are assessed according to their use, but a change in use results in a land-use-change tax.

The annual tax bill on a residence with an actual market value of $100,000 varies from $1,087 to $7,938, depending on where you live in Rhode Island.

Dates of assessment and payment: Property is assessed according to its value as of December 31. The dates on which payments are due are prescribed by the ordinances or resolutions of each city or town. Each city or town is required to offer the option of paying taxes in quarterly installments.

Assessing officials: Initial assessments are made by the assessors and boards of assessors of the towns and cities.

Appeals: Taxpayers may appeal to the assessors, and further appeals may be taken to the superior court.

Assessments based on: Fair cash value, which is generally defined as equivalent to market value. There is no statewide assessment manual, and computer programs are generally not used.

Source of statewide tax information: Property tax division, Rhode Island Department of Administration.

SOUTH CAROLINA

What is taxed: All real estate and tangible personal property, unless expressly exempt. Mobile homes are taxed as real estate.

Exemptions for personal property include: Household goods and furniture used in the home of the owner. A separate exemption applies to wearing apparel. In practice, household items that are not attached to the structure or land are not assessed for taxation. There may be exceptions, however. For example, in some counties, kitchen appliances, even if free-standing, may add to the assessment.

Homestead exemption or other tax relief: The homestead of a veteran with total service-connected disability, or of the unremarried surviving spouse of a person killed in action, is exempt. The homestead of a paraplegic or his/her un-remarried surviving spouse is exempt. Homesteads of persons who are age 65 or older, or who are blind or totally disabled, are exempt to the extent of $20,000 of fair market value.

Unique exemptions: Property of the Palmetto Junior Homemakers Association is exempt. So is property of eleemosynary theatre companies, and carnival equipment that is in the state less than six months of the tax year.

Tax burden for residential real estate: Property is classified into seven categories, each with different rates of assessment. Owner-occupied residential property (a house and up to five acres of land) is assessed at 4 percent of its true value in money.

Rented residential property is assessed at 6 percent of its value. After these adjustments are made, the tax rate is the aggregate of all lawful levies. There is no state levy, but the General Assembly may enact one under a constitutional provision requiring it to levy a tax sufficient to cover any budget deficiency. The annual tax bill on a residence with an actual market value of $100,000 ranges from about $500 to $1,500, depending on where you live in South Carolina.

Dates of assessment and payment: Property is assessed according to its value as of December 31. All taxes become due between September 15 and January 15. Counties, towns, and cities may allow discounts for early payment, or payment in installments.

Assessing officials: Initial assessments are made by the county assessor in each of the 46 counties. Cities and towns use the county values.

Appeals: Appeals may be made to the county Board of Appeals. Further appeals may be taken to the Tax Commission, then to the courts.

Assessments based on: A percentage of true value, as described above. True value is generally considered to be equivalent to market value. There is no statewide manual, and computer programs are generally not used.

Source of statewide tax information: Property division, South Carolina Tax Commission.

SOUTH DAKOTA

What is taxed: All real estate, unless expressly exempt. Mobile homes permanently affixed to realty are taxed as realty.

Exemptions for personal property include: Personal effects, household furnishings, home appliances, sporting and hobby goods, pets, grain and seed, honey, and sugar beets. In practice, household items that are not attached to the structure or land are not assessed for taxation.

Homestead exemption or other tax relief: Homesteads, other than mobile homes, are exempt from the state tax but not from county taxes. Persons with low incomes who are either disabled or age 65 or older may receive refunds and tax reductions on the taxes paid on their homesteads. The percentages of refund and reduction are based on an income schedule.

Tax assessments may also be frozen for such heads of household if income guidelines are not exceeded. Tax reductions, also based on income, are available to paraplegics and other persons who have lost use of both legs.

Unique exemptions: A three-year tax credit is allowed to offset the cost of a renewable energy system installed as a residential improvement. There is an eight-year moratorium on any tax increase resulting from restoration or rehabilitation of registered historic property. For each occupied dwelling on a parcel of agricultural land, $10,000 of the value of agricultural structures is exempt.

Tax burden for residential real estate: Property is assessed at its true and full value in money, but the taxable value is a percentage—not to exceed 60 percent—of that figure. The state tax rate is limited to two mills per dollar of taxable value. The annual tax bill for a residence with an actual market value of $100,000 ranges from about $2,040 to $3,400, depending on where you live in South Dakota.

Dates of assessment and payment: Property is assessed according to its value on January 1. Payments are due in equal installments, by April 30 and October 31 of the year following assessment.

Assessing officials: Initial assessments are made by the county assessor.

Appeals: Assessments may be appealed to the local Board of Equalization. Further appeals may be taken to the county board, then to the state Board of Equalization, and then to the circuit court.

Assessments based on: True and full value in money, which is generally defined as equivalent to market value. The *Marshall Valuation Service Handbook* (published by Marshall and Swift) is used statewide. Computer programs, based on Marshall and Swift, are used in some but not all counties.

Source of statewide tax information: Dennis Hanson, property tax director, South Dakota Department of Revenue.

TENNESSEE

What is taxed: All real estate and personal property, unless expressly exempt.

Exemptions for personal property include: There is a specific exemption for household goods, furnishings, wearing apparel, and other tangible personal property valued up to $7,500 for an individual or $15,000 for a married couple. But don't worry if you have personal property that exceeds those values. Another section of law specifies that tangible personal property is considered to have no value for tax purposes unless it is public utility property or industrial or commercial property.

In short, household items that are not attached to the structure or land are not assessed for taxation.

Homestead exemption or other tax relief: The Tennessee Constitution does not provide for a homestead exemption as such, but reimbursements are made to certain qualified homeowners.

Reimbursement is made to low-income persons age 65 or older, or to totally and permanently disabled homeowners, for taxes paid on the first $15,000 in actual value of their residences. The annual income limit to qualify is set by the legislature. A qualified disabled veteran may receive reimbursement from the state for taxes paid on the first $120,000 of actual value of his/her residence.

Also, counties and cities are authorized to defer part of the residential property taxes of low-income elderly or disabled homeowners.

Unique exemptions: Property of nonprofit artificial breeding associations is exempt. So is a residence owned by a college or university, if its chief executive officer is required to live there. Property used for airport runways and aprons is also exempt.

Tax burden for residential real estate: Residential and farm properties are assessed at 25 percent of actual value. Qualified agricultural, forest, or open land may be assessed according to its

273

value for current use. Owners of qualified residential property zoned for commercial use may apply to have their property assessed according to its value for residential purposes. There is no state levy.

The annual county tax bill for a residence with an actual market value of $100,000 ranges from $397.50 to $1,412.40; the average city tax bill for a residence with the same value ranges from $32.50 to $1,065, depending on where you live in Tennessee.

Dates of assessment and payment: Property is assessed according to its value as of January 1. Reappraisal and equalization are to occur at least once every five years, unless the Board of Equalization determines that this is not necessary for a particular county. County taxes are due the first Monday in October.

The due date for city taxes is set by ordinance in each city. Counties and municipalities may allow a 2 percent credit if taxes are paid within 30 days after the due date, or 1 percent if paid within 60 days after the due date.

Assessing officials: Initial assessments are made by the county assessor, or, in cities that collect their own taxes, the city assessor.

Appeals: Complaints may be taken to the county Board of Equalization. Further appeals may be taken to the state Board of Equalization, then to the courts.

Assessments based on: The property's "sound, intrinsic and immediate value, for purposes of sale between a willing seller and a willing buyer without consideration of speculative values." This translates roughly to what other states call fair market value. A statewide manual, prepared by the Division of Property Assessments, is being revised as of this writing. A computer program created in-house, the *Computer Assisted Appraisal System III*, is used for assessments.

Source of statewide tax information: William S. Carman, director, Tennessee Division of Property Assessments.

TEXAS

What is taxed: Real estate and tangible personal property, unless expressly exempt.

Exemptions for personal property include: Household goods and personal effects. In practice, household items that are not attached to the structure or land are not assessed for taxation, unless they are used for business purposes.

Homestead exemption or other tax relief: For county purposes, the first $3,000 of assessed value of a homestead is exempt from any special county taxes that are used for farm-to-market roads or flood control. For school district purposes, the first $5,000 is exempt, and an additional $10,000 is exempt for persons who are age 65 or older or disabled. Also, once a person first qualifies for the over-65 school district exemption, his or her total tax bill to the district can never be increased, unless an improvement is added to the house.

A larger general homestead exemption—up to 20 percent of the assessed value—may be adopted by any local taxing unit.

In addition to the exemptions listed above, local governments may, at their option, exempt another $3,000 or more from the assessments of homesteads owned by persons age 65 or older or disabled.

There are also additional exemptions available to disabled veterans and their families, adjusted according to the percentage of disability, and to surviving family members of an individual who dies on active military duty.

Homestead exemptions in Texas are applied to an owner-occupied residence, plus up to 20 acres of yard.

Unique exemptions: Solar or wind energy devices for on-site use are exempt. So are implements of husbandry used in producing farm or ranch products, and livestock for human or animal consumption.

Tax burden for residential real estate: Property is to be assessed at full market value, except that the following categories of land may be assessed at use value: agricultural, timber, recreational, park, and scenic land. The tax rate is the aggregate of all lawful local levies; the state is prohibited by the Texas Constitution from levying an *ad valorem* property tax.

The annual tax bill for a residence with an actual market value of $100,000 varies from about $1,500 to $2,090, depending on where you live in Texas.

Dates of assessment and payment: Property is assessed according to its value as of January 1. All property must be reappraised at least once every four years. By statute, the tax bill becomes delinquent on February 1 of the year following assessment. In some counties, if one half of the property tax bill is paid by December 1, the remaining half may be paid, without penalty, by the following July 1. Localities may allow discounts for early payment.

Assessing officials: Appraisal districts are established in each county. The chief appraiser of each district is responsible for initial appraisals. Assessors for each taxing unit base their assessments on the appraisal information.

Appeals: Appeals can be made to the Appraisal Review Board. Further appeals may be made to the district court within 45 days of receiving notice that an order was entered.

Assessments based on: The state issues a *General Appraisal Manual*, although use of the manual is not mandatory in all of the 253 appraisal districts. Most of the districts use computer programs. Taxpayers have the option of "rendering" their own properties, i.e. listing the estimated value of their properties on rendition forms available from the appraisal district office. If the chief appraiser disagrees with the figure, or if the taxpayer chooses not to render, the appraisal district will make its own appraisal. Business properties are assessed by the state.

Source of statewide tax information: Texas State Property Tax Board.

UTAH

What is taxed: Real estate and tangible personal property, unless expressly exempt. Mobile homes are taxed as real estate if they are on permanent foundations. Those not on permanent foundations are taxed as personal property.

Exemptions for personal property include: Household furniture and furnishings. In practice, household items that are not attached to the structure or land are not assessed for property taxation.

Homestead exemption or other tax relief: The assessed value of residential property (a house and up to an acre of land) is reduced for tax purposes by 25 percent.

Residents age 65 or over with incomes of less than $10,000 may receive a homeowner's credit of up to $300 against property tax liability, or half the tax bill, whichever is less, on a sliding scale based on household income. The same credit may be granted by counties to other low income persons, if additional criteria are met.

The first $30,000 of taxable value is exempt if the homestead is owned by a disabled veteran, or his/her surviving spouse and orphans.

The first $11,500 of taxable value is exempt if the homestead is owned by blind persons, or his/her surviving spouses and orphans.

Unique exemptions: Property used for irrigation is exempt.

Tax burden for residential real estate: Assessments are based on full market value. However, to account for the fees associated with the sale of a house, assessors base valuations on 80 percent of the estimated sale price. The value is adjusted again to account for the 25 percent homestead exemption. The net result of this equation (100 percent x 80 percent x 75 percent) reduces the assessed value of residential property to 60 percent of the full market value.

There are statutory limitations on the maximum tax rates that can be enacted by the state and by counties. The annual tax bill on a residence with an actual fair market value of $100,000 ranges from $670 (Brigham City) to $1,170 (Sandy), depending on where you live in Utah.

Dates of assessment and payment: Property is assessed according to its value as of January 1. In general, taxes must be paid no later than November 30, but county governments may choose to extend the delinquency date to December 20.

Assessing officials: Residential assessments are made initially by county assessors.

Appeals: Appeals may be taken to the County Board of Equalization, then to the State Tax Commission, whose decision is final.

Assessments based on: 60 percent of fair market value, as discussed above. There is no statewide manual. Computer programs are used for assessments in most counties.

Source of statewide tax information: Office of Standards and Training, Property Tax Division, Utah State Tax Commission.

VERMONT

What is taxed: Real estate and personal property, unless expressly exempt.

Exemptions for personal property include: Household furnishings and wearing apparel. (The personal property tax applies primarily to business equipment. Municipalities also have the option of taxing business inventory.) In practice, household items that are not attached to the structure or land are not assessed for taxation.

Homestead exemption or other tax relief: Homesteads of Civil War and Spanish War veterans are exempt. Disabled veterans of other conflicts and their families may qualify for an exemption of the first $10,000 of assessed valuation.

Property tax rebates are available to residents whose tax bills on their homesteads exceed a particular percentage of household income (3 percent to 5 percent, depending on level of income). Rebates must be applied for when state income tax forms are filed. This relief program is available to renters as well as homeowners.

Unique exemptions: Fallout shelters, mechanics' tools, motorized road-building equipment, and farm property used to store manure are exempt. Municipalities are authorized to exempt alternative energy sources (such as solar collectors or windmills) if the energy produced is not for sale or exchange.

Tax burden for residential real estate: By law, real estate is listed at 100 percent of its market value. If assessments, on the average, fall below 80 percent of actual sales prices, municipalities may lose state aid for schools. However, a few of the "wealthy" towns, which don't qualify for much school aid anyway, have assessments well below that percentage.

An owner of farmland or other open-space land may apply to be taxed only on the use value of the land. In that case, the state pays to the municipality the difference between use value and fair market value.

In practice, the annual tax bill on a residence with an actual market value of $100,000 ranges from about $400 to $3,300, depending on where you live in Vermont. The statewide average tax bill for a residence with that value is $1,580.

Dates of assessment and payment: Property is assessed according to its value as of April 1. Payment dates are determined by each municipality, and payments may be in as many as four installments.

Assessing officials: In smaller municipalities, responsibility for initial assessments lies with an elected Board of Listers. In larger municipalities, the responsibility often lies with an appointed city assessor.

Appeals: Initial appeals may be made to the listers or to the city assessor. Further appeals may be made to the local Board of Civil Authority, and then either to the state Division of Property Valuation and Review or to the superior court of the county where the property is situated.

Assessments based on: Fair market value, as determined by the local listers and assessors. A statewide manual is available, but its use is not mandatory. The State Division of Property Valuation and Review operates a computerized assessment program that is used by many municipalities. In communities that do not use the state system, most assessments are performed manually, but the general trend is toward computerization. Where the state computer system is used, the figures may be overridden manually by the local listers or assessors.

Source of statewide tax information: Vermont Department of Taxes, Division of Property Valuation and Review.

VIRGINIA

What is taxed: Localities may tax real estate and tangible personal property. Categories of property not subject to local taxation may be taxed by the state. (For example, Virginia is authorized to tax intangible personal property, but does not do so at present.)

Exemptions for personal property include: Household goods and personal effects are defined as separate items of taxation. Counties, cities, and towns may exempt all or any of the classes of household goods and personal effects. In practice, throughout most of the state, household items that are not attached to the structure or land are not assessed for taxation. However, there are reportedly at least two localities that have not exempted all household goods. It may be a good idea to check the policy of your local government before beginning a building or remodeling project.

Homestead exemption or other tax relief: Localities may exempt or defer taxes on dwellings owned by residents who are age 65 or older, or disabled. There are limits on allowable household income and assets for those qualifying for an exemption or deferral.

Unique exemptions: Localities may exempt, for up to ten years, the increase in value of real estate rehabilitated for residential, commercial, or industrial use. Certified solar and other alternative energy equipment may be exempted. Special assessments are allowed for property that is encumbered by a deed with a perpetual easement permitting inundation of the property with water.

Tax burden for residential real estate: Property is to be assessed at 100 percent of fair market value. Localities may impose different rates for levies on real estate, personal property, and merchants' capital. The annual tax bill on a residence with an actual fair market value of $100,000 varies from $310 to $1,690, depending on where you live in Virginia.

Dates of assessment and payment: Real estate assessments are made according to value as of January 1, except that counties, cities, and towns may opt to assess as of July 1.

Assessing officials: Real estate is assessed under the direction of local boards of assessors or professional appraisers. Personal property is assessed under the direction of the commissioner of revenue.

Appeals: The first level of appeal is to the professional or the board responsible for the assessment. The next appeal may be filed with the Board of Equalization or taken directly to the circuit court. Within the state tax system, the highest public official authorized to grant relief is the commissioner of Revenue. The commissioner's order, however, may be appealed to the circuit court, then to the Supreme Court of Virginia.

Assessments based on: Market value. There is no statewide manual, and computer programs are not generally used for assessments.

Source of statewide tax information: Property Tax Division, Virginia Department of Taxation.

WASHINGTON

What is taxed: All real estate and personal property, unless expressly exempt.

Exemptions for personal property include: Household goods, furnishings, and personal effects that are not for sale or commercial use. A separate head-of-family exemption applies to personal property used in a business (other than motor vehicles or motor homes) up to $3,000 in value. Business inventory held for sale is also exempt. In practice, household items that are not attached to the structure or land are generally not assessed for taxation. However, certain borderline items, such as a wood stove, may be included in an assessment of real estate.

Homestead exemption or other tax relief: Full or partial exemptions, based on household income, are available for residential property of persons who are age 61 or older, or disabled. When a person who qualifies for an exemption dies, the exemption remains available to a surviving spouse, if the spouse is at least age 57. Tax deferrals for property tax, or special assessments, are also available to residents age 61 or older or disabled, and to surviving spouses age 57 or older. Surviving spouses must be enrolled in the program if they are to take advantage of an exemption or deferral.

Unique exemptions: A physical improvement to an existing single-family dwelling is exempt for three years, if the value of the improvement does not exceed 30 percent of the value of the structure. This exemption cannot be claimed more than once during a five-year period. In order to take advantage of this exemption, it is necessary to file a notice of intent to construct, prior to the time the improvement is made.

Also, any new facility used to manufacture alcohol fuel is exempt for six years. Another exemption exists for agricultural produce and crops, including animals, birds, and insects.

Tax burden for residential real estate: Property is assessed at 100 percent of true and fair value. Owners of agricultural, open space, or timber land may apply for valuation according to current land use. The annual tax bill for a residence with an actual market value of $100,000 varies from $843 to $1,579, depending on where you live in Washington.

Dates of assessment and payment: Property is assessed according to its value as of January 1. Taxes may be paid in two equal installments, which become due April 30 and October 31.

Assessing officials: County Assessors are responsible for initial assessments.

Appeals: Assessments are subject to equalization by the county Board of Equalization. Appeals of the Board's ruling may be made to the state Board of Tax Appeals.

Assessments based on: True and fair value, which is generally interpreted as being equivalent to market value. There is no statewide manual. Computer programs are generally not used for assessments.

Source of statewide tax information: Joseph D. Simmonds, appraisal supervisor, Western Region, Washington Property Tax Division.

WEST VIRGINIA

What is taxed: All property, real and personal, including intangibles, unless expressly exempt.

Exemptions for personal property include: Household goods and personal effects that are not held or used for profit. Household goods that are used for profit are exempt up to the value of $200. In practice, household items that are not attached to the structure or land are not assessed for property taxation in most localities, but assessment practices vary.

Homestead exemption or other tax relief: For residents age 65 or older, or permanently disabled, the first $20,000 of assessed value of a homestead is exempt. For the same category of taxpayers, additional tax relief may be available if income guidelines are met.

Unique exemptions: Property used for the subsistence of livestock is exempt.

Tax burden for residential real estate: Under current statutes, property is assessed at its true and actual value, and categorized into four classifications. Residential property and farms are considered Class II property, and by statute, taxed at a maximum rate of $1 per $100 of assessed valuation. However, that limit does not apply to taxes for debt service, so in many localities actual taxation exceeds that amount.

Assessment practices vary widely from locality to locality. Some localities use old state appraisals and cost factors, with effective dates ranging from 1956 to 1979. In some localities, assessments are based on percentages of sales prices.

A 1982 constitutional amendment provides for a statewide reappraisal of all West Virginia properties that are subject to *ad valorem* taxation. The results of this reappraisal are to be phased in over a ten-year period, following a complex procedure. However, as of late 1988, the West Virginia legislature had not yet chosen to implement the statewide reappraisal.

In the meantime, assessments vary so greatly that we were unable to obtain a reliable estimate of the range of annual tax bills for residences with an actual value of $100,000.

Dates of assessment and payment: Property is assessed according to its value as of July 1. Taxes are paid to the sheriff in two installments: the first is due September 1 and delinquent October 1; the second is due March 1 and delinquent April 1. If taxes are paid on or before the due dates, there is a discount of 2½ percent.

It is up to property owners to be certain that assessors and sheriffs have their proper mailing addresses, for the purpose of receiving tax tickets. Failure to receive a tax ticket does not exempt a property owner from the obligation to pay *ad valorem* taxes.

Assessing officials: The county assessor and his/her deputies are responsible for initial assessments.

Appeals: Appeals may be taken to the county court, then to the circuit court. If there is a question of valuation exceeding $50,000, a further appeal may be made to the West Virginia Supreme Court.

Assessments based on: True and actual value, with local variations as discussed above. Statewide appraisal manuals are available. Computer programs are used to produce the tax rolls and books, but not to generate assessments. However, if the statewide appraisal is implemented, it will be computerized.

Source of statewide tax information: West Virginia State Tax Department.

WISCONSIN

What is taxed: Real estate and personal property, unless expressly exempt.

Exemptions for personal property include: Personal ornaments and jewelry, family portraits, private libraries, musical instruments, radio equipment, household furniture, equipment and furnishings, apparel, bicycles, and firearms. In practice, household items that are not attached to the structure or land are not assessed for taxation.

Homestead exemption or other tax relief: All property taxpayers receive credits. The amount is determined by applying the percentage of the taxpayer's assessment to the dollar amount of property tax credits allocated to the municipality by the state. Also, low-income taxpayers are granted property tax relief through income tax credits. In addition, loans of up to $1,800 are available to defer property tax payments by qualified persons who are age 65 or older, or who are disabled.

Unique exemptions: Perennial plants that produce annual crops are exempt. Other exemptions include: property owned by youth hockey associations, solar and wind energy systems, nuclear attack shelters, camping trailers, manure storage facilities, and temporary structures used to provide shade for ginseng plants.

Tax burden for residential real estate: Real property is assessed at full value at private sale. The average annual tax bill for a residence with an actual market value of $100,000 is $2,464. The range of tax bills for such a residence is $1,351 to $4,045, depending on where you live in Wisconsin.

Dates of assessment and payment: Property is assessed according to its value as of January 1. Taxes may be paid in a single installment by January 31, or in two installments due January 31 and July 31. A city may, by ordinance, provide for payment of real estate taxes in three or more installments.

Assessing officials: Initial assessments of residential real estate are made by local assessors.

Appeals: Assessments are reviewed, and may be revised, by the local Board of Review, then by the Department of Revenue. Appeals from decisions of either body may be made to the circuit court.

Assessments based on: A statewide procedural guide known as the *Wisconsin Property Assessment Manual.* Computer programs are used for most assessments.

Source of statewide tax information: Glenn L. Holmes, director, Wisconsin Bureau of Property Tax.

WYOMING

What is taxed: All real estate and tangible personal property, unless expressly exempt.

Exemptions for personal property include: Personal property held for personal or family use. Business inventories are also exempt. In practice, household items that are not attached to the structure or land are not assessed for taxation.

Homestead exemption or other tax relief: A homestead tax credit, formerly allowed, has been discontinued. A veterans' exemption is available, up to a maximum tax benefit of $800, with additional exemptions for veterans with service-connected disabilities.

Unique exemptions: Lands from which minerals are being extracted (up to a limit of 40 acres per site), industrial development projects, and personal property of nonresident military personnel are exempt.

Tax burden for residential real estate: Property is assessed at a percentage of fair market value, either current or as of a past year. The percentages vary, but currently, residential and commercial structures are assessed at 25 percent of their 1967 market value.

Non-farm land is assessed at 8 percent of current value. Farm land is assessed at 8 percent of current value based on productive capacity. Taxable personal property is assessed at $11\frac{1}{2}$ percent of current replacement value less depreciation. The annual tax bill for a residence with an actual current market value of $100,000 varies from about $700 to $800, depending on where you live in Wyoming.

Dates of assessment and payment: Property is assessed according to its value as of February 1. Taxes are payable in two equal installments: the first is due by November 10, and the second is due by the following May 10. However, there is no penalty if taxes are paid in full by December 31.

Assessing officials: Initial assessments are made by county assessors.

Appeals: Equalizations are made by the county Board of Equalization. Decisions by the county board may be appealed to the state Board of Equalization. A further appeal may be made to the county district court.

Assessments based on: Values and procedures prescribed by the State Board of Equalization. A statewide manual, the *Wyoming Cost Manual*, is used. A computer program is used for most assessments.

Source of statewide tax information: Robert E. Williams, supervisor of local assessments, *Ad Valorem* Tax Division, Wyoming Department of Revenue and Taxation.

Glossary

Builders, assessors, and municipal bureaucrats have vocabularies of their own. Following is a representative sample of the words you will encounter during discussions of your dream house. If they roll off your tongue easily, the people you're dealing with may treat you with more respect.

ABATEMENT: A reduction in property taxes, following a grievance or appeal.

AD VALOREM: A term sometimes used by assessors and lawyers. An *ad valorem* tax is a property tax.

APPRAISER: A professional who estimates the fair market value of property.

ASSESSED VALUE: The value assigned to property for the purpose of computing property taxes. Usually, the assessed value is either fair market value or a percentage thereof.

ASSESSMENT CARD: A card used by assessors when physically inspecting properties, usually with boxes to check the quality, quantity, and condition of each feature of the property. It is usually only a data collection card, which does not include computations of the assessment or the tax bill.

ASSESSMENT DATE: A specific date set aside each year for assessments. The assessment for the year is based on the condition of the property as of that date. The person who owns the property as of that date is responsible for property taxes for the entire year. (In practice, if the property is sold, at closing the buyer usually pays to the seller a proportionate share of the tax bill for the year. However, as far as the tax collector is concerned, the person who owns the property on the assessment date is responsible for the bill.)

ASSESSMENT SHEET: A sheet, compiled manually or by computer, that lists the valuation of each component of a piece of property and explains how the valuation was determined.

ASSESSOR: The person who determines tax assessments of individual properties. In some localities, the assessor is an elected official. In others, the assessor is a professional appraiser who is hired by the elected officials.

BEADBOARD: Expanded polystyrene.

BFH: Big (expletive deleted) hammer. Builders' term for a tool used to make technical adjustments during rough framing.

BLUEBOARD: Extruded polystyrene. The largest manufacturer of this product dyes it blue. Other manufacturers make "pinkboard" or "greenboard."

BOCA: Building Officials and Code Administrators International, one of three major model building code groups. BOCA's *Basic/National* codes serve as the model for most state and local building codes in the Northeast and parts of the Midwest.

BUILDING INSPECTOR: (1) A municipal or county official who views structures to determine whether they are built and maintained in ways that are consistent with permit, codes, and other legal requirements. (2) A free lance inspector who, for a fee, will analyze the condition and problems of a structure prior to purchase.

CABO: Council of American Building Officials, an umbrella organization consisting of the three major model building code groups (BOCA, ICBO, and SBCCI). Among other things, CABO publishes the *One and Two Family Dwelling Code*. This document serves as a model for most of the state and local codes for single-family houses and duplexes.

CHASE: A space or groove in a wall for plumbing pipes and/or electrical wiring.

CHLOROFLUOROCARBONS: Volatile, inert, saturated compounds of carbon, fluorine, chlorine, and hydrogen, often referred to as CFCs or the brand name *Freon*. They are useful as blowing agents in the manufacture of rigid foam insulation, but harmful to the environment.

CLAPBOARD: A type of wood siding. A long thin board, thicker on one edge than along the other, applied horizontally.

CLERESTORY WINDOW: A high window overlooking the roof of an attached structure, such as a garage. The term is often misused to describe any high window. It is also often misspelled.

CLOSING: The ceremony that makes official any real estate transaction. Deeds are transferred, mortgage loans are finalized, and large sums of money are paid to attorneys and real estate brokers during a closing.

COLD PANTRY: An unheated room in some older houses, used for storage of foods that should be kept cool but don't fit in the refrigerator.

CONTRACTOR: A person who performs, or arranges for, work to be done at an agreed-upon price or rate. A general contractor makes arrangements for an entire building project. A subcontractor takes on responsibility for a portion of the contract, such as the foundation, drywall taping, etc.

COST APPROACH: One of the standard approaches to assessment. The cost of construction of an equivalent structure is estimated, according to today's prevailing prices. Once that basic value is determined, "depreciation" is subtracted.

DEPRECIATION: The lessening of the value of a structure due to aging and wear and tear.

DESIGN FACTOR: A multiplier used by many assessors to increase or reduce the overall valuation of a structure. If a structure has many corners, angles, levels, slants, and curves, it will receive a design factor that will greatly increase its assessment. A two-story house that approximates a cube in design will be assigned a low multiplier, usually "1" or less.

DESIGNER: A professional who designs custom houses, usually for a fee slightly below that charged by an architect.

DRYWALL: A common wall material that emulates plaster; often referred to as gypsum board or by the brand name *Sheetrock*.

EQUALIZATION: The process of accounting for the differences in assessments among structures and among localities. If assessments are 30 percent of fair market value in one locality and 80 percent in another, the assessments may be "equalized" in order to make taxation more equitable.

ESTIMATE: A ball-park price, submitted by a contractor. If you hire a reputable contractor, the final price should come close to the estimate unless unexpected snags occur or unless changes are made in the scope of the project.

EXEMPTION: A classification of items that are excluded from property taxation.

EXPANDED POLYSTYRENE: A type of rigid foam insulation, commonly referred to as "beadboard" or "EPS." It is generally the lowest-cost type of rigid foam, and contains no chlorofluorocarbons. However, EPS has a lower R-value per inch of thickness than polyisocyanurate or extruded polystyrene.

EXTRUDED POLYSTYRENE: A type of rigid foam that is commonly used to insulate the exteriors of basements and other masonry walls. "Blueboard" is an example. It is durable and has a high R-value per inch, but contains chlorofluorocarbons.

FAIR MARKET VALUE: An estimate of the price that would be paid by a willing buyer to a willing seller, in an arm's-length transaction. Tax assessments are usually either fair market value or a percentage thereof. Some property tax systems use other terms that mean essentially the same thing as fair market value; e.g., "full cash value" or "true value in money."

FASCIA: A board that runs the length of a roof, covering the ends of the rafters. A fascia board is a cosmetic feature on most but not all houses. If a house has a gutter, it is mounted to the fascia.

FIBERGLASS: Fine filaments of glass woven into fabrics. The most common form used in house building is insulation batts. *Fiberglas*, with one "s," is a brand name.

FINISH CARPENTRY: The careful work done to make a structure look good after all the rough carpentry is completed. Casing and trim around windows and doors, molding, drywall, siding, and finish flooring are examples of finish carpentry.

FOOTING: A mass of concrete, poured below the frost line, supporting the foundation of a house.

FORMICA: A brand name, often used as a generic name for plastic laminates.

FROST LINE: The depth below which the ground does not freeze in winter. According to conventional building theory (challenged by some), the footings of a foundation must be below the frost line. In the cold climate where I live, the frost line is about four feet beneath the surface. In warmer climates, it's closer to the surface.

GOVERNMENT WORK: Builders' term for the minimum passable standards. A piece of work that is acceptable, but not a source of pride for the builder, is often described as "good enough for government work."

GRIEVANCE: The first level of appeal to protest a tax assessment. In most jurisdictions, a grievance is made to the tax assessor or to the government official who is responsible for the initial assessment.

GYPSUM BOARD: Another name for drywall.

HALF BATH: A bathroom without a tub. In some jurisdictions, a bathroom with a shower stall but no tub is listed as a half bath. In other jurisdictions, a shower stall bumps the listing up to a "three-quarters bath." The distinction is significant: a half bath is assessed at half the value of a full bath of equivalent quality.

HALFLAP: Double-coverage asphalt rolled roofing. This is a low-cost roof covering that provides better protection from leaks than you can get from more expensive coverings. However, some people (including my wife) believe that it doesn't look as attractive as asphalt shingles.

ICBO: International Conference of Building Officials, the largest of the three major model building code groups. ICBO's *Uniform Codes* serve as a model for most of the state and local building codes in the West, Southwest, and much of the Midwest.

IMPACT FEE: A fee charged by a municipality or county in exchange for granting the right to develop a piece of land. The fee helps pay for schools, roads, parks, fire stations, and other services and infrastructure that will be made necessary by the development.

INCOME APPROACH: A standard approach to assessment of business property. Under the income approach, valuation is based on the amount of income generated by a business, rather than the attributes of the real estate.

INTANGIBLE PERSONAL PROPERTY: Property such as stocks, bonds, and bank accounts.

INTENTIONAL: Builders' term for a project that turned out better than expected. For example, if ugly paneling is covered with wallpaper and it looks beautiful, the builder might say: "That almost looks intentional."

JOINT COMPOUND: The plaster mix used to cover joints, nail holes, and defects in drywall. It is also often used to mask blemishes in other materials. Do-it-yourselfers often call it "goop." However, if you wish to win respect from building professionals, you must call it "mud."

JOIST: A horizontal 2x8 (or 2x6, or 2x10, or whatever) used to support a floor.

LISTER: A person who gathers data for an assessment. In a few jurisdictions (including the one where I live), the elected assessors are called listers.

MANUFACTURED: Anything that is built off-site is "manufactured." Examples include pre-hung doors, stock cabinets, and structural wall panels. A manufactured house is one for which most of the components were built off-site.

MARKET APPROACH: A standard approach to assessment. A market approach determines fair market value of a property by comparing it to other properties that have sold and the prices that were paid for those properties.

MILL RATE: A mill is a tenth of a cent. In the good old days, property tax rates and electrical rates were expressed in mills. A few jurisdictions still use mills in their property tax formulas, although the formulas usually specify a very large number of mills.

MOUND SYSTEM: When the soil at a building site is not sufficiently porous to pass a percolation test, it may be necessary to bring in additional soil for proper drainage of the septic tank. This is called a mound system.

MUD: Any thick compound that becomes hard when it dries out. For example, drywall tapers refer to joint compound as mud. Masons refer to mortar as mud.

MULTIPLIER: In many assessment systems, a base value is assigned to property, then adjusted by multipliers. For example, if a building lot is in a "good" neighborhood, the base value might be multiplied by 2.2. If it's in a "bad" neighborhood, the base value might be multiplied by 0.73. Other multipliers might be used to account for the design factor of the house, the view, road frontage, the shape of the lot, soil drainage, and other factors that can affect the market value of the property.

NEIGHBORHOOD FACTOR: A multiplier used by assessors to account for price differences among lots in different neighborhoods.

OUTGASSING: The gradual release of toxins into your house or into the atmosphere. The formaldehyde in your plywood or carpets may outgas and threaten your health; the chlorofluorocarbons in your rigid foam insulation may outgas and threaten the environment.

PB PIPING: Polybutylene piping, sometimes used as a substitute for copper supply pipe where codes allow.

PERCOLATION TEST: A test to determine whether soil is porous enough to support a septic system. Test holes are dug, and an engineer fills them with water, then records the drainage time. A poor "perk" means that a typical household septic system would stink up the neighborhood.

PERSONAL PROPERTY: Anything that you own other than real estate. There are two classifications: "tangible" and "intangible," described separately.

PIER: A vertical support for a structure, usually made of concrete or pressure-treated lumber. Piers often serve as a foundation for a porch or deck, but can also provide a low-cost foundation for an entire house.

PIGGY ROOM: A modern cold pantry. Located just off the kitchen, a piggy room is a low-cost, convenient pantry that is ideal for food storage because it remains naturally cool.

PINK TRAILER: Any house or parcel of land that can be purchased at low cost, because it has characteristics that turn away other potential buyers. Often the defects can be overcome, and a pink trailer can be converted, economically, into a dream house.

POINT: A bank fee, paid at the time of closing. One point is 1 percent of the amount of the mortgage loan.

POLYISOCYANURATE: A type of rigid foam, often used in stressed-skin panels. It has a high R-value per inch of thickness, but contains chlorofluorocarbons. Practice saying this word out loud: people who pronounce it correctly in casual conversation command respect wherever they go.

POLYURETHANE: A versatile polymer that comes in many forms; most commonly, a clear coating for wood floors and trim. It is also the plastic sheeting usually used for vapor barriers, but this form is more often referred to as "plastic."

PVC PIPING: Polyvinyl chloride piping, commonly used as waste pipe; sometimes also used as water supply pipe.

QUOTE: A price that is guaranteed by a contractor in advance of a project.

R-VALUE: A measure of the resistance of a material to heat flow. The higher the R-value, the more effective the insulation.

RADIANT BARRIER: A thin material, usually reflective foil, designed to block the flow of radiant heat into or out of a house. To be effective, a radiant barrier must face an air space.

REAL PROPERTY: A synonym for real estate, often used by tax assessors. Another frequently-used synonym is "realty."

REAL ESTATE: Land, and anything attached to land. For example, a house and all items that are attached to or built into a house are classified as real estate.

ROMEX: A brand name of the most common type of electrical wiring, often used generically.

ROUGH CARPENTRY: Framing, sheathing, and all other carpentry work except application of finish materials.

SANDWICH PANEL: A building panel with insulation sandwiched between two surfaces. An example is a stressed skin panel with waferboard laminated to the exterior and drywall laminated to the interior, for use in a timber frame house. A structural sandwich panel has waferboard laminated to both sides.

SBCCI: Southern Building Code Congress International, one of the three major model building code groups. SBCCI's *Standard Codes* (often referred to as "Southern Standard Codes") serve as the model for most state and local codes in the South and Southeast.

SHAKE: A specific type of wood shingle, formed by splitting thin sections of a short log with a hatchet. The word is often misused to refer to any cedar shingle used for siding or roofing

SHEETROCK: A brand name for drywall, often used generically. When used as a verb, it is sometimes shortened to "rock," e.g., "We have to rock the wall today."

SITE-BUILT: Any component of a house that is constructed at the building site is site-built. A site-built house is one that is constructed primarily at the site.

SLAB: A concrete floor, poured on grade, over (or inside of) frost walls that extend below the frost line.

SOFFIT: Technically, a soffit is the horizontal underside of any building component, such as a stairway or an arch. However, the word is most commonly used as a reference to the boards that enclose the underside of a roof overhang. This can be confusing if you look up the word in a standard dictionary. In the parlance of most builders, a house has no soffit unless the underside of the overhang is enclosed.

SPACE HEATER: An individual heating unit. This is an old-fashioned term, but is still used to describe units that are outdated, inefficient, or of inferior quality.

STICK-BUILT: Site-built, using conventional stud construction.

STRESSED SKIN PANELS: Panels of rigid foam insulation, laminated to a sheathing material, usually waferboard. Sometimes called stress skin.

STUDS: The uprights in a conventional wall frame, usually 2x4 or 2x6 lumber.

STYROFOAM: A brand name, often used generically (and incorrectly) as a reference to various types of rigid foam insulation.

SUBCONTRACTOR: Anybody who contracts to do, or to take responsibility for, a specific part of a construction project. The contract may be written or implied.

TAKE-OFF: A list of materials used for a particular portion of a construction project.

TANGIBLE PERSONAL PROPERTY: Furniture, socks, underwear, cars, boats, tools, jewelry, golf clubs, camcorders, etc. Your tangible personal property consists of all the items you own except for (a) real estate and (b) intangible items such as money, stocks, etc.

THERMAL MASS: Any dense material, such as masonry, that serves as a heat bank. Thermal mass can soak up heat from erratic sources, such as solar gain or a wood-burning stove, and release it gradually over an extended period.

TITLE INSURANCE: An insurance policy paid for by the person who purchases real estate, to protect the bank against losses if the lawyer missed something in the title search. For an additional fee, purchasers have the option of buying title insurance to protect themselves as well.

TITLE SEARCH: A search through old deeds and related documents to confirm that the title is clear. Usually, a purchaser is responsible for searching the title prior to closing. If the property is mortgaged, banks insist that a title search be signed by a lawyer.

U-VALUE: A measure of heat flow through a material. The lower the U-value, the better the insulation. R-value is a more common measure, but window salesmen sometimes discuss energy efficiency in terms of U-value.

VAPOR BARRIER: A thin barrier, usually plastic film, covering the interior side of walls and ceilings, to protect the structure and insulation from moisture damage caused by condensation.

WAFERBOARD: Any of several types of sheeting manufactured by gluing wood particles together under pressure. Most waferboard, like plywood, comes in 4 x 8 sheets. Types of waferboard are not interchangeable. Some types, such as oriented strand board, have great structural strength and are frequently used for subflooring or structural sheathing. Other types have no structural strength, and serve primarily as underlayment to provide a smooth base for carpeting or plastic laminates.

WALL FURNACE: A modern, efficient space heater, usually fueled by gas or kerosene. It is mounted on the wall, draws combustion air from outside, and vents its fumes outside. The temperature is controlled by a thermostat, similar to that used for a central heating system.

Index

A Note to Readers:

I expect to update this book periodically. Therefore, I'd like very much to hear about your building or remodeling projects. What cost-cutting steps did you take? Which of those steps have produced the most satisfactory results? What has been your experience with local tax assessments? Please pass along any comments or insights that might be helpful to others who are planning their dream houses.

Thanks in advance. I look forward to hearing from you.

Steve Carlson
c/o Upper Access, Inc.
P.O. Box 457
Hinesburg, Vermont 05461

Upper Access, Inc. publishes nonfiction books to improve the quality of life. Please call or write for our catalog.

Upper Access, Inc.
One Upper Access Road
P.O. Box 457
Hinesburg, Vermont 05461

802-482-2988
1-800-356-9315